Big Data and Ethics

Health Industrialization Set

coordinated by
Bruno Salgues

Big Data and Ethics

The Medical Datasphere

Jérôme Béranger

First published 2016 in Great Britain and the United States by ISTE Press Ltd and Elsevier Ltd

ISTE Press Ltd
27-37 St George's Road
London SW19 4EU
UK

www.iste.co.uk

Elsevier Ltd
The Boulevard, Langford Lane
Kidlington, Oxford, OX5 1GB
UK

www.elsevier.com

Notices

Knowledge and best practice in this field are constantly changing. As new research and experience broaden our understanding, changes in research methods, professional practices, or medical treatment may become necessary.

Practitioners and researchers must always rely on their own experience and knowledge in evaluating and using any information, methods, compounds, or experiments described herein. In using such information or methods they should be mindful of their own safety and the safety of others, including parties for whom they have a professional responsibility.

To the fullest extent of the law, neither the Publisher nor the authors, contributors, or editors, assume any liability for any injury and/or damage to persons or property as a matter of products liability, negligence or otherwise, or from any use or operation of any methods, products, instructions, or ideas contained in the material herein.

For information on all our publications visit our website at http://store.elsevier.com/

British Library Cataloguing-in-Publication Data
A CIP record for this book is available from the British Library
Library of Congress Cataloging in Publication Data
A catalog record for this book is available from the Library of Congress
ISBN 978-1-78548-025-6

Printed and bound in the UK and US

Contents

Acknowledgements

My ideas were realized by working closely with (the company) Keosys, a leading firm in IT-applied Medical Imaging for Clinical Research and Medical Diagnosis. This has given us both the means and the skills necessary to make this analysis possible.

Finally, I would like to express my appreciation to Mr Jérôme Fortineau who was involved right from the beginning of this venture and who has always considered the subject of ethics as an essential and fundamental part of digital technology within the health sector. He has provided me with both moral and intellectual support throughout my research on the subject. For that reason, I dedicate this book to him.

Foreword

Some time ago, I took on the task of writing a book about Big Data. My aim was to explain some of the generic notions clearly, which would, out of necessity, profoundly alter the world in which we are evolving. The concise work that I had initially wished for proved sufficiently staggering for my editor, to cut it down to keep it within 250 pages, an upper limit which it was right not to exceed. Although I was satisfied with the result and seemingly my readership is, it is no less true to say that I took from this work, a strong sense of the saying "Do not bite off more than you can chew". Wanting to cover the whole of a discipline causes it to change completely. It is difficult to be precise about every point.

The work that you are now holding in your hands seems to have succeeded in avoiding this fault. By clearly resolving to restrict the field of study to the medical world and, more specifically, to ethical issues in this sphere, the pitfall of fragmenting has been skillfully evaded.

As regards health, the digital issues are certainly technological but not uniquely so. With respect to technology, this book sufficiently emphasizes that the technological revolution is here. Evidence of this includes patient–social networks, testing new opportunities, data processing through mass epidemiological models, etc. However, beyond that, all of this has significant implications regarding applications. Are we returning to an era where it is agreed to accept a level of transparency regarding personal data, which is unequal and beyond anything that we might have conceived? Will the absence of a trigger (machines detecting correlations and offering solutions although incapable of explaining the origin of the event) become the norm, plunging our society into a post-dialectic era in which the so-called "learning machines" are superior to humans when making medical decisions? Is it acknowledged that we should review public health policies from the viewpoint of a model, which has the datum at its center and therefore, an entirely different patient relationship?

In reality, there can be 'n' number of questions of this type and, moreover, this book evidences this. This is why it is important, from now on, to initiate the debate as widely as possible. For the silence in which these technologies are developing is deafening. While our world instigates a technological, and therefore epistemological, revolution the like of which has been heretofore unknown, the incompetence of the intellectual sphere, and especially the body politic, to instigate appropriate thinking is astounding. We can therefore simply, by means of this book, promote the merit of posing numerous essential questions while suggesting the methodological tools to deal with them.

Gilles BABINET
February 2016

A French entrepreneur in the digital sphere, Gilles Babinet is also a Digital Champion, that is to say that he is France's representative in Digital Economic issues with the European Commission. He has written two books, in January 2014 and February 2015 respectively published by Le Passeur with the titles, *"L'Ère Numérique, un nouvel âge de l'humanité"* ("The Digital Age – a New Age of Humanity") and *"Big Data, penser l'homme et le monde autrement"* ("Big Data – an alternative Way of Thinking for Man and the World").

Introduction

Introduction

In a general way, by procuring increasingly improved tools for himself, technology allows Man to build his own socioeconomic universe and to innovate in tandem with this configuration. New technologies favor the circulation of information of every kind. The latter necessitates less space and makes it easier to move, share and even sell this information. From Morse code, via wireless telegraphy, we are henceforth propelled into the digital era where JPEG and MP3 meet in Internet networks, where information has become more ethereal than ever.

According to Moore's Law (1985), technology since that date has allowed us to process millions of pieces of information just in seconds. Every day on the Web we disseminate dozens of small digital stones, which both design and strengthen the so-called Big Data[1] edifice. Like a "pyramid of knowledge" suddenly appearing one fine day in the Egyptian desert, here is a new universe in the process of taking shape before our very eyes. Moreover, unlike the monuments to the Pharaohs, this sector grows both limitlessly and exponentially.

Indeed, with the growth of the Internet, the use of social networks, mobile telephones and Cloud Computing[2], connected and communicating objects, the automation of information exchanges, data is nowadays more abundant than ever and each day its growth becomes ever more rapid. Big Data processing is updated every day so as to process an enormous quantity of data, which is often unstructured, in record time. Consequently, the firm Ericsson predicts that there will be 50 billion connected objects globally between now and 2020. In two days, the world thus creates as much data as the whole of humanity has created over 2000 years. Each day, we generate 2.5 trillion bytes of data. To the point 90% of all global "data" has been created in the last two years. The increase in raw data produced by individuals, firms, public institutions and scientific actors offers new perspectives on monetization, analysis and treatment of data. Big Data results in a major transformation in digital application by businesses across all economic fields. The latter have considerable repercussions in terms of development, research, service improvement, management and job creation [WE 12].

---

1 The word "data" is the Latin plural of *Datum*. We have decided to keep the noun in plural in this book.

2 Cloud Computing designates a model for telecommunication, which was instigated at the beginning of the millennium which is constantly changing. This model offers free access to services from any digital device, which is connected to the Internet. The services range from file storage to content management via the operation of online applications. The term "Cloud" comes from the metaphoric representation of these services.

This leads to a world in which new information and communication technologies (NICT) play a pivotal role, particularly in the health discipline.

As a result of the intrinsic development of medical information concerning patient privacy, our work formulates an ethical analysis of Big Data, mainly within the health ecosystem. However, you may note that all of our considerations, methods and tools flowing from this book can be adapted and extrapolated to other related sectors implying the production and spread of other types of personal data such as commerce, transport, finance, distribution, manufacturing, services, utilities, telecommunications, the public sector and education.

Nowadays, it has become almost inconceivable that digitized personal data should not have an application within modern medicine. The emergence of e-health, telemedicine, m-health, NBDC (Nanotechnologies, Biotechnologies, Data Processing and Cognitive Sciences) and Big Data modifies the health benefit, the doctor–patient relationship, and the scientific understanding of the human body and illnesses. The exploitation of personal data is a sensitive subject, as the latter affects each individual's privacy directly. The situations where difficult strategic choice issues arise, as regards management of personal data, become more copious every day.

In this context, the world's interaction with NICTs represents an unstable or even precarious system. Thus, the issues associated with Big Data are significant, as much economically, as for guaranteeing a secure digital space to protect both our private lives and fundamental liberties.

Moreover, the revolution of these immense volumes of raw and heterogeneous data goes hand in hand with the development of a new data science. The development of Big Data has entailed the setting up of sophisticated analyses, genuine "scaling up" in the conception and application of analysis models and the implementation of algorithms. From now on, software must have the capacity to detect interesting data so as to achieve optimum data processing. This is called "Data Mining". This approach uses an inductive, and no longer a deductive, method in seeking to establish correlations between several data items, without predefined hypotheses. It should be mentioned that this technique has only a descriptive value scientifically, as it identifies a link between two variables, but does not explain it.

Finally, techniques of "advanced analytics"[3] rely upon these large volumes of data to find the so-called "weak signals"[4] within a directory structure having identified categories.

From these tools, structures may henceforth detect and optimize, plot and target, even predict and forecast accurate data [IDE 14]. The flow and intersection of "data" in real-time allows a more detailed understanding of the environment. Decision-making is improved and actions or services may run more efficiently. In addition, the graininess and the large spectrum of data sources studied authorize the discovery and monitoring at a very detailed level.

In this context digital technology changes the health ecosystem completely. Whether it is a question of prevention, diagnosis or care, scarcely a day goes by without an innovation, which contributes to transforming medicine to become public. What appears for health professionals to be the ultimate provocation in the digital era resonates as the promise of a more precise and quicker diagnosis, indeed a totally personalized patient treatment.

However, the significance of Big Data does not stop with individual health. In terms of public health, the exploitation of massive amounts of data may contribute to new health products, detection of missed signals during epidemics, serious undesirable effects, etc. However, such a revolution also carries ethical risks around health data of a personal nature, such as integrity, trust, security, respect for private life and individual freedoms [GOO 14], reputation, regulation, etc.

On this basis, our book is structured according to the following triptych:

– It defines the applications for Big Data within the health sphere. It also shows in what respects Big Data constitutes a new phenomenon, a medical paradigm shift and with what social and technical evolutions it is associated.

---

3 The term "advanced analytics" includes the techniques and methods like non-parametric statistics, dimension reduction, association rules, network analysis, cluster analysis and genetic algorithms, etc.

4 The signal is not weak by the nature of the information source (whether it is formal or not) but by the linkages between this source and an entity, which is able to take a decision having related the signal and a given scenario. A weak signal is hardly decipherable, informal and unlikely but generally heralds an upcoming event.

It then details the applications and possibilities offered by the analysis of large volumes of data and the positive applications, which flow from these. The work endeavors to indicate the principal risks and issues relative to these applications. The analysis of Big Data may increase anxiety as a result of the intersection of large volumes of data. Thus, a number of questions surrounding necessary conditions, particularly, the right to privacy [SCH 12] and data security arise.

– Then, this book sets out the ethical value of the medical datasphere via the description of a Big Data ethical analysis modeling. On the one hand, this chapter describes the principles of selective ranking of health data and "ethical data mining", while it sets out the Big Data the ethical evaluation tools within the field of health on the other.

– Finally, this text makes recommendations and sets essential stages for successful management and governance of personal health data, and establishes the conditions necessary for the development of studying of Big Data.

The characteristics of Big Data

The term Big Data refers to a new discipline, which is located at the intersection of several sectors such as technology, statistics, databases and professions (marketing, finance, health and human resources, etc.). In practical terms, this approach is a response to the dramatic rise in unstructured data, as observed sometimes in multi-structured data, within the data universe (for example the Internet, RFID chip, mobile, etc.). This activity allows for the capture of digital data, for high-speed processing and thus to make them available for exploitation by organizations, businesses and public institutions, whatever the nature of this data may be. Big Data is, above all, a technological structure whose objective is to transform raw data (for example, location, navigation, metadata, stemming from social networks or administration) knowledge which is directly exploitable, entirely founded within a structured scientific method [GUI 11] that regains a wide diversity of data processing, which is implemented with the help of self-learning techniques, predictive or pre-emptive analysis and by fusion or data research. These NICTs all have the aim of giving "data" a meaning.

The tools to use during this process are the real innovation of recent years. Big Data has been made possible thanks to a technological power (examples being Cloud Computing and tools like Hadoop, MapReduce or Cassandra), which have made possible applications and services which, up to that point, were simply theoretical. This is principally associated with two issues: data volume and its complexity [BEN 14].

Behind Big Data is the source material: the "data". This data comes from different media, the Internet, RFIF sensors or Smartphones, expressed by more and more different and complex forms via videos, discussion forums and social networks. Hadoop has rapidly become the reference with regard to parallelization of Big Data. The American "Big Four" known as GAFA (Google, Apple, Facebook and Amazon) the three Chinese giants known as BAT (Baidu, Alibaba, and Tencent) and the four large symbolic data "disruption" firms namely NATU (Netflix, Airbnb, Tesla and Uber) implement promotional and targeting technologies for users. Editors were employed to adapt the initial offer Open Source Hadoop as a business solution, which has been customized according to customer applications and performance indicators. Nowadays, the principal offer which is found on the market, either through Cloud Computing solutions or the medium of devices (body hardware integrating Hadoop technology) and the development of means of high-performance calculations (for example MapReduce[5]). Other technologies (such as Pig, Cassandra, Hive, etc.) supplement Hadoop so as to make data processing more specialized.

These software programs are non-relational distributed database management systems using NoSQL access[6] (Not only SQL), which thus exceed the codifications of the SQL language (Structured Query Language). Besides, this NoSQL approach is one of the other principal characteristics of the emergence of Big Data. Generally, these NoSQL databases are classified according to the way they store "data". One thus finds categories such as future-orientated foundation core values, the document, the column or even structuring databases based on graph theory. One may give, as examples, solutions such as:

– SenseiDB; Voldemort (LinkedIn);

---

5 MapReduce is a technique which segments data operation (known as a "job" at Hadoop), of which two are elementary, so as to facilitate the parallelization of data treatment, i.e. Mapping and Reducing [COR 12].
6 The term "NoSQL" designates a category of systems database management (SDBM). These SDBM are no longer based upon the classic relational architecture.

– Cassandra; Hive; HBase (Facebook);

– Dynomo; S3 (Amazon) – CouchDB (Ubuntu One);

– MongoDB (SourceForge.net);

– MapReduce; BigTable (Google);

– No Database SQL (Oracle);

– Storm; FlockDB (Twitter);

– Hadoop; S4 (Yahoo).

Ultimately, these technological tools allow the processing of different types of data in considerable quantities and in a short period of time. Big Data allows for reconciliation, harmonization, unification, interconnecting and growth of important volumes of digital data, in a world which is henceforth digitized. It particularly allows for numerous data flows, for example, tracking CRM data (Customer Relationship Management), tracking of user interactions on the company website and within the newsletters sent. Moreover, the issue of real time is increasingly powerful in editor offers, whether it concerns the processing on dedicated servers or in-memory processing (within the computer memory).

Furthermore, there is not just one but several measures, which characterize Big Data. Historically, this phenomenon was defined by three words, the so-called three Vs (Volume – Velocity – Variety), by [LAN 01], an analyst at Gartner Research. Ever since that time, this concept has been enriched systematically. We have also included three additional factors which are namely: Veracity, Visualization and Value. Consequently, it is the interaction and the combination of "6 specific Vs" which define these "mega data" rather than the size of a specific database. These six characteristics which are unique to Big Data are defined as follows:

– Volume: the increased use of NICTs (smartphones, social networks, connected objects, etc.) encourages us to produce increasing amounts of data while performing our everyday activities, which are as much occupational as personal. Nowadays, the world produces a considerable amount of data of all kinds. The first is the so-called "Moore's law" (1965), which empirically observed that the "number of transistors in a circuit of the same size, doubled every eighteen months without any increase in their cost". This observation has not been refuted up to now and has since been extended to data storage memories.

According to the United Nations (UN), more data was created in 2011 than during the entire history of humanity[7]. The volume of digital data went from 480 billion gigabytes in 2008 to 2.72 zettabytes in 2012. By 2020, this volume will continue to increase at an exponential rate [BAI 14] reaching 40 zettabytes. [ABO 13] According to the study report, by Global Investor (Crédit Suisse), produced in June 2013, the digital world will have grown in 2020 to 300 times its size in 2005, particularly due to the emergence of connected objects. Thus, the volume of data produced globally each year will have multiplied by a factor of 44, by the year 2020. The quantity of archived information will increase four times faster than the world economy, during which time data processing capability will grow nine times quicker. It is estimated that 90% of all available data today was created during the last two years [BRA 13]. According to Dr Laurent Alexandre[8], the total volume of e-health data doubles every 73 days. This significant amount of data opens the field consequently to systems experts.

– Variety: Big Data represents a wide diversity of contents or formats (text, e-mails, videos, logarithms, images, sound, etc.) and sources of data (Machine To Machine, smartphones, etc.). We thus speak of unstructured or multi-structured data. Market data is, indeed, omnipresent; it comes, more uniquely, from internal sources but also from discussion forums, social networks or other external sources, which favor application data in real-time. This notion of multiple sources is one of the fundamental concepts of Big Data. Henceforth, it appears illusory to make a decision, which is based on a single truth-possessing data source. We are forced into the need to cut across several sources to draw usable conclusions. It is worth noting that efficiency logic desires that we seek to reduce the time needed for such processing considerably so as to make it more frequent in real time.

Health data may be issued from research institutes, epidemiological centers, pharmaceutical laboratories, imaging centers, hospital reports, insurance companies, client files but also social networks and forums. The types of data source are numerous. They can come from data, being either

---

7 Robert Kirkpatrick, Director of UN Global Pulse, on the Value of Big Data, theglobalobservatory.org, 5 November 2012.
8 A panel discussion titled: "What is the distance between secrecy and transparency?" during the Convention on Health Analysis and Management (CHAM) on 26 September 2015.

social, via networks and other media, personal (for example, tracking device data) or transactional or administrative probes [KIN 09]. Naturally, approaches centered on Big Data depend upon the intrinsic quality of the data which underpins them. Speed (or Velocity): Big Data is generated and evolves very quickly. Accelerated processing is able to occur in real time. This imposes the need for rapid processing, almost on a just-in-time basis, so as to be able to use accurate information and draw relevant conclusions. According to the report from the Institut Montaigne[9], "Grötschel's calculation" establishes that "the speed of calculating algorithms progresses forty-three times quicker than micro-processing capability. Algorithms may be defined as operational and instructional sequences of a computer program". Decision-taking by humans, concerning, in particular, a given purchase, is of the order of around ten minutes. This allows time for decision processes, cross-referencing information and to reach a decision. With the dawn of the Internet, this process has seen its points of reference completely turned upside down. Henceforth, everything is done very quickly! The order of magnitude of a few minutes has given way to a few seconds. Indeed, the interaction between the Internet user and his environment is directed progressively from the slower cognition sphere towards the motivation sphere, even the realm of the short-lived emotion. With respect to social psychology, the phenomenon is increased further by the speed that information spreads within the connected communities. From now on, in several hundred seconds, information may be communicated to millions of Internet users, potentially changing their behavior patterns. The acquisition of information is not enough. Its social impacts must also be anticipated. The equation, which links both speed and its contribution, is vital in community life. The whole of society lives through this unstable equilibrium between division and competition. It was with the same sense of purpose that algorithms, allowing for instantaneousness, were developed.

– Truth (quality of source information): although the data stemming from core applications within an Information System (IS) are restricted in number, but controlled in terms of both quality level and consistency. *A contrario*, public data associated with behavior or feelings, may be abundant but subject to distorting prisms. In the use that is made of such information it appears essential to be able to neutralize these phenomena without

9 A report from the Institut Montaigne titled: "Big data et objets connectés. Faire de la France un champion de la révolution numérique" ("Big data and connected objects. Making France a digital revolution champion"), pages 1 to 228, April 2015.

modifying the source data. The management of the criteria for both veracity and origin of the "data" manipulated is becoming fundamental. Big Data presents uncertainties, which are attributable to a lack of coherence, ambiguity, latency and the incompleteness of information. Decision-making processes should take into consideration this varying degree of uncertainty. For this purpose, these mechanisms must have the capacity to distinguish, evaluate, balance or sort out different categories of data so as to retain a particular authenticity.

– Visualization: data visualization is one of the basic requirements for success in the treatment of big data. This dataviz (an acronym for data-visualization) developed at the junction of design and statistics. It makes up a structuring and collaborative approach in the accompanying data which has been produced by connected objects. Its added value lies in the representation or the personalization of data and the diffusion of its contents to operational decision-makers and to the public, so that the latter consider Big Data useful. This data-visualization comes from both analysis and graphic formatting which is particularly readable via dashboards or radar representations. The real issue for this Big Data market is to make tools, which are linked directly to the perception of the recipient of the information received. It is by working out ergonomics which are adapted to their user that dataviz may be set up on a long-term basis both within the communicational and decision-making sphere of firms and organizations [HAM 13]. Finally, this dataviz must respond to two requirements: on the one hand, being sufficiently complete to manage complex inter-relationships within large data sets while being able to translate these correlations into pertinent visualization correlations, which are fairly simple so as to emphasize decision-taking truly within a structure, on the other.

– Value: coherence, trust, predictability and data quality have become essential criteria in the processing of large chunks of data. Big Data is, indeed, defined by data development, that is to say transforming the latter into information, which will subsequently generate important benefits *through* the uses which are made of it [GFI 12]. If it is difficult to consider *a priori* the value of raw data, it seems decisive to endeavor to integrate data sources which are likely to generate information which has a recognized added value. Big Data have both intrinsic data values (relating to conception) and extrinsic data values (relating to usage). The positive or negative significance of a piece of data must never be under-estimated. A data source, which has not been used internally, might have a monetizable value for a collaborator. Moreover, another data source, which *a priori* has no value, may, transpire, in a partnership framework, to bear a distinguishing signal.

What is ethics?

The word "ethics" takes its origin from the Greek term "ethos" signifying "manners" (Cicero), and "customs" (Plato and Aristotle). Ethics concerns the "environment" and the "nature" of an individual. Thus, the manner in which we live in the world represents the manner which makes us somebody. The expression "to be lived in" makes perfect sense and is of symbolic value. Viewed from this angle, ethics are the customs, which it is necessary to acquire so as to make a space habitable. Ethics thus involves calling into question the values which underpin action. This favors a conflict of values in a world of ideas. It "naturally finds its source of consideration in taking action" [HER 97]. Its objective is therefore to give actions meaning. Ethics is an individual tendency to act honestly in a given situation, so as to make the right decision. It only makes sense in a situation in which it acknowledges arguments, discussion and paradoxes.

Ethics refers to the requirements for a good life, both for oneself and others. It is "the desire to have an accomplished life, with and for others, within a fair institutional framework" [RIC 91]. It is the order of interpretation and/or practice. An ethical action is firstly a response (from the Latin *respondere*: to respond to ..., to answer for ... hence responsibility) to an extreme and complex situation. Ethics assumes three principal functions, which include the determination of what is morally right, knowledge of the reasons justifying an individual's effort to live in a moral way and the practical application of the outcomes achieved in the first two tasks.

Everyone seeks the values that drive them, chooses principles of action which should prevail, ensures the right conditions to implement them and becomes aware of their reality. Above all, ethics is an adventure, a compass, seeking an appropriate interpretation and position in relation to our personal reality. We are confronted with reality through the prism of our feelings, emotions, of our objectives, of our thought patterns, and our representations, which both concern and galvanize us. The interpretation and analysis comprise both a proportion of intellect and affect. It is the entirety of these two components, which gives value to reality and is articulated with ideas or idea processes in which it finds a coherent meaning. It is this complex mechanism of development and decline, between the rational and the sensible, which is important for us both to learn and to adapt to ourselves. Out of necessity, this passed through a system of mediation playing a role in developing meaning so as to both condition and direct the meaning that is produced. In this context, ethics may be defined as "a means of regulating behavior which comes from the individual and emphasizes co-constructed and shared values to give meaning to both his decisions and actions, thus calling upon both his personal judgment and his responsibility" [BOI 03].

In this book, our framework of ideas partly takes its source and inspirations from the ethical classical theories, which we would normally skim through. Namely from the Greek model of virtue[10], where ethics is primarily concerned with the individual (the agent) who carries out an act, or with so-called relational theories (such as utilitarianism[11], social contracting[12] and within ethical frameworks[13]) whose main concern is the nature and moral value of the actions carried out by the agent. More holistically, our thought process is based upon ethics directed towards the individuals creating, or receiving, the action involving Big Data and subject to its effects:

– for this purpose, we apply universal principles, which are both consensual and regulatory paving the way for social cohesion. In ethics, the principle constitutes the bedrock which presents itself "in the form of a commandment" [COZ 07]. It is unchanging, universal and intangible; and its value is not influenced by the course of history. This is why all societies working towards this universality illustrate this uniqueness which surrounds us. The so-called "universal" principle exists within the so-called multiplicity of things and therefore, human beings. The term principle comes from the Latin *principia*, itself borrowed from the "original" Greek which translates into two meanings: firstly, it designates "what comes first and what is at the source" [COZ 07]. We return to the origins of cultural architecture, moral foundations, rules of law, customs and traditions of a given society;

---

10 The moral principle of trying to be virtuous and of universal casuistry questioning.

11 The universal moral principle of maximizing consequences.

12 The universal moral principle which affirms that the whole of society is based on social contracting.

13 The universal moral principle of the categorical imperative (Kant). This ethical theory asserts that every human action should be considered according to its conformity (or non-conformity) to certain duties. It focuses upon the respect of rights and obligations.

– secondly it signifies "who gives authority" referring to the "prince" who "comes first" and in whom is vested supreme legitimate authority.

Upon consulting international bioethic literature, we note that four constants return persistently according to the country. Thus, references to the principles of "autonomy", "charity", "non-maleficence" and "justice" [BEA 01] appear consistently in related works whatever be their country of origin, its culture, its beliefs, its philosophy or its religion (see Box I.1):

– Autonomy

This designates the fact that an individual allows himself to have his own rules of behavior, as the Greek terms "autos" and "nomos" respectively mean "himself" and "law or rule" The purpose of this principle is to involve the patient in the decision-making process.

– Charity

It contributes to the well-being of others. It must fulfill two highly precise rules. The action undertaken must be beneficial and useful, that is to say have a positive cost-benefit relationship.

– Non-maleficence

This aims to avoid harm to the person to whom you owe the responsibility (the patient) and save him from the harm or suffering which would make no sense to him. Its aim therefore, is both to do good and abstain from doing harm. This principle appears in the Hippocratic maxim *primum non nocere*[14], the consequence of which is to do good to patients and to stop them from being harmed and subject to injustice.

– Justice

Its purpose is to share available resources between all patients.[15] This principle is strictly linked to the notions of equality and equity, which play a part in the process of making fair decisions directly. Ideally, all actions may tend towards a perfect equality, but according to the circumstances and the nature of the individuals involved, equity is often essential both to establish priorities and a particular hierarchy in the actions to complete. This principle includes a scope concerning all patients which may be designated as "macro-ethic" while the three previous principles have a far more individual and relational dimension and may be considered as "micro-ethic".

Box I.1. *Vocation of the four ethical principles*

---

14 "Above all, do no harm".
15 Time, money and energy resources.

Human and social sciences are obviously involved in ethical aspects: lawyers, sociologists, scientific philosophers, philosophers, researchers in information and communication sciences, cognitive sciences, psychologists, geographers, managers and economists, anthropologists, ethnologists, users and patients, whose accounts are invaluable. All parties bring essential views and arguments to ethical thinking upon the application and expansion of these new tools which will modify the existing society and each of our lives profoundly, particularly within the health framework.

It is in these conditions that we develop the idea of ethics being developed within a dialog. From this flow, a deliberative approach where the most appropriate ethical view emanates from a discussion between all of the actors who are concerned with the conception, implementation and application of an IS which is intended for the delivery of care. Our code of ethics serves as a vehicle for a vision for medical decisions which is both standardized and algorithmic, disassociated from a personalized and synthetic clinical approach, which is elaborated around patient needs.

Finally, ethics may be defined as a reflection upon action for which we must seek the appropriate direction. The "How" of a given action changes to "Why". Ethics then becomes the search to justify the standards that we establish. These standards are not a prerequisite for the ethical solutions to practical dilemmas, but rather the result of the actual decision-taking process [SPA 13]. In this regard, it is essential to identify and characterize the conditions and the method which allows us to go in search of the four ethical principles seen previously, being able to give a sense of the choices whether to act in one way or another.

Ethics in the digital sphere

Is there a code of ethics which is appropriate for digital technology? This question arises time and again and is the subject of debate, indeed, so much that it seems unnatural to associate a human science with a technological science given that they are almost total opposites. Yet, digital technology creates contradictory injunctions on all sides, which, as a consequence, has specific ethical repercussions for information and communication technology (ICT). Big Data may be ethically neutral but its uses are not! Individual behaviors give rise to applications of this new space and time, which digital technology generates. NICTs are a cultural, and indeed an anthropological, phenomenon. They produce new behaviors, new world views and new social norms.

We can take the example of anonymization, which poses the question of the responsibilities of individuals whose invisibility might free them from certain rules of decorum. The instantaneousness and ubiquitousness, which the Internet allows consequently irreversibly reverberates our actions in our words and thoughts. From now on, ethics and technology should not be linked in line with a two-stage mechanism. Ethical issues should be an integral part of their brief and thus constitute focused ethical thinking. Consequently, we no longer speak of an interdisciplinary approach but rather of a fusion ending up with a veritable digital ethic where the question of social and moral implications is integrated within NICTs.

In these conditions, it becomes essential to establish expectations and specific ethical predictions in the digital world; and reify new ethical and legal value systems, while always keeping in mind this question: might digital technology pose a threat of misuse to our ethical behavior?

In ethics, the term "value" is a necessity. It is a yardstick, which allows us to judge the facts. It indicates the ideals to strive towards. This word has a general and dynamic connotation. It has, primarily, a philosophical evocation before having an ethical consequence. One of the foundations of ethics is this imperative to appeal to actor rationality. This idea is achieved through an understanding in coordination, exchange and sharing between the protagonists. Each person contributes to seeking cross-comprehension of the situation analyzed. This therefore, presupposes a certain consensus and solidarity between the interlocutors who share the same aims. If ethics is always, by its very nature, complex to define, putting it into perspective with digital technology constitutes another challenge. Ethics demands a vision, a design and an ambition, which takes shape in a given direction.

Internet and Big Data are becoming omnipresent in our daily lives, the ethical preoccupations around information security have become one of the hottest trends in the whirlwind of research and practice of Information technology [TAH 11]. This is principally due to technological progress which has allowed the production, collection, storage, processing and transmission of data at an unprecedented consequent pace from diverse sources [HAM 07]. Numerous studies conducted on Information and Communication Technology (ICT) aim to clarify if the ethics of ICT is different from ethics in other fields.

[MOO 85] asserts that NICTs have created "unique" ethical problems; as these technologies are "logically malleable" and offer new possibilities for ethical behavior. Technological application has devolved new ethical behaviors, thereby favoring the generation of unique and new ethical problems. Ethical questions associated with ICT and the emergence of applications have been called "information ethics" [MAS 86].

Moreover, all technology defines the relationship between human beings and their environment, indeed as much their human as their physical environment. The concept of technological dynamics charting its own course remains very strong. McLuhan's legacy, in line with which technologies develop and influence the world, still resonates [BAD 15]. ICT has the power to hypnotize society; "All new technology thus reduces the interaction of both the senses and human conscience, and more precisely, within the new sphere of innovations where a type of interdependence between both the subject and the object occurs" [MCL 77]. No technology may be considered as purely instrumental. This applies, particularly, when it is a question of major automatic ISs developed so as to contribute to both the management and integration of large organizations, for example health structures. In such a context, the environment is made up mainly of human beings. By forcing ISs to develop, human factors simply control technical factors. Even though the satisfaction of the latter is compulsory, they are never really enough. Within the entire Big Data edifice, the human factor and interactions between humans and computers become critical. However, in a context of simultaneous multi-users, human interaction is the principle issue to resolve. The evaluation of large-scale digital data sets, such as those found in the health sphere is upon the concept of "human interrelationships" [FES 01], which underpins the conception, implementation and the application of Big Data. In such conditions, these "mega data" mainly appear as a social system with psychological, sociological and ethical features. The gap between the room for maneuver and the representation of a given action is greatly reduced. An ambiguity takes hold between genuine digital action and its representation; or between continuous motion and discreet management of such a motion. Consequently, digital technology is a place with limitless freedoms, owing to the fact that everything operates in a continuous motion. At the same time, by being discreet in the end, this movement is therefore, easily controllable. Digital ethics should "attempt to think through the relationship between the gesture and crystallization of the gesture" [VIT 12]. It is from this approach that the reasoning of our ethical thinking must start and lay down ethical principles which are specific to digital operations. The ethics of NICTs may be divided into three main themes:

– data ethics: defining the ethical principles which guarantee the fair processing of data and the protection of individual rights, while applying Big Data to both scientific and commercial ends;

– algorithmic ethics: translating the study of ethical problems and the responsibilities of the inventors of scientific data as regards both unforeseen and undesirable consequences, as well as lost opportunities for the invention and application of autonomous complex algorithms; and

– practical ethics: this represents the identification in an ethical framework which is appropriate to shape a professional code of ethics upon data governance and management, favoring both scientific data progress and protecting the rights of those concerned.

Before returning directly to the issue itself by describing the crucial issues and ethical risks which fuel our thinking around Big Data in the health field, it seems essential to explain their individual ends, their aims and more generally their *raisons d'être*: that is to say to benefit individuals. Henceforth, business leaders evoke a refocusing of their strategy upon individual needs (for example, within the medical sphere, health service users). For Dr Channin, "the number one priority of an IS is the patient". [CHA 09] The technological revolution with respect to the information sector must be led both in the best interests of patients and to ensure better care. In other words, the only value to take into account, with a view to retaining this, is the human individual considered as a dignified moral being. This human dignity constitutes an absolute value when given to an individual. Thus, ethical principles, practices, techniques and ergonomics must be imposed so as the patients and their families remain the main recipients of this technological evolution. This is all the more true when all ethical thinking becomes a conflict between human values whatever our religious beliefs, cultures, political influences or sphere of activity may be, our emotions which reveal our deepest values. As Pierre Le Coz emphasized in 2010 on the occasion of the first ethics day on "Cancer and fertility" at l'Institut Paoli-Calmettes[16], "…if there are no emotions, there cannot be any formal values and therefore no ethics".

---

16 This is a cancer care center based in Marseille.

Indeed, every major ethical principle may be associated with a particular emotion. We can make the following connections:

– respect for the principle of autonomy;

– compassion for the principle of charity;

– fear for the principle of non-maleficence;

– indignation for the principle of justice.

For [DAV 12] "Four elements are defined, both for individuals and organizations, which may be considered within the ethical framework of digital data:

– identity: what is the relationship between our "offline" and "online" identity?

– confidentiality: who controls access to data?

– ownership: who owns the data and the rights to transfer it and what are the obligations of the individuals who both generate and use this data? Is our existence built up of creative actions for which we either own the copyright or other rights relating to their creation?

– reputation: how can we determine which data is trustworthy?

– within the technological framework, medical ethics has to deal with actions, which have an incomparable social causal consequence for the future. These are accompanied by forward-looking knowledge, which, regardless of its incomplete nature, extends beyond everything that we have previously experienced. It may be defined as a mechanism for reflection upon the moral meaning of the relevant action. This definition is intended to be extensive and critical and to integrate several components of data-processing ethics. [WAS 96] In the main, we consider that there are five ICT-related situations where ethics have a bearing as follows: the ethics of "empowerment": such ethics are associated with the patient actor (e-patient) who is entitled to autonomy and dignity (respect for his rights);

– the ethics of access: these involve fundamental rights and transparency (the concept of "Universal Design");

– the ethics of dissemination: these relate to an evolutionary transformation from computerized monitoring towards a medical informatics service (involving both centralization and distribution of information);

– the ethics of data recapture: these are focused upon transformations which are seen as potential opportunities (digital literacy);

– the ethics of collaboration: these encompass information-sharing (on the Web with, in particular, online forums or social networks).

Generally, on the one hand digital ethics lead to lines of questioning upon both the behavior and use by individuals who are faced with NICTs, while the increasingly upon autonomous behavior of technological tools as such on the other. Most often these technologies are programmed with the aim of leading to many actions, which are independent of human intervention (such as algorithms for both recommendations and decisions). Within this framework, ethics, as such, constitutes a means to regulate behaviors based upon respect for values, which are both judged to be essential and should have prevented this human objectivity and supply a framework for data application [EYN 12].

It is necessary to add to this the long term order of magnitude of actions, and also, very often, their irreversibility. All of this places the responsibility at the core of ethics, including both the horizons of space and time, which correspond to those of ethical principles. It is thus the responsibility of a business, ethically-speaking, to know how to use digital technology and data. In these circumstances, the Information Systems Manager must ensure that Big Data projects are ethical.

It should be noted that the majority of professional practices around Big Data are controlled by laws, which differ both according to culture and country mentality. On the whole, the latter aim to warn us against inappropriate behavior and to preserve the ethical order of society. However, these laws only cover those situations where ethics come into play.

In this regard, since in this world information prevails and entities are built upon it, our ethics also turn to the dominant intellectual thinking of data communications ethics. This was instigated by Luciano Floridi, a professor at the University of Oxford. It focuses upon on what is ethical in an information society and its characteristics are more closely matched to our sphere of analysis [FLO 98]. Contrary to the classic models which are intrinsically anthropocentric, individualistic and of a social nature, above all, data communications ethics is interested in the environment (also called the "info-sphere"[17]) where information is created and spreads, particularly Big

17 Dan Simmons coined this word (1989) to designate an informational environment.

Data. This info-sphere represents a digital space that is constituted by a heritage which is both persistent and ever-changing within a geographical space which is often indeterminate. In essence, it is an intangible and ethereal environment, which, for all that, does not make it, any less real or indeed less essential [BER 15]. This information environment is made up of all information processes, services and entities, including information officers, their interactions, their responsibilities and their mutual relationships.

Connected to this info-sphere are all of the software programs and other technological tools overseen by this manager [CAR 00] as well as its every legitimate user. This info-sphere consists of a set of subjects and objects which revolves around computer devices. It also includes all of the data, which belongs to an individual (or legal entity) and all of the data which pertain to it, but which are outside of its center of gravity (examples being security, politics, etc.). In summary, the info-sphere of a healthcare facility group together all structural communicating objects, being all of the data and connections associated with the IS [BER 15].

For this purpose, the Italian philosopher bases his argument upon the information theory, and more particularly, upon the concept of information entropy, introduced by Shannon[18] in the mid 20th Century. For the author, information entropy, measures, by analogy with thermodynamic entropy, the degree of disorder within a given system, or more precisely, the knowledge, which we possess. Indeed, if we know something perfectly, we can understand it and locate all related details. We can enumerate its sequence in order. It therefore appears to us to be arranged in order. There is, therefore, a direct correlation between a system's organization and our knowledge of it. In that way, the weaker the entropy, in other words, the more organized it is, the greater the level of knowledge in relation to it will be. Moreover, vice versa, the greater the entropy, the less organized it is considered to be, the lower the level of knowledge about it. Starting from this premise, Luciano Floridi develops his thinking around "information ethics" taking as the

---

18 Claude Shannon, an engineer with the telephone company Bell determined information as an observable and measurable magnitude (1948); the latter became the essential pillar of the communication theory which he worked out with Weaver. This concept of information was the object of the theory known as "the theory of information". This was a mathematical theory that was applied to telecommunication techniques. This mathematical theory, derived from technical preoccupations with telecommunication, remains to this day the basis of the concept known as scientific information.

criterion informational global entropy, which he applies to his notion of the "info-sphere" that is to say the environment in which information develops. He states, "Ethical behavior would diminish the entropy since it would make the information more significant, while a growth in entropy would be harmful to everyone". Thus action, which is said to be "right" or considered to be ethical, would lead to a diminution in the overall entropy and an increase in the knowledge which we all have.   Conversely, incorrect information or data already known would increase the level of entropy by disorganizing the info-sphere.

Thus, data communication ethics marks out good from evil, what must be achieved and the obligations of the moral agent, based upon four fundamental laws which must be complied with: not to cause entropy in the info-sphere, to guard against the production of entropy in the info-sphere, ensuring the exclusion of entropy from the info-sphere and ensuring that the right type of information is favored by data expansion (quantity), its improvement (quality) and its broadening (variety) within the info-sphere [FLO 98].

In this context, ethical issues[19] that this digital universe gives rise to are better learned and understood, if we associate them with concrete events or facts from a real-life context [FLO 02]. For example, the concept of confidentiality may be linked to presence or absence in the Big Data processing tool with parameters allowing the concealment of the identification of the patient to whom the medical information relates. In respect of the accessibility to medical information, the latter may be associated with the existence within the IS of a platform for sharing and exchanging to which the user may have access to depending upon his status, his profile and level of clearance.

In addition, according to [FES 01], the concept and the word "info-ethics" may be examined upon two levels:

– human relationships which exist within all Big Data health systems;

– health structures having a supplementary dimension concerning the individual. These are aimed at human changes.

---

19 Examples being confidentiality, professional confidentiality, protection of medical data, respect for privacy, accessibility of medical information, shared responsibility, respect for and maintenance of patient autonomy, etc.

As we shall see, information becomes the primary purpose of moral action. Introducing ethics into the digital world is unnatural owing to the fact that ICT systems will have no social and human value. This idea comes from a common thinking, which considers that all technology is neutral ethically as only a human being may contribute reason to his actions. However, we acknowledge that Big Data also disseminate values inasmuch as they both impact upon and condition the way that their users behave. As a consequence, no digital data is ever neutral [FIS 14]. That is why we must not reduce digital ethics to an expression of extrinsic values for best technological practices but also intrinsic values for these. Finally, with the advent of digital and "massive data", there is an entire set of ethics to invent because NICTs design a new relational and sociological paradigm [DOU 13]. We cannot claim to be able to make up a new set of ethics but rather rethink and reinvent the existing ethics so as to develop it towards "algorithmic ethics" applied exclusively to digital. This new approach has the aim of integrating ethical values and principles upon the conception, implementation and application of Big Data, especially within the field of medicine.

Lines of questioning around Big Data in the health sphere

Via an ethical approach, pondering collection, storage, application and availability of personal health data, is not difficult and may even amount to added value quickly, in the sense, even of an explosion of a return on investment. Every technology performs practices, produces values and behaviors and, as a consequence, interferes with new social norms. Big Data imposes new considerations upon our values and how we carry out our actions and the fact that it gives a larger number of people more means to communicate and interact with each other. In this case, we might ask ourselves, if these "massive data" pose their own ethical problems. For example, does privacy have the same value on the Internet as in our daily lives?

In the exercise of their daily activities, in relation to health "data", individuals are subject to multiple, successive and complex questioning, where respect for human values which are considered to be universal and the restrictive limits of positive decisions taken, constantly confront each other. Numerous questions related to the consequent volume of data and its collection, storage, particularly using information tools, which do arise within a wide variety of sectors.

In these conditions, this work aims to reflect ethico-technological aspects upon design, management, control and application of Big Data in the health field. We propose to articulate our thoughts around a series of questions, such as:

– what are the changes that Big Data and data analysis will bring to healthcare? How does "massive data" impact medical practice? What changes might be anticipated for patient services and for health?

– where are both health data and the means to use them to improve care to be found?

– should we be guided in opinions and medical decisions merely by processing Big Data in the health field?

– should we inform individuals of the risks they run of particular illnesses owing to their genetic heritage?

– all of this accumulated data has a value. How or where can we find this value so as to improve treatment?

– how do we combine the essential requirements both of sharing data and ensuring privacy, while storing data within a Cloud Computing system?

– how do we unite both the public interest and the protection of individuals?

– is it necessary to adapt the organization of health care systems to these technological developments?

– from a legal point of view, how can each country make its health data secure?

– to what extent should professional practices around digital health data respond to an objectiveness, neutrality and/or rationality criteria?

– to what extent is it possible to develop both the approach and ethical commitment to the application of Big Data within the health field? What is the value of medical data ethics? how should these ethics be passed on to both information and communication professionals and/or health professionals? How can we gain an awareness of ethics? Will there be an increase in demand?

– how should the ethics of NICTs be viewed in the health sector? Is ethics inherent in the emergence of so-called "mega-data?" Is it a mechanism with a specific significance? How should ethical values spread? How should global digital technological change be expressed through ethical principles? How should Big Data and ethics be reconciled within a firm?

– is there a recognized system of reference for good ethical practices for these enormous volumes of data?

– how should the data that we produce be classified?

– will large-scale DNA and human genome analysis help to treat illnesses? Alternatively will this simply end in a new wave of medical inequalities and injustices?

– will the study of Big Data make user access to health information more efficient and effective?

– what should be done to set informational limits in respect of data which may be completely insignificant when taken individually?

– what might be done to ensure that the new technology for Big Data processing uses existing data and technology?

– how might new types of analysis and applications for the exploitation both new and old data become possible?

– how will these new actors interact with current actors within monitoring and processing segments such as pharmaceutical laboratories and medical components manufacturers? Will it be more of an issue of competition than of partnerships? What responsibilities will actors have in data application? accountability seems to be a somewhat feeble response to digital junctions and limitless processing! When, in tomorrow's world, everyone will have the ability to start their own online searches and data extraction, what will actor regulation mean? When will systems be able to retrieve anyone's data online so as to build a medical profile?

– will there ever be an interdependent financial model to fund Medicine 4.0[20] based around personalized risks?

– who will regulate companies who are likely to search the Web so as to refine our recruitment profiles? What authorities should run them, by authorizing access and assuring the optimum efficiency and security whilst

20 The concept of Industry 4.0 was expressed for the first time during the Industrial Technology Exhibition in Hanover, in 2011. It corresponds to a new means of organizing production methods from technological foundations such as the Internet of objects, technology relative to Big Data and even cyber-physics systems. The objective is to put in place so-called "intelligent" firms ("smart factories") capable of a greater production adaptability and more efficient resource application.

guaranteeing the democratic and transparent nature of Big Data management?

– how will we manage to create wealth through Big Data, while creating an economic confidence, which is necessary so as to develop new Big Data applications.

There are so many questions, which deserve examination and debate so that these determining issues around Big Data in the medical field have clear choices. This is why it is essential to favor a technical–ethical approach to these issues so as to provide rich, open and fruitful consideration around the subject.

The objectives and contributions of this book

The development of digital technology and its omnipresence in our modern society creates a mounting need to establish ethical reference points. In this context, we may question the specificity of Big Data to create new ethical problems or even to reinforce certain moral classic dilemmas. The present book aims to provide tools for ethical reflection around development, set up and application of "mega-data" in the health field.

The objective of this book is to give actors concerned with such Big Data the main tools so as to allow readers to acquire an ethical approach to NICTs. To define a social and moral framework which manages the public interest and individual personal health data rights and to define a new space for data confidentiality, while concentrating more upon accountability for data application than individual, clear and informed, consent during the collection of the latter [FIS 14].We wish to bring a certain equilibrium and harmony between both human intentions and the purpose of technological tools which are associated with Big Data. The issue is to reinforce the meaning of our actions so as to allow the reader to be aware of, even to validate, preliminary guidance for a balanced and controlled integration of "massive data" volumes within the medical ecosystem. In summary, the expectations concerning our work are diverse, making possible:

– the identification and characterization of the issues associated with these extremely large volumes of data; to gain a clear perspective upon the Big Data lifecycle to understand the ethical-technical expectations of the players who are, directly or indirectly, associated with this data;

– understanding organizational models, actors, methods and data-linked approaches;

– to work out a model and ethical evaluation of Big Data analysis intended to lead to both positive and selective actions of good practices and reduced risks;

– introducing a ethical-technical methodological guidance which makes coherent alignment of technological actions with moral values possible, through connecting risk ontologies and the ethical objectives associated with Big Data exploitation;

– helping organizations to elaborate a framework both for discussions and explicit ethical consideration so as to strike a balance between the commitment to practical technological innovation and the risk of data processing prejudice;

– listing prescriptive rules of conduct for the ethical treatment of Big Data;

– building "algorithmic ethics" around both recommendations and developments introduced concerning personal digital health data;

– increasing awareness of all actors and promoting a culture orientated towards awareness-raising, involvement, appropriateness and accountability around "massive data";

– assisting firms to develop an aptitude so as to both cast doubt and undertake an ethical analysis which is explicit in this new Big Data context.

The ultimate interest is therefore to assist the reader to have a precise knowledge of ethical issues that such a subject provokes. This is, in our opinion, the essential condition for a human approach, which nowadays goes beyond financial and material considerations.

By highlighting a background based upon innovative ethical-technical thinking, our book aims to introduce the fundamentals of substantial mind set change, as well as an environmental transformation of the "human face" of Big Data and its applications to the medical field. The objective is to find a certain coherence and direction, in this landscape, which is undergoing perpetual technological evolution so as to provide the best care possible for the health service user [BER 15].

1

The Shift towards a Connected, Assessed and Personalized Medicine Centered Upon Medical Datasphere Processing

Today's world corresponds to a universe where digital data is omnipresent, thus opening up prospects around reality that we have never known before. Hence, we are witnessing the emergence of the process of "datafication" which consists of digitizing and assessing everything, so that data emerges from written works, locations, individual actions or even fingerprints. Such a phenomenon contributes to transforming our ecosystem by providing the possibility of analyzing infinite quantities of increasing amounts of data, the acceptability of both approximation and disorder and the search for correlations rather than relationships between cause and effect. It may be observed that this notion of "correlations" stemming from biology has been used for a long time in economics.

Big Data, which nowadays appears to both optimize processes and to participate in diagnosis and health care delivery, will clearly emerge into a metamorphosis, not only of the health system as we know it today, but also of medicine. We are thus returning to the post-industrial era. As Bell said in 1973, "A post-industrial revolution society is based on services. What counts is not raw muscles and power or energy, but information". We are now in a new world which is centered upon digital data and where "Hippocrate's medicine has given way to e-ppocr@te" [BER 15] all being linked, measured and personalized. [FLO 09] characterizes this new ecosystem based upon the information philosophy as the fourth revolution[1] after Copernicus[2], Darwin[3] and Freud[4]), allowing the reconciliation of nature (derived from the Greek word physis) and technology (derived from the Greek word technè) through a philosophical interpretation of the info-sphere.

1.1. The digital gap and the medical paradigm shift

The paradigm notion is revealed when a society takes a gamble that a model is sufficiently pertinent to be able to be substituted for reality. Once established, this model, which is hoped will open up a large field of discoveries, becomes exclusive and leads, *de facto,* to the overshadowing of the entire complex scope that fails to comply with it. As soon as this paradigm reaches breaking point, the new model generally assumes ownership of previous achievements, within a broader perspective. A paradigm shift is complex and always takes time. In 1977, Edgar Morin said, "It is difficult to change the starting points for reasoning, both associative and repulsive relationships between some initial concepts, but upon which the structure of reasoning, and indeed, all possible discursive developments depend". This revolution not only changes our understanding of the outside world but also our notion of what we are as living beings.

In a world of ever-increasing data, where perceptions are becoming infinite, where everything will become a sum of infinite values, organizations are attempting to understand how to extract the value of all of this data that they are retrieving. This new mass of data, which has never been seen before, generates new knowledge. This causes a paradigm shift in health data, whose value lies in both sharing and pooling it. The best-known health applications fall within the personalization of the doctor–patient relationship.

---

1 Luciano Floridi proffers the idea that Man may be categorized within informative organisms (so-called "inforgs") [FLO 07], amongst others, which are not radically different from entities, natural or intelligent agents, or indeed, modified connected objects.

2 Nicolas Copernicus (1473–1543) highlighted heliocentric cosmology which has moved the earth, and therefore humanity, away from the center of the universe.

3 Charles Darwin (1809–1882) proved that all living species have evolved over the course of time, through natural selection, thus shifting humanity from the center of the biological world.

4 Sigmund Freud (1856–1939) showed the importance of Man's unconscious, thereby moving Man away from a Cartesian perspective which is clear to us.

Consequently, the digital turning point appears to be an epistemological revolution, since data IS are no longer positioned within categories of reason, but we are able to make use of it one piece at a time, in both a singular and differential way. For the philosopher Gaspard Koenig[5], this has repercussions on science (moving from deduction to correlation), on language (with the identification of each object through its own characteristics), on knowledge (based upon the fact that reasoning because of its ability to conceive will lose its status and that knowledge becomes quantitative and not qualitative), on politics, on philosophy (with the field of immanence, if all objects are connected), and on insurance, politics and war (through cyber-crime), and also other associated fields. Subsequently, we are witnessing a convergence of data which is all homogeneous, digitized and that can be integrated, and therefore, have more meaningful correlations. "Data" is not the product of knowledge, but the material of such knowledge.

Thus, this new data science has been able to materialize, from the simple fact that in the last few years, databases, processing tools, server management and large-scale storage have been re-evaluated entirely, which has allowed their operational performance to be favored considerably. This data input for everything provides the means for mapping the world progressively in a quantifiable and analyzable way. Hence, these digital technologies may precisely emulate the behavior and habits to an increased extent, which, has not, as yet, been achieved [MAR 14].

This digital revolution represents as much a change in our ecosystem as the elaboration of new realities in which digital (based on the silicon chip or online technology) expands and is increasingly linked to analogical (carbon-based or offline technology), to both absorb it and amalgamate with it in the medium term. Stemming from this transformation, the concept of the "info-sphere" will be displaced as a means of referring to the information space till it becomes synonymous with reality. Consequently, real-time analysis is gradually becoming a major issue. The analysis of Big Data may be conducted using two data measurement indicators:

– at the individual and personal level, where we focused on the collective and aggregated data before;

5 "L'utopie numérique est-elle dangereuse pour l'individu?" *Les Assises de la Securité et des Systèmes d'information,* Monaco, 1 October 2015.

– on a real-time basis, whereas we worked with retrospective statistics previously.

The convergence of these two components, both individual and real-time, is the cornerstone for these "massive data".

We do intend to define this digital data conversion in the sense of a rupture; there is no continuity. Telemedicine digitization distinguishes itself as a "transformational space", even if it is still achieved around a "perceptive structure" by symbols, images and writing [GHI 00]. This change may accentuate a digital gap between individuals as a result of:

– the inability to access the method, the processing algorithm and the logic of the decision-making criteria which are used in Big Data analysis [TEN 13];

– the difficulty for individuals and organizations to have access to or to buy data [MCN 14];

– the complexity involved for actors in modifying data [BOY 12];

– the possibility or impossibility for the individuals concerned to be informed as to the traceability of the data during its lifecycle [COL 14];

– the difficulty of understanding both when and why specific processed Big Data have been classified in a particular category. This understanding is essential so as to reinforce self-monitoring of the latter [LYO 03].

Lastly, algorithmic knowledge has also progressed allowing both faster search and structuring of databases. From both chemical and post-traumatic health care, we are moving progressively towards preventative and personalized health care.

In the past, business data was seen as a management activity by-product, analyzed by "Data Mining" teams whose influence within the business was, as a consequence, reduced. Nowadays, we are at the beginning of an era where all professional and personal services and activities for individuals are becoming digitized. The attitudes of company directors are changing regarding recognized data as a significant innovation lever, which is likely to cause both new economic models and significant productivity gains. Only organizations and bodies with the knowledge to adapt their ISs to new perspectives of multifaceted data will really attain optimum value.

In just a few years, a large amount of other data, the so-called "unstructured data" or "semi-structured data"[6] has been grafted onto structured data and run within traditional data processing applications (ERP, CRM, SCM and other applications). Thus, we may list several types of unstructured or semi-structured data:

– electronic messages (e-mails and instant messaging), data entries and evidence placed on the Web, digitized contractual documents, and conversations with call centers and websites;

– mobility-linked data: web browser history, identifiers (SIM cards, ID numbers such as IMEI, UID etc.) and location-based positioning;

– data generated by connected objects: machines, sensors, home automation, "smart" cars and meters, set-top boxes (Internet operator gateways, cable TV boxes or other similar devices) and personal biometric systems;

– data which are created and shared outside of traditional business communication circuits through Internet social networks.

This data will be identified and designated as unstructured, once they require a more complex transformation, before their significance is revealed. Processing of such data (particularly, in real time) irretrievably through powerful algorithms. Lastly, these new types of "data" may have the purpose of enriching other types of "data". However, they may also constitute, in certain cases, the core data being processed [BEN 14]. Subsequently, in this context, there are different analytical approaches around digitized data (see Figure 1.1).

Traditional approaches to health research may be noted, with hypotheses based on deductive reasoning, generally relying on a small quantity of data, collected in highly controlled circumstances, such as randomized clinical trials. With Big Data, new additional possibilities appear in terms of scope, flexibility and also data visualization. Techniques such as the extraction of large amounts of data facilitate inductive reasoning and an exploratory analysis of data is revealed. This allows researchers to identify data models which are independent of specific hypotheses [ROS 14].

---

6 Examples of semi-structured data include e-mail messages, logs and other such forms, and types of unstructured data are photo, video and sound files.

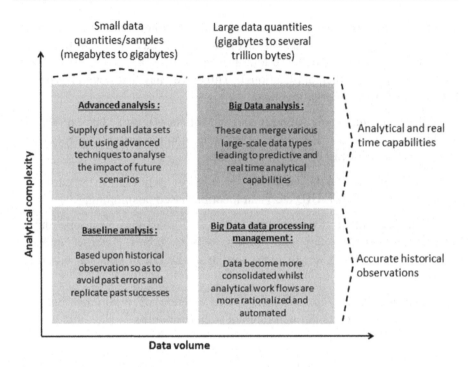

Figure 1.1. *Analytical approaches to data according to analytical complexity and digital data size*

In this context, data clustering is justified by the concept that says "It is possible to learn things from a large volume of data which cannot be learned from a small volume" revealing the implicit link between Big Data and complexity [MCN 14].

Thus, the complexity around the treatment of large volumes of data refers as much to the inherent difficulty in analyzing the latter as is does to complicated reasoning or algorithmic justification (or analytical processes) [MIT 15]. Consequently with Big Data, we come back to a system of total immanence, which does not make the distinction between reality and its representation. The intermediation layer that the statistics were representing has been deleted. Inductive reasoning allows us to generalize an observed phenomenon, even if only on one occasion. This approach, however fundamentally human, remains foreign to engineers and scientists attuned to Cartesian epistemology. Reasoning depends on the previous inductions and detected singularities; it cannot be replicated. Inductive reasoning does not demand having at one's disposal complete and coherent parameters, as, in any event, the brain will only process them partially, as it will concentrate on what it concludes are the main aspects of the situation. As a result of this speed of delivery, it is possible for errors to appear.

Moreover, inductive reasoning allows algorithms to reproduce observed situations, by using them beyond their specific field, so much that they remain effective, without seeking to break them down. Promptness allows algorithms to concentrate on the essential aspects so as to maintain the equilibrium between their contribution and competition from others. The study in Big Data clearly falls under the constructivist epistemology. That is to say that each process develops its own baseline that participates in the overall system without ever entirely understanding the latter. This is a continuous and constant learning process which never stops that creates an imperfect but useful knowledge, a little like the human brain.

An algorithm which is constructed during an inductive approach may be designed according to a certain purpose; which is to say its "products". For example, the graphs achieved by this algorithm based on analyzed data have a practical application. Data which comes from an algorithmic application is invaluable knowledge so as to assess its own efficiency. This may, in particular, be helpful for plausibility calculations. The most optimum inductive algorithms are therefore evolutionary. Their data processing becomes more refined according to the most pertinent use which may be achieved. We are witnessing a paradigm change in data understanding. It seems as if it has become practically pointless to identity in a given situation, the "Why", as the "What" suffices, to the point that we sometimes become incapable of explaining a causal relationship, for example, the reasons for a dysfunction [MAY 14]. Thus, if data are analyzed by processing algorithms, without "human controls" [HOF 13], the variable quality of data does not take account of the context, the meaning, the interpretation and therefore, the causal effects so as to explain complex phenomena.

According to Irving Wladawsky-Berger [WLA 14], "Relating data directly to action, drastically changes traditional governance patterns which are based on the ability of experienced leaders to link effects to causes and to act according to proven models". There is a clear distinction between statistics (which are used for explanation) and data science (which is used for prediction). The first is generally, used so as to validate models or explain phenomena, while the second is concerned with directly data into action transforming, typically by making predictions or taking decisions, leading to a major cultural change within organizations.

Subsequently, actors are liberated from everything that relates both to the average and to the norm, since *a priori*, we no longer select data. We may take into account all points relating to all data, including the most insignificant. This emancipation promotes radicalization of actuarial logic, to the detriment of social justice. All distinction in the individual treatment which would be economically justified becomes automatically legitimate. In their work, [MAY 14] explain future practices for both considering and acting, whether such practices both result in and examine harmful effects of both figuring out solutions and of the "data" that Internet operators will be able to work with. For the authors, "Everything changes when the data become massive, may be processed quickly and have a certain tolerance level for inaccuracy. Decisions may be taken by machines and no longer by human beings". In future, correlations coming from Big Data will be used to refute intuitions of causal links, by showing that often there is simply nothing but a statistical relationship between the effect and the presumed cause.

That is why, at present, we are witnessing a multiplication of applications, services and processes which are data-driven. Big data should be considered as a technological revolution in the ability to collect, store and use data. Having appeared on the west coast of the US, following the massive development of digital applications, nowadays, "massive data" constitute a technological response to a new analytical paradigm. Data analysts are metamorphosing into genuine computer scientists with new skills and know-how in methodologies quite analytical. Nowadays, the use of data is far more documented, far more instantaneous and far more relevant, becoming the major issue of businesses commercial activity within businesses. Thus, data favors not only transactional management, but also interactions and events and, as a consequence, discovery, modification and favors new behaviors or questions received ideas.

Consequently, Big Data marks a triple rupture in IS evolution: the explosion of the number of ideas available, the growing variety and the permanent renewal of this data. The processing, obviously of such data, demands much more than the processing power. It requires a break with Cartesian reasoning, to rediscover the so-called non-scientific face of human thought that is inductive reasoning [MAL 13]. This avalanche of data renders ineffective the basic data storage tools and the management of databases (such as MySQL), the preprocessing phase, which relays upon human expertise (indexing) and semantic analysis (for example modeling and decision-making intelligence) tools.

We are witnessing the use of new solutions such as:

– the investment in new storage technologies to deal with data growth;

– user access to a Big Data solution in production;

– application and testing of a Big Data solution within Cloud Computing;

– use of a database device[7];

– the application of Big Data to integrate social information;

– the application of Hadoop;

– the construction of Hadoop pilots;

– other new solutions.

Big Data creates artificial intelligence (AI), which no human can understand. From now on, algorithms and codes rule cyberspace. As these tools are updated, the nature of cyberspace changes. The application of Big Data is the perfect example of this! With processing algorithms, APIs (Application Programming Interface[8]), and "mega data", everything on the Internet becomes more complex. As data, junction points and applications multiply, become more complex and complicated, transparent regulation becomes ever more fluid.

A Big Data project consists of two parts, which are tightly interwoven, that is storage and data analysis. Analysis relies upon storage by facilitating access, storage relies upon an analysis by decreasing the volume. The inductive criteria and the promptness with which analytical solutions possess respond entirely to the demands of this operational process. These subjacent technologies which implement these changes constitute technological ruptures with the world of relational databases (see Figure 1.1).

---

7 This term designates a product, hardware or software program which allows us to respond to a need with a turnkey solution.

8 The purpose of API is to establish a connection between an application and its user. It is also in-charge of controlling the program and ensuring the interoperability of different programs and platforms.

One may thus:

– accede to limitless data, quickly, while allowing the optimization of operational mechanisms;

– use new and future data sources (connected objects, sensors, data stemming from discussion forums, social networks open-data and other such data sources;

– accelerate decision-making;

– have the ability to provide new services and applications to customers, partners and/or the general public.

Furthermore, such a phenomenon also imposes a genuine cultural revolution, owing to the fact that actors must accept the need to work with available, incomplete and quickly accessible data. In return, this imposes a need to consider, "data" as a consumable product, indeed a perishable one, which cannot necessarily be retained. Users may even be driven to modify them for a new application. This poses a number of doubts on data legitimacy, questions around its source and its traceability.

Finally, these technological ruptures change individuals' relationships with their health, by allowing everyone to become a player in it. It amounts to citizen empowerment, implied not only in the monitoring and control of health indicators, but also in the exchange and sharing of information with health service users and doctors. For health professionals, Big Data generated by patients becomes a new source of information, likely to both enrich diagnostics and sustain monitoring for observation purposes. Nowadays, connected objects, sensors and smartphones reinforce observation and reduce therapeutic inertia for individuals suffering from chronic illnesses. These NICTs develop a new doctor–patient relationship, the doctor now having to consider this new source of information whilst increasingly electronic patient files allow the recovery of this data. By improving distance monitoring, digital health data contribute to rethinking the relationship with the one's doctor, which henceforth goes beyond the traditional framework of a straightforward medical consultation. We are witnessing a sociological change, from the fact that it becomes difficult to be unaware of what is happening to the patient in the period between two medical procedures. This paradigm shift is, particularly, visible concerning chronic illnesses [POS 14].

1.2. The medical datasphere and its ecosystem

In less than two decades, the Internet and the mobile telephone have revolutionized our means of communication. Nowadays, the health sector is confronted with an important transformation, fed by the explosion of knowledge in biomedical sciences, biomechanical sciences, nanotechnology, in the field of the so-called "cyborgization"[9], in hospitals, and by the standardization of some technologies such as human genome sequencing. Henceforth, health data produced, collected and stored during the course of a patient's treatment are literally massive. These Big Data power the medical datasphere. Coupled with progress, achieved in ICT[10], this evolution around these large volumes of data looks likely to become a revolution. Key innovations and transformations are considerable, likely at the same time to reduce health expenses and to open up the way to a more connected and personalized medicine which improves both the prognosis and diagnosis of diseases.

Health professionals and patients are always looking for data relating to observed diseases, treatments and appropriate care provision or around preventative action. For such data they mainly consult websites for both information and to make enquiries. We are seeing the emergence of patient communities but also increasingly of health professionals through community platforms (whether in one or several domains) and active groups on public social networks such as Twitter, Facebook and LinkedIn. From the perspective of care facilities, the Web has become an essential tool in the doctor–patient relationship. This is happening by means of both website tools and services and an increased presence on social media such as YouTube, Twitter or on Facebook. These communities of health professionals favor sharing, particularly clinical cases or expertise, multidisciplinary collaboration, or similar activities between colleagues and fellow professionals.

Moreover the digital era has contributed to the convergence of well-being, prevention, care and drugs pathways, thus enlarging the health

9 This term translates the implantation within patients' bodies of neuro-prosthetics to fight against neuro-degeneration or tetraplegia.
10 Cloud Computing, search engines, Data Mining techniques, very large databases, data centers, Open Data and search engine spiders. Multi-agent automatic spider data systems, CRM (Customer Relationship Management), profiling, and innovative approaches to data acquisition, semantic Web tools, connected objects, bioinformatics, biometric mechanisms, and informational nanotechnologies represent essential elements upon which Big Data rests.

ecosystem to new arrivals such as Big Tech (Samsung, Philips, Apple, etc.), big Internet players (Facebook, Google, Twitter, Amazon, Apple, and so on), and start-ups stemming from the so-called "Quantified Self" (Glooko, iHealth, Withings, Bodycap, Scandu and others – see Figure 1.2) [ENG 13]. To these players, we may add all of the other Big Data pathway protagonists, namely;

Within the Information Technology sector:

– specialists in Data, Big Data solutions being MapR, Teradata, EMC, Hortonworks;

– historical solution suppliers being Oracle, IBM, HP, SAP, and similar integrators;

– integrators being Atos, CapGemini, Accenture, Sopra, and others.

Within the Big Data analytical sector:

– specialist suppliers being Zettaset, Datameer and others;

– BI editors being Qliktech, SAS and Micro-strategy and similar.

We note that numerous PME specialists within Big Data have emerged. Historically, the first were: Captain Dash, Criteo, Tiny Clues, and Squid (for data analysis), Dataiku and Hurence (concerning Big Data equipment and software), and Ysance (for data advice).

This reshuffling of the cards around these new actors favors the perspective of a product lifecycle which is much longer than previously. The so-called Big players and Big Tech companies are developing a multitude of mobile platforms which rely upon health or well-being data[11]. In the United States, the number of partnerships between Apple and American hospitals focused upon this type of data platform does not stop multiplying across the territory. Value creation in the spread and provision of digital interfaces and the flows through these operators will both promote and ensure that further fruit is borne from the "data" within the digital health ecosystem.

---

11 For example: Microsoft HealthVault, Samsung Digital Health Initiative, Apple HealthKit, Google Fit, Google Android Wear, Nike+ and others.

The market for connected applications and objects has seen exponential growth through the dynamism of Big Techs and the trend for digital health services which are accessible from anywhere, anytime. The development of smartphones and the scaling-down of sensors have made improvements possible in both the monitoring and sharing of health data using applications which are increasingly ergonomic and adapted. Thus, better support is available, especially for chronic illnesses making health care, dosage adjustments and control of side-effects more efficient.

These connected objects produce data (also called "Small Data" which both power and enrich Big Data, and at the same time the medical datasphere. They comprise various forms and applications (pedometers, scales or online blood pressure monitors) and are accessible to a large number of people. We are witnessing an increasingly significant automation of numerous physical, biological or clinical parameters, like blood pressure, weight, movement, oxygen saturation, heart rate, body temperature, forced exhalation, walking, glycaemia and sleep, etc. Consequently, new technologies offer the opportunity of providing support to the patient, on the one hand during observation and monitoring, monitoring his illness, coaching, education therapy, and on the other hand to the health professional during medical practice while making a diagnosis, tools to assist medical decision-making, medical prevention, epidemiological treatments and screening, treatment adaptation, trends in health care utilization, training, among others. As a consequence, the relevance of data gathered varies significantly according to user profile and the context.

In these circumstances, the global volume of mobile health and well-being applications has gone from 6,000 in 2010 to 1,00,000 in 2013. Irrespective of function, on average a shop such as the AppStore has approximately 500 new applications every month. These health and well-being applications are intended more largely for the general public than for health professionals. However, this trend may be reversing markedly. As regards connected objects, there are approximately 15 billion worldwide. This figure may reach figures between 80 to 100 billion between now and 2020 [CNO 15]. Consequently, all of this technology associated with Big Data in the health sphere is an opportunity to work out a less traumatic and expensive, and far more preventive, participative and personalized form of medicine.

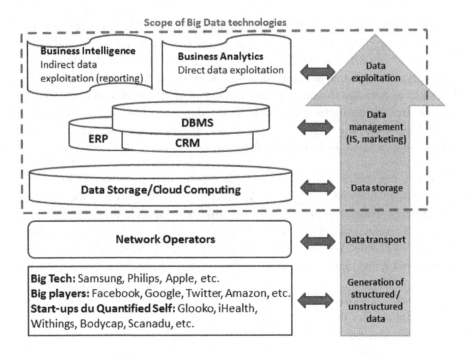

Figure 1.2. *Scope of Big Data technologies and actors*

1.2.1. *Medicine 4.0*

One of the main sources of change within the health system is the computerization, digitalization and technical networking affecting management, organization, care provision and service delivery at one and the same time. The technological progress achieved makes it possible to process, store and disseminate information, in all its forms, written, oral or visual, thereby being increasingly unencumbered by all constraints of distance, volume and time. Started in the majority of industrial countries from the beginning of 1980s, the implementation of ICT relies increasingly evidently upon the diverse changes which continue in the health field [CAR 01].

Health data may be generated by HISs (Hospital Information Systems), smartphone health applications [BOY 12], health social network platforms [COS 14, LUP 14], monitoring technologies [MIT 11, MIT 13], home-based sensors [NIE 10], forums and online clinical trial monitors. Other data are produced by the so-called "data brokers" who collect, analyze, store and sell data based on a variety of medical data coming from social media, insurance declarations, online Internet purchases, clinical data from public health organizations or other health services and medical devices [TER 12]. This new world of Big Data is permanently examining the real world with the objective of creating both foreseeability and predictability of its individual aspects. We are confronted with a future in which everything will be predicted by others, through processing and analytical algorithms and the way in which we interact through the Internet. This observation applies right across the health sector. Connected medicine provides a much better understanding of infectious illnesses than chronic illnesses at population level, innovative approaches for patient diagnosis and treatment, improvement in disease research and related their corresponding treatments, as well as the optimization of illness monitoring and risk factors. We may use the example of the so-called "extended nervous system" which is capable of detecting the first signs of an illness and carrying out the appropriate treatment or just-in-time medicine.

Hence, we are coming into the medical era known as "Version 4.0", relying upon Big Data, algorithms and expert systems so as to pave the way towards a more individualized, personalized and predictive medicine. This new medicine follows in the footsteps of the ancient medicine of Hippocrates[12] and Medicine 2.0 (also called Internet-connected medicine), seen during the period between 2000–2009.

We can use the examples of the visit to the cardiologist, which has henceforth become a "virtual consultation"; the form for monitoring dialysis data has given way to on-screen data or X-rays which have gone from "analog" to a "digital" format. Support to complete the diagnosis is no longer by way of a physical surface (the human body or a document) but a set of "superimposed computational layers" [GHI 00]. The study of digital health data, may be completed for purposes, such as clinically useful predictive models [CHO 14], personal health data monitoring [BOY 12, MIT 14, NIE 14, POL 13], and efficiency and interaction of horizontal and longitudinal health products [TEN 13].

In Los Angeles, it is thus possible to call a doctor at his home, a single click away, in less than an hour, thanks to the application "Heal". In a few

---

12 It is worth noting that the text of the Hippocratic Oath invites the doctor to perform his job with the best knowledge of the technologies of his time.

minutes, the platform connects the patient with the doctor who is closest to his home, who will come out 24 hours a day, seven days a week. We are witnessing a progressive "Uberization" of medicine where the dominance of NICTs in the delivery of many services offers greater power and opportunities to the consumer. This phenomenon has gathered pace with the emergence of Internet intermediaries and the digitization of part of the added value, which connected objects and software programs give doctors.

In the sphere of health insurance, we may proffer the business known as Oscar which captured 10% of the market share in the New York–New Jersey region in a few weeks owing to considerable understanding of technological tools through its website which is simultaneously ergonomic, clear and simple. This business offers a new model to its insureds, for example by offering connected free bracelets to its customers, by promising to reward those, who exceed 10,000 steps per day or who develop an important care network, as a result of using the Web.

Beyond the approach of the "6Vs"[13], which is both useful but highly descriptive, we may give additional clarification in terms of the destination of Big Data through what we have called the 5Ps (Prediction, Personalization, Prevention, Participation and Prognosis), which emphasizes, in a very original way, the role played by large data volumes in certain applications which are particularly relevant in medicine. These characteristics encourage us to ask a whole series of questions such as what is the added value of the term *Big* in Big Data. How can we draw maximum benefit from buying a large volume of information and what might we then extract from it? How might we handle data so as to help health professionals and researchers? Other questions arise.

The application of Big Data makes it possible to have the ability to personalize at the most detailed level of the interface offering the solution. It is a question of a thorough knowledge of a medical environment which makes it possible to configure the entire health care system, for a group specifically, of health care service users, indeed for an individual patient. The accumulation of data makes it possible to identify at risk patients, to select the best therapeutic and diagnostic strategy with the aim of optimizing early diagnosis (thus covering both the predictive and prognostic side of medicine). This form of medicine also has the aim of avoiding medical

---

13 Please see the general introduction to the book.

complications, particularly with heart and vascular diseases, which affect quality of life and patient prognosis (this being the preventive aspect more than the curative aspect of medicine).

In these circumstances, the field of possibilities is considerable and, nowadays, we can foresee only the significant transformations that the advent of digital within the health sphere will produce. This convergence between technological innovation and scientific research, between digital, mathematics and medical progress, will have direct repercussions upon medical practice which up to now has been based predominantly around medical procedures.

In addition, the image of people spending time on information websites through frequent use of health applications on smartphones, is progressively as common as health service users increasingly wishing to become responsible for their own their health (the participative aspect of medicine).

The emergence of this connected and predictive medicine cannot survive without:

– the standardization of exchange formats between medical devices;

– the development of a sector of businesses and start-ups linked to connected objects and Big Data in the health sphere the alteration of medical protocols to support prevention within the health sector;

– working out how trained medical professionals can be alive to NICTs within the health care sector; and

– the growth of health data terms of use regulation.

Consequently, this personalized medicine brings into play numerous clinicians and researchers, particularly in chemistry and molecular biology. It particularly is based on the analysis of an enormous quantity of data, for example biological and genomic data[14], medical imaging, texts and unstructured data, which features in medical reports, questionnaires, and other hospital registers, non-genetic markers such as biomarkers, bone density or the body mass index, and even data linked to the environment, reporting symptoms by Tweets through social networks.

---

14 It may be noted that the human genome is not the only one to be taken into consideration but also the genome of the bacteria found in intestinal flora.

To this, we may add the "Small Data" of the "Quantified Self" which supply physiological and environmental information through mobile patient probes. The integration of biological data, for each individual, gives hope to both health researchers and professionals, who wish to improve the treatment of the patient, but also boost disease prevention. The consolidation of data, indeed, will make possible better monitoring and improve the knowledge of the impact of different factors and optimize patient care from prevention to long-term monitoring. We are in an era of "disease management".

This trend around personalized medicine evolved jointly with the appearance of new analytical technologies, such as new generation fast and low-cost DNA sequencing; NICTs have also made the interpretation of large quantities of data possible. From now on, the idea of expert systems processing in record time approximately 10,000 billion pieces of data from DNA sequencing emanating from a tumor, introduces the concept for any given patient, of an entire team of experienced doctors, now being unequal to the task.

We may take the case of the Danish bioinformatics specialists who have produced a stratification of patients based upon their medical history, for cardiac diseases or diabetes, by means of patient monitoring over several decades. To do so, they use processing algorithms which were not based on causality but around correlations which were, hitherto, not been observed. The objective here was not to understand the "Why" but simply the "How". IBM estimates that continuous analysis of an individual's personal health data reduces his chances of death from a given condition by 20%.

Moreover, Big Data improves danger or risk recognition and, if possible, prevents it. Thus, beyond the concept of forward-looking, the objectiveis to define what the risk is or what represents a potential danger, so as to apply in real-time both a clinical scheme and modified behavior. We can cite the example of the American actress Angelina Jolie who successively in May 2013 underwent a double mastectomy, then in March 2015 ovary and fallopian tube removal, having learned, after genome sequencing, that she was carrying a mutation in the gene BRCA1, leading to a risk of greater than 90% of developing a cancer in the following ten years. In Texas, the business Seton Healthcare Family put in place a predictive analytical algorithm so as to limit the risks of patient re-hospitalization. The private hospital group indicated "decreased risks, costs and even mortality rates but did not supply exact figures" [HIS 15][15].

The Khoo Teck Puat hospital in Singapore is able to predict patients presenting a significant risk of readmission by studying patient hospital readmissions on more than two occasions within a period of 26 month. This analytical model makes it possible to anticipate a meticulous care-burden by targeting the program of hospital home visits in a more effective way. The researchers are resorting to Big Data so as to study genetic and environmental factors entailed in multiple sclerosis so as to research personalized treatment. The hospital group Aurora Healthcare established in Wisconsin, in 2012, commenced a Big Data program to identify secondary effects of therapeutic treatments. These studies show that there would be a 10% lower readmission rate and a six million dollar economy with treatment costs reduced by 42%.

In France, we are witnessing the emergence of Big Data-related partnerships particularly, seen at the end of 2014:

– between *AP-HP*[16], Quinten[17] and Le Laboratoire Roche[18] with the intention of better understanding and recognizing the disparities within the same illness;

– currently in 2015, between the prestigious École Polytechnique and the CNAMTS (*Caisse Nationale d'Assurance Maladie des Travailleurs Salariés*)[19], with the development of algorithms around public health issues, by drawing from the thousands of terabytes which the Caisse Nationale has available. The objective is to detect both missed signals and anomalies in pharmaco-epidemiology, and identify practical factors so as to better analyze health pathways and fight against fraud and abuse.

---

15 *Des Systèmes d'Information Hospitaliers et de la E-santé* ("Hospital Information Systems and e-Health").

16 This is the *Assistance Publique Hôpitaux de Paris* – the group of hospitals within the Ile de France region.

17 This is a company which ensures the implementation of effective customer data strategies.

18 This is a world-leading company in health sector R&D.

19 The organization's aims include ensuring the availability of health insurance legal frameworks for all illnesses and accidents at work, while promoting awareness of the same and the control of medical expenditure by health professionals.

Such applications are becoming integrated into a new style of medical practice and a "business model" which is centered on preventive procedures, the reduction of health expenses, in favor of outpatient treatment and by reducing long-stay hospital care.

However, Big Data should not just be used with a view to reducing costs but represent an important lever for continuous improvement in health care. The collection and mass utilization of clinical parameters and physiological data thus, has the potential to profoundly transform the health insurance markets.

This is why from the end of 2013, the-then Executive Chairman of Google, Eric Schmidt, during a conference predicted, "Insurance is the industry which is, most apparently, on the brink of seeing Big Data uses exploding". In reality, nowadays, insurance as an industry is simply in the process of exploding. Big Data and data interpretation, particularly genetic data, has completely overturned traditional models of health insurance. Predictive medicine and algorithms have made it possible for insurers to reduce the risks by becoming experts in personalized health prevention. This is why insurance professionals have promoted programs encouraging individuals to equip themselves with sensors and to subscribe to personal genetics projects, thus saving thousands of lives as a result of the trial "Pre-emptive Strikes against Illnesses" [CNI 14]. This is why Google has invested in the health sphere through, for example, the recent updating of its medical encyclopedia comprising more than 900 references to diseases. The investment fund, Google Ventures, nowadays manages two billion dollars worth of assets and has notably taken under its wing start-ups such as 23andMe (which specializes in genetic testing), Foundation Medicine (which specializes in genetic cancer profiling) and further DNAnexus (specializing in exchange and analysis of genetic data).

That apart, regarding support with medical decisions, IBM has launched the Artificial Intelligence IT program "Watson", which is capable of analyzing all patient medical information. It also cross-references such information with millions of other files to make a diagnosis and prescribe the best treatment, which the software ensures is the least costly for the health insurance organization. This IT program has the ability to understand speech and to find the issue within a processing time, which compares to that of a human being. It uses the software Hadoop to cover a large quantity of content. Watson evaluates the probability that the response that it expands upon is the right one responding only if such probability is considered high enough. Watson is, for example, useful within the sphere of medical diagnosis. By analyzing symptoms and medical data supplied by a doctor (through speech) and accumulated knowledge (medical dictionaries, scientific literature and case studies, etc.) by using "Machine Learning" technology which makes it possible to learn from previous diagnoses, Watson offers a medical diagnosis which is both evaluated on the basis of probability and with clarified reasoning. For patients, such an expert system resonates as the promise of a quicker and more precise diagnosis, even of entirely personalized treatment. Henceforth, doctors will be able to analyze billions of pieces of data where nowadays they make their diagnosis on a handful of data. A tumor genome requires the analysis of thousands of billions of pieces of data which only expert systems can process. In these circumstances, we might of course envisage that tomorrow's doctors will sign prescriptions completed through treatment algorithms, as Dr Laurent Alexandre, the founder of DNA Vision predicted. It is worth noting that IBM announced, on 6 August 2015 that it had acquired Merge Healthcare, Cloud services editor specialized in the management of medical imaging for a billion dollars. As a result to this, the Watson supercomputer will soon be able to manage medical images via its AI platform on top of health data which it continuously stores up and analyzes, particularly within cardiology or orthopedics. As a consequence, IBM announced the creation of a specialist entity Watson Health which brings together around 2,000 individuals in Boston in collaboration with Johnson & Johnson[20] Medtronic[21] and Apple.

Finally, the American giants Apple and IBM joined forces to launch in collaboration, the Watson Health Cloud platform, intended to host anonymous data gathered by the Apple HealthKit software and by the Apple ResearchKit module with the aim of including users who wish to be involved in scientific research and clinical trials [JAC 15]. Moreover, Apple led discussions with two insurers, so as to use information collected by users of its application "Health", to draw up tailor–made insurance contracts.

The company Flatiron Health[22] conceived a Big Data solution called "OncologyCloud" based upon the idea that 96% of data potentially available around patients affected with cancer had not yet been analyzed. The aim of

---

20 A company which produces, innovative health care solutions among others.
21 This manufactures health technology products.
22 This US start-up collects oncology data with a view to providing data pipelines, infrastructures and software to cancer centers, doctors, researchers and patients.

this service is to take data collected during both diagnosis and treatment; and make it available to clinicians working on cancer-based studies.

In addition, according to the edition of the French daily newspaper *Le Figaro*, 18 July 2015, the Food and Drug Administration (FDA) started consultations with the search engine Google recently, the information being current as of June 2015, so as to use its data to identify unknown secondary effects of drugs. Millions of patients research the Internet concerning both their symptoms and appropriate treatments. Moreover, among these health-assistance users many make requests about problems other than the diseases for which they are being treated. These are investigations which are of interest to the American agency as they can inform them about unidentified secondary effects at the time of clinical trials. The latter are only carried out on a few thousand patients before these treatments are placed on the market and they do not thus find every problem. The FDA is also interested in other projects such as those of Microsoft, which runs the search engine Bing. In 2013, its researcher Eric Horvitz and scientists from Stanford[23] revealed that using the anti-cholesterol medication Pravachol and the anti-depressant Paroxetine, could often lead to a problem with hyperglycemia. Their study led to six million requests from Internet users over a one-year period. It showed that the Internet users, who made both requests for the anti-cholesterol tablet and the anti-depressant, were doing twice as much research upon hyperglycemia than who only searched for one of these treatments.

Furthermore, the two companies Apple and IBM collaborated recently around a major health data platform which will make it possible for Apple iPhone users to monitor the data-sharing with the Watson application. The objective is to discover new medical perspectives of potential user real-time activity for biometric data. However, the issue of Big Data does not simply end the concept of individual health. In terms of public health, the exploitation of these massive volumes of data contributes to the development of new health products, to the detection of missed signals during an epidemic or serious undesirable effects and other health-related aspects.

This metadata makes the analysis and exploitation of the behavior of thousands of individuals possible through the overlapping of complex correlations, and anticipating certain phenomena such as, for example, flu.

---

23 Stanford University, California.

Indeed the analysis of this volume of data makes it possible to put into place predictive algorithms. The large scale processing of Big Data permits, for example, the anticipation of a flu epidemic. Google Flu Trends achieved this by combining research terms in the search engine Google and relating them to current health predictions. According to [VIK 13], "Google's software found a combination of 45 research terms which, when used together within a mathematical model, form a strong correlation between both predictions and official figures". Thus in 2009, Google helped the American health authorities, as a result of a model which made it possible to predict the development of the epidemic of the flu strain H5N1 precisely.

Google, through its Google Flu Trends tools, takes all searches carried out on the search engine and then measure how many times the term "flu", "gastro-enteritis" or "chickenpox" has been researched and the number of times; the search engine measures this by reference to both the largest possible number of years and the largest possible number of countries. They, in fact realized, by measuring such aspects, that people had a tendency to search for information upon influenza or another illness when they thought that they had similar symptoms. In the large majority of cases, they did have them. What is noted, in practical terms, is that when Google announced a particular concentration of searches about a flu pandemic, it was thought that this concentration happened approximately two weeks too late. In summary, Google succeeds in anticipating, predicting and foreseeing two weeks in advance the health monitoring alerts for medical organizations. In the short term, a permanent Internet connection makes it possible to identify health risk factors according to our behaviors and browsing habits. Big Data thus, authorizes large-scale non-commercial dissemination of public health messages so as to warn of the risks of chronic illnesses worldwide. We may predict a scientific study involving very large-scale analysis of the Internet behavior of individuals affected with chronic illnesses such as diabetes so as to identify thepossibility of correlations between surfing habits and risk factors. We might also be able to identify which types of diseases will come to light if, as individuals, we consume given food types.

Moreover, a permanent geo-localization of connected applications and supports (telephones, tablets and computers) may favor a more precise understanding of Internet users' lifestyles[24] and invite such users to

_____

24 In this way, receipts might include purchase nutritional values and our telephone applications might guide us towards healthier habits.

download health applications on smartphones encouraging people to undertake a sport activity, briefs upon food calorific values often being underestimated or little-known.

Twitter also decided to capitalize on its role as a public utility by making it possible to plot the spread of the influenza virus in January 2013. With more than 500 million tweets per day, Twitter has numerous data threads from which we undertake extract studies.

Big Data also contribute to the fight against the spread of epidemics. In Africa, mobile telephone geo-localization data have been shown as highly invaluable as a means to track population movements through actual population shifts, and thus to anticipate disease development at national level. This made it possible to predict the spread of the Ebola virus. These strategies also tried to follow the Haiti earthquake where they were used to help plan intended victim disaster relief shipments.

Consequently, "massive data" implying a large cohort of patients, also has the potential to accelerate scientific research and experimental protocols for many diseases and treatments. For example, researchers particularly used the social network site Facebook to establish a map of Americans with the greatest leaning towards obesity. Such wide-ranging research would take considerable time and would cost a fortune through a classic investigative survey on the scale of millions of individuals.

In addition, the start-up Flation Health aims to collect data upon cancer treatment and to provide essential knowledge to cancer centers, practitioners, researchers and the sick which is necessary to take the right medical decisions. Data gathered correspond to population statistics, refunds and treatments provided which are gathered by health centers, doctors' practices, hospitals and insurance companies through a Cloud Computing system. This data is made available to hospital and independent practitioners, researchers, and care centers so as to assist with treatment decisions. Health professionals may thus have access to relevant data and high-quality statistics to take better informed decisions upon the appropriate treatments. It may be observed that the overlapping of DNA sequencing data, declared diseases and living environment (profession type, dwelling and other factors) will specifically allow for improved understanding of epigenetic mechanisms[25]. The analysis of this data will achieve its full potential as long as it can be cross-referenced with other sources, for example stemming from treatments, diseases and possibly even genetic information.

Moreover, "clustering" which is the ability to make up homogenous groups following a given criteria may become one of the important commitments of Big Data within the health sphere within the years to come. We can cite the case of the start-up CardioLogs (which was recently chosen in the Global Innovation Competition) which developed an automatic diagnostic tool to interpret ECGs (electro-cardiograms) using the principles of Big Data. The originality of this approach stems from the technology used: The algorithms used learn from highly voluminous ECG "Datasets" whose analysis and interpretation is carried out beforehand and digitized by cardiology teams. They represent classification algorithms for cardiac diseases. Based upon the analysis of the entire signal from all of these ECGs and associated diagnoses, the tool will build groups (or clusters). These consist of "normal" ECG patients, those presenting with a given disease, and other aspects. Thereafter, whenever it is presented with a new ECG reading, the CardioLogs tool is able to say to which category it belongs or whether it does not belong to any category. Finally, the algorithm is capable of revealing its interpretation according to category, that is to say, setting out a diagnosis, even formulating hypotheses on the patient's condition which should be remedied by further examination (for example an ultrasound scan, blood test or another test).

This solution, offering cardiovascular diagnostic assistance, functions in real time from technology uniting medical knowledge to "Machine Learning". The purpose of the service thus consists of optimizing patient care for cardiovascular disorders.

Consequently, the majority of Big Data rests upon Big Data and uses the concept of forecasting. How should, the data, be exploited so as to anticipate conditions better. How might data and knowledge be sufficiently accumulated so as to be able to predict needs, problems and behaviors, and other such issues?

---

25 Epigenetics is the diverse expression of genes according to the environment. In other words, two individuals carrying the same gene may or may not develop an illness depending on the influence of the environment upon this gene.

Thus, personalized medicine does not only define what the most appropriate patient treatment is but also makes it possible to detect risks and offer a preventive solution. Generally, Big Data favors the understanding of health problems, diseases, treatment efficiency and organizations. This massive data favors detailed studies of the health system so as to optimize, even overturn preventive medicine to predictive and participative medicine particularly with increasingly detailed prognoses. This will only contribute to the creation of standards which are intended for public health and research based on the "data" [SAF 06, STE 13].

Certain Net giants such as Apple and Google are starting up within this niche market through the mobile Health application and the Google Fit platform, making "data" centralization of many health applications which are available on Smartphones possible. By centralizing health data collected, the latter may well be essential as the main future intermediaries between health users and traditional actors in the health market. This context will both create and bring in new professionals, so-called "data scientists", within the medical sphere thus signaling a resurgence of the medical function in future years.

1.2.2. *The "Quantified Self" and Small Data*

With the advent of health applications on smartphone, the use of an automatic digital measuring system linked with the trend of the "Quantified Self", being a type of biological "selfie" which increasingly invades our daily life. This trend was established in 2007 in the United States by two journalists of the magazine *American Wired*, Gary Wolf and Kevin Kelly. It is regarded as understanding oneself thanks to the aggregation of these physiological data coming from interconnected objects. We are witnessing a real data flood, carrying a data quantity which may be close to several hundred billion bytes. Data interacts and swirls around us so to become part of us. Collection, analysis, understanding exchange and sharing of data lead the individual irremediably towards the active process of analysis bringing together both data and information technology. Data produced by mobile health applications are known as "Small Data". Contrary to telemedicine or self-measuring, the Quantified Self is not born of protocols validated by clinical studies but of the fruitful meeting between technological innovations. It thus involves the availability of sensors and portable information processing systems such as smartphones, and citizen needs, which combines social networks and "patient empowerment". This technological tendency is not neutral simply from the fact that it transforms our relationship with the world and with people, and influences our habits, our daily ways of life and as well as our uses.

Thus, with Big Data and the Quantified Self, it might be envisaged that the continuous accumulation of data produces consciousness. Thus self-conscientiousness no longer exists, as such, as it is no longer understood and is simply the sum of our perceptions.

At present, there are more than 97,000 conventional mHealth applications in online stores, and around 1000 new applications are brought out each month [BEC 14]. In the following years, it is estimated that there will be 3,000,000 free downloads and 300,000 downloads sold which will relate to mHealth applications in the United States [VIG 14].

Certain health applications may be intended for health professionals so as to achieve a large number of daily medical tasks such as calculating medical doses, consulting medical files, accessing clinical referrals and supporting medical decisions [PAT 12, MAR 15]. According to Mobin Yasini and Guillaume Marchand (2015), six major categories of professional use may be listed as follows:

– medical consultation around reference data (such as medical manuals, health news and other forms of reference);

– educational tools such as *Serious Game pour la Formation*[26];

– communication and/or sharing of information (for example, an application in a discussion forum, a consultation platform for doctors and other such means);

– management of professional activities (such as researching job vacancies, calculating tax and other such activities);

– in response to a contextual need (for example, using the mobile device as a diagnostic tool, a reminder in the decision aid system and such other contextual needs);

– health management (such as management of the stock of medication, locating the nearest health service, and other forms of health management).

---

26 "Serious game for training".

Other health applications concerning the wider public in particular the average health user are defined in [GAR 14, CAR 13]. Consequently, mHealth has introduced an anthropological communication transformation in their *couplage au corps*[27] program with a use threshold which is much more accessible than the computer [BOU 06]. These solutions, mobile applications and connected objects contribute to:

– facilitating daily monitoring of patient health indicators, screening, the prevention of complications for individuals by chronic illnesses and autonomy and keeping the dependent elderly in their own homes;

– maintaining a practice over time (self-regulatory behavior);

– being able to compare their data with that of other users, so as to place themselves in relation to the rest of the population;

– completing clinical research trials without forcing the "guinea pig" to be hospitalized for three days, measuring heart rates, body temperature and other tests may be achieved from a distance, which creates more patient comfort and even makes the study more realistic so patients may go about their business;

– reducing the "white coat effect", such as for example increased tension during a medical consultation;

– favoring exchanges, communication and cooperation between professionals and health teams;

– reducing the number of appointments and relieves congestion in surgeries;

– improving the communication, the contact with and patient education upon treatment. The patient will thus will thus be more knowledgeable about his disease and better prepared to speak with the doctor, hence a better understanding on the part of the health user;

– favoring data access, knowledge, the training of health professionals and research.

The principle of the Quantified Self[28] is to be able to both collect and download measurements, data and health condition parameters (the rate of oxygen in the blood, temperature, tension, weight, nutrition, and other parameters). This new practice has made possible the generation of automated

---

27 "Connection to the body".
28 This is the Socratic promise of "Know you, know yourself" of the modern age.

and continuous personal data, and constitutes a form of massive data collection around individual practices heretofore unseen. These digital self-measurement systems represent a major challenge, especially in the health-sphere, where it contributes to the development of personalized medicine. The "quantification" tools aim to put into figures the maximum information relating to the human body, whether this relates to physical performance, behaviors, emotions or even Man's capacity to understand [CNI 14]. The Quantified Self represents an aide to understanding through data, how we both improve and correct potential shortcomings or problems, which the individual may encounter. Self-evaluation by means of technology focuses for many on medical self-monitoring. Self-evaluation translates into a reflexive attitude, which makes both an awareness of one's actions and critical self-evaluation possible. This approach which forces the subject to look at and analyze himself, to search within his own problems makes it possible to identify avenues for future action and to develop reflected and autonomous behavior.

Digital self-evaluation may be the source of personal and professional progress, as long as the user of the connected object pushes its own limits, and excels itself. The discovery of learner autonomy is inextricably linked to self-evaluation. Acquiring autonomy involves having self-confidence, taking responsibility for our own actions and reassuring the individuals who surround us. Consequently, comparisons may be inferred both from the examination and personal interpretation of data. These comparative measurements reveal rules which have a social common ground. This quantification represents an actual management tool for the individual, which relies on standards, criteria and benchmark data.

In these circumstances this new practice and approach to medicine has the consequence of providing the health service user with both a personalized and targeted understanding of his state of health. Data constitutes a mediation tool, which makes it possible for individuals to be both self-reliant and reliant upon others. This quantification is not limited to an individual action, but is also achieved through user interactions. The qualitative angle is preponderant in both the acceptance and significance of this approach. The communicating dimension is vital for the product user through both efficient and effective use. In other words, the connected object must include, on the one hand, a technological purpose based around accounting for the mechanism in place, while a human purpose focused upon suitability, adoption and use of the object on the other. In the light of these observations, it appears vital that cross-consultations take place between inventors, businesses, institutions and users to ensure that this personalized medicine is focused around the processing of personal digital health data. With the advent of connected objects and digital links [CAS 10], the patient is becoming active in his own health increasingly, as a result of the processing of this new type of personal data, which will modify the doctor–patient relationship directly, particularly with respect of the Knowledge–Power duality. By processing his own health data, the user has the feeling of having self-control and gaining autonomy, quenching a thirst for knowledge and once again, being in control of his health care decisions. It might be presumed that this relationship between patients and careers is directed towards a shared medical decision which is both preventive and predictive, based on examining collected quantities of medical data.

Consequently, the integration of an object-based mobile application makes it possible to synchronize and incorporate health data into a dashboard (DB) so as to obtain:

– historical data (for observing the development of a parameter);

– the interpretation of "data";

– showing correlations between the different types of data collected;

– sharing data measured and having the possibility of comparing it with other data.

Contemporary medicine will henceforth undergo the use of connected health objects so as to measure parameters such as weight loss, blood pressure, respiratory exchange with the skin, heart rate, physical activities, or chronic illnesses (these being diabetes[29], chronic fatigue, stress, etc.). Smartphones natively integrate many modern sensors [BEN 13], especially biosensors, which are specific to the medical field which record biological and clinical parameters. It is the era of the so-called "Internet of Things" integrating probes, connectivity and infrared, with communicating terminals (the iPhone, iPad, laptop computer, Google Glass, or similar devices), Machine To Machine (for example, servers and objects), and the Internet of things (for example cars, home automation, distribution, etc.). According to

---

29 Glooko is a medical application that allows us to link a smartphone with a blood glucose level self-measurement tool. The data which flows from this mobile health application are aggregated and then stored on Glooko's servers. Practitioner data consultation is predicted using a dedicated interface.

[MIC 14], it is possible to identify four key capabilities of connected objects associated with Big Data being remote control, optimization, monitoring and autonomy. The mechanisms make it possible to collect data, analyze them, and to display them with a clear explanation, and cross-reference this data with other data, detecting potential anomalies, while improving analysis models and algorithms along the way.

Communicating objects have the ability for data exchange with other objects. They were able to develop rapidly thanks to constant progress within wireless telecommunication and microelectronics. According to predictions, their numbers could reach 25 billion (Gartner), 50 billion (Cisco & Ericsson), or even 75 billion (Morgan Stanley) by 2020. It was estimated that the potential market for mobile Health application users would go from one billion in 2012 to 3.4 billion in 2017, according to the American institute Research2guidance. By 2017, it is estimated that each smartphone user will have acquired at least one downloaded application. In its report "Disruptive Technologies", the consultancy firm McKinsey considers that the health field will represent between a third and a half of the global economic impact of connected objects by 2025.

The latest 2014 barometer from the partnership organization Vidal-French National Medical Council[30] shows us that the use of the smartphone as a doctor's prescription-aid has grown considerably from 34% of doctors in 2012 to 64% in 2014. Health-assistance professionals can no longer ignore these digital technological advances, and should henceforth run with them by integrating them into their medical practices. The next generation of health professionals will entirely favor the use of NICTs and digital medical data for preventive, or even predictive, interventions and no longer simply curative interventions. Thus, after processing and correlation by appropriate algorithms, part of this unstructured raw data, might provide highly interesting data and indicators to improve care and the optimization of patient quality of life. According the report by the market research firm Suisse Soron Research which was published in October 2014, so-called "Wearable" connected objects can save approximately 1.3 million lives between now and 2020. Nearly 700,000 lives will be saved, thanks to accessories used in health establishments, so as to supervise patients' states of health and any disease developments.

---

30 Vidal specializes in prescription support services and benchmark information on health products and the French National Medical Council (FNMC) regulates the French medical profession.

By improving his knowledge of the patient, the doctor is placed better to bring about more appropriate and personalized treatment choices. A diabetic will no longer enter his blood sugar level in a log book which will, instead, be measured using a connected sensor that will store the data, send it to the health professional and release an alert signal if the evaluation is too high.

In addition, these connected objects take different forms and are known as intelligent objects, such as sensors, watches, bracelets, mobilephones, glasses, etc. which recognize, build up and exchange data between them, through telecommunications devices and sensor networks. Smartphones and touch pads set up as new hubs, having the function of a remote control for connected objects but also as primary interface for data consultation. Each month around 3,000 connected objects applications come onto the market. Until now, the major actors in electronic and data "devices" have predominantly been focused around fitness and well-being data, not wholeheartedly buying into the highly regulated world of health. However once their technology is sufficiently accurate and reliable to be tested by the *Agence Nationale de Sécurité du Médicament et des Produits de Santé* (ANSM)[31] and/or the FDA (Food and Drug Administration), and when their data collection, centralization and storage platforms for digital data conform to health regulations, they can really take on the medical devices market. An example of this is Toshiba which was not slow to do so with its tracker intended for use by doctors.

It is possible to identify several types of applications and connected objects in the field of health:

– therapeutic and good practice guides (InfectioGuide, Médicaments, OrcaHealth, Natom Viewer, etc.);

– medical procedure costs (Fees);

– calculations and medical scores (MedCalc Pro, Gaz du sang, Withings, and others);

– well-being applications (RunKeeper, Runtastic Pro, Nike+, Endomondo, and others);

31"National Agency for Medical Safety and Health Products".

– first aid and emergency first aid (*Arrêt Cardiaque*[32] 2.0, Urgences1clic, and others);

– applications which monitor weight, stress, blood sugar levels[33], oxygen, heart rate, blood pressure, sleep, remote patient treatment, children's lung capacity, and other health issues (Zeo, Tactio Santé, WakeMate, Samsung Gear, Fitbit Flex, Jawbone Up, Withings Pulse, MyBasis, Smart Body Analyzer, Scanadu, Sony Smartband, NeuroOn, iOximeter, Imedipac, Do-Pill SecuR, Medsecure Sivan, My Spiroo, and other such organizations);

– prevention applications (for example, against the risk of AIDS);

– connected objects which allow older people or handicapped individuals to stay at home (robotics and so-called "exoskeletons" or similar);

– pacemakers, thermometers (MyThermo), glasses (GoogleGlass), connected lenses (Google/Novatis), watch (Apple Watch[34]), connected glasses (AuxiVia), connected toothbrushes (Power Toothbrush or Kolibree), bracelets measuring physical activity (Bitbrick band), good walking posture (Arki), or calories consumed (GoBe);

– geo-localization systems (electronic devices, mobile telephones, etc.) for confused older people or those suffering from Alzheimer's disease (Aloïse IGL tag, Columbia Medical Intelligence bracelet, Locate Box, MobilAlarm (which is a European project));

– the surgical robot developed by Google and the pharmaceutical group Johnson & Johnson offers surgeons less invasive and more precise tools;

– the smart key Pill'up which attaches to medicine boxes to remind patients to take their treatment;

– systems of artificial intelligence capable of analyzing all patient medical information, and to cross-reference them with millions of other files to make a diagnosis and prescribe the best treatment. Software ensures that it will be the least costly as possible for a partnering health care insurance company (for

---

32"Cardiac Arrest".

33 New interpretations of glycemia used within the context of treatments for diabetes of course make it possible to measure patient sugar levels but also to regulate insulin injections through regular control supervised by a doctor.

34 Apple Watch is involved in health research projects through wrist sensors so as to measure and monitor physical activity and heartbeat.

example IBM's software for Watson); and other technology similar to those mentioned above.

Starting from connected objects, health applications and data, that is retrieved, the patient is led to ask a series of socio-cognitive questions around the relationships and gaps between the user, technology and the data flowing from them:

– what are the repercussions of ICT on the health user throughout his lifetime?

– should our habits and our body movements which both distinguish and personalize us be dependent upon values and master data which are common to everyone?

– can the user fall into a type of so-called "normopathy" (a norm-related illness)[35]? who is the rightful owner of this data?

– how can personal health data which is exchanged through connected objects become anonymized?

– where are "data" actually stored?

– do health application users have any real control over their data?

– is the patient aware of the potential resale of his data?

– does the Quantified Self risk discriminating against followers who will never be as successful and optimal?

– are the averages resulting from algorithms legitimate?

– how are the new reference values, which serve as a guide for user's daily actions, both constructed and validated?

– is our data a projection of ourselves?

– do they sum up our identity?

– what do we learn from them?

– how might we make sense of them?

– how should we set about doing it?

---

35 Language, thoughts and standardized behaviors, in view of performance and efficiency lose all capacity for challenge as soon as life itself becomes a program that is integrated into an immense headless machinery itself [BUI 03].

– how might we convert this data into self-initiative?

– how might we modify our habits according to this data?

– does this multiplication and flood of health applications on smartphones truly take account of the needs and demands of users?

– should decisions made by e-health platforms prevail over human decision-making?

– how can we trust this raw data, which is produced "from the bottom up" in large quantities, if it is not based upon a prescriptive and conventional framework of both proven and recognized recording?

For the most part, users of Quantified Self devices, have a lack of knowledge related to problems surrounding personal data protection owing to a disinformation and the low level of information around how such things work. In these circumstances, general confidentiality and medical confidentiality remain the main parameter for a particular reticence towards the development of connected devices in the health sector. Self-evaluation associated with a quest for achieving perfectionist normativity leads to an increasing exposure of everyone's private life, even everyone's intimacy. A lot of sensitive health data, which is produced by sensors or smartphone applications, should remain confidential and only be accessible to its user and the authorized health care professionals. Confidentiality, therefore, remains one of the user prerogatives. By way of necessity, this leads us to question the means of data storage, their re-use for other purposes, even their appropriation by the publishers of mobile applications or other connected objects [SAV 15]. This is the reason why connected objects should integrate secure gateways (through cryptography) between the "data" source and destination which they both disseminate and receive.

For Jacques Lucas [LUC 15], "...we need to ensure that we do not see new reasons emerging to depend on these connected objects. It is important that the sick or even the healthy do not end up surrounded with "health sensors" which could provide them with all sorts of data with that they would not know what to do or which might, quite wrongly, make them worry. We need to be conscious of the possible development of a kind of 'cyber-chondria'".

According to the French attorney Omar Yahia, [YAH 14], "...this data should be subject to a particular legal regime" giving rise to the following questions:

– what will be the role of health data hosts? In view of sharing, traceability and accessibility for all, do health data mean that organizations may re-use data as they see fit?

– is it necessary to lay down data use restrictions?

– is it necessary to obtain free and informed consent from health application and/or connected objects users, so as to exploit these data commercially?

– so as to guarantee data confidentiality [HAM 13], would it not be necessary to institute a password-based or certificate-based authentication, indeed even voice recognition trusted by the relevant connected object?

– does reduced manufacturer data access encounter RFID chip deactivation or equivalent mechanisms which equip these objects?

As many unanswered questions mark the paradox of the Quantified Self which advocates, on the one hand citizen autonomy and individualization, and is susceptible to lead, on the other hand, to a standardization of both the body and human behavior.

We are definitely at the core of a fragile equilibrium between confidentiality and data transparency where both ethical and legal lines of questioning take on their full meaning. For Dr Laurent Alexandre, the founder of Doctissimo and DNA Vision, "…the externalization of intimacy has taken hold with health data now featuring on social media". Social and community networks have broken down the barriers around data sharing, making the latter both utterly visible and accessible to everyone.

From this observation, manufacturers pay particular attention to ergonomics, comfort, the design of user-friendly interfaces, precision and trustworthiness of data recording, thus placing all questions around confidentiality and security, of secondary importance by developing a sense of trust and closeness with users.

The importance factor is not so much the actual data but the act of measuring it, which has the effect of both developing and transforming it. This self-evaluation is, consequently, synonymous with appreciating one's personal development and taking responsibility for one's actions. It becomes really beneficial when done as a matter of routine.

Self-evaluation is not about quantification. It not only consists of integrating more data into metacognitive systems, but also reintroducing order by formulating an info-communicational report which is qualitative in and of itself. This is why, it appears necessary for us to learn, examine and understand the various cogs, which constitute these NICTs so as to use ethically, usefully and, especially, in a personalized way these connected objects.

It would be judicious to build a reference system of health smartphone applications so as to present guarantees of independence and objectivity with both clear and efficient criteria. Work must be completed so as to define criteria and indicators, to classify and record applications to make it possible for doctors to prescribe them for the right health user at the right time. For that, it becomes necessary to have a pragmatic approach, where NICTs must be easily understood by health professionals.

Finally, the use of the Quantified Self will depend directly on the possibility of processing Big Data for which it will be one of the major suppliers, with, at issue, the aptitude of discovering the "motives" which allows the mass conversion of unstructured data into useful and relevant information to clarify the action needed. In order that this highly personalized approach might end with personal development, in other words towards a real so-called "Modified Self", it would be necessary to give everyone the tools to discover their own "pertinent motives".

1.2.3. *Open Data*

Following the example of Big Data, in recent years Open Data has been an inescapable set of themes. The term Open Data appeared for the first time in 1995 in a document of an American scientific agency introducing environmental and geophysical Open Data. Open Data developed well before Big Data; in this sense it preceded it. However, it is also an intrinsic part of Big Data by the volume of data that it conveys. Consequently, Open Data is asserted as a significant breeding ground for Big Data, as the data it holds are considered as trustworthy, integrated, free of defects, which acknowledges the recurrent issue of data quality [HAM 13]. This practice consists of making digital data accessible to all, easily and freely (without legal, technical or financial restrictions), worked out, either by a public institution or a community. This freedom of access and the opening up data to third-party use is therefore, integrated in a trend that regards public information as common property, the dissemination of which is both in the public and general interest. The theory of the American sociologist Robert King Merton brings to light the benefit of scientific Open Data. Each researcher should contribute to the common property and all must give up all intellectual property rights with the aim of advancing knowledge. It is the convergence of this scientific idea with the ideals of free software programs and Open Source, which shapes Open Data such as is being implemented nowadays. Value creation which, rather than through a form of volume effect, is undertaken more through sharing data, making it available to third parties, involvement and collaboration. Open Data attempts to introduce an inversion of logic. By default, data and public information must be published on line, before even before a third party demand such data. This marks a mental cultural shift.

Open Data is the fruit of its era, where the imperatives of transparency and "accountability" are increasingly important. Transparency is perceived here as the response to an era of scorn, even defiance, regarding institutions and their representatives. This movement is in response to a set of issues which are as much economic as political. We expected democratic benefits from Open Data (better transparency in public action, citizen participation, a response to the lack of confidence concerning both elected officials and institutions) but also the creation of economic value by the development of such new Open Data activities.

In the research and public health sector, Open Data represents the commitment to increased medicine indications (http://www. lagazettedescommunes.com/232095/donnees-de-sante-pourquoi-lopendata-est-une-necessite-et-comment-y-parvenir/-fn-232095-2), safeguarding public health by identifying of major events or, on the contrary, missed signs such as the beginning of epidemics or biochemical attacks. It also represents the commitment to managing public health policies with an almost surgical precision so as to adapt them to the local and national population needs, or to ensure that health is protected according to the use of particular health products. Consequently, Open Data favors, on the one hand, better health monitoring at national level while highlights the risk factors at different levels and of working on both the detection and treatment of epidemics, on the other. On the economic front, Open Data within health makes possible better management of costs, which inevitably undergoes the recommendation of appropriate, reliable and quality care. Finally, the champions of Open Data insist on the democratic aspects of this practice and upon the importance of public organizations demonstrating transparency.

However nowadays, Open Data is confronted with 'n' number of challenges and questions, as much at demand as supply level. The data supply still remains largely to be developed; as a priority most data owners have made data available that is easiest to obtain (as much technically and legally as politically). Data that is perceived as sensitive, or that with a strong social or societal impact, remains largely outside of the Open Data sphere.

Certain data is complex to understand if its primary use context is unknown. Is it not therefore, a risk to make it accessible to all? Will we not distort it in the interpretation process? Data appropriation by the largest number of individuals quickly, indeed, collides with the difficult question of data culture. Skills from various sources are necessary such as knowing how to locate data sources, being capable of processing and manipulating them, casting a critical eye over the requirements of their production and their being made available and controlling basic statistical concepts, among other factors.

Confidentiality and abuse in the use of this sort of data should not be overlooked within this type of debate. We may fear a possible "indirect re-identification of individuals" by intersecting and cross-referencing a lot of data as well as the use of this information by private actors with the potential abuse that may ensue from this. The aspects of data security are therefore, highly important elements of using such Open Data.

Moreover, the private sector's interest in health data is not completely unselfish. One may even envisage high economic stakes in a world where money ought to remain a discreet issue. Politicians worry about the growth of health costs. Beyond that, a better circulation of data between players, including within the public sector and the creation of new services should allow for clarification of player policies, optimizing the operation of the health system, health alerts, better clarity of the care offered as well as the fight against health inequalities, and therefore achieving more during times of severe economic strain.

Would this openness make an equality concern between actors essential? Moreover, if Open Data in the health sphere does not make it possible to reduce or curb expenditure, does it ensure greater savings throughout the overall system? Health expenses correspond to essential economic activities in terms of employment, technological progress and production.

Finally, from a more general point of view the main problems around the exploitation of Open Data are of technical nature as the volume of data is such as to not be able to be processed by humans alone. Open Data are only controllable by those producing them (for example, the control of updates) and truly exploitable by others only if it:

– is possible for the data to exist on a network through a URI[36] (this includes URLs[37];

– reduces the cost of data transformation by supplying standard machine-readable formats; improves data quality to avoid its alteration during processing for data provision. Having an error-containing data warehouse is preferable to a distorted warehouse. Thus, through a specific request service for the given data, processes for frequency and automation of updates by data producers is possible.

The availability of these types of data has numerous impacts upon the ISs of the businesses producing them. Several aspects may be studied such as:

– pooling of structure tools to exploit these data being decision tools for extraction, storage and altering data and MDM[38] tools for cleaning and formatting (see compare data interoperability); implementation of the architecture to ensure the dissemination of data including identification and extraction, consolidation and storage and processing and dissemination;

– the choice of means of publication according to how new the data is. The operation will vary according to whether one wishes to process data in real time or whether the data does not need being refreshed frequently;

– the selection of the means of storage of the publication platform. So as to guarantee data security, it is necessary, either to generate a new internal infrastructure, or to use an external host (see Cloud Computing);

---

36 Unique Resource Indicator.
37 Uniform Resource Locators.
38 Master Data Management.

– control of data logging so as to rationalize the volumes processed. Data may be replaced by the last version at warehouse level and a log kept at publication level only.

1.2.4. *Clinical research based upon medical Big Data*

Medical research has always relied on the analysis of significant data volumes. Clinical trials are scientific studies, which allow the measurement of both the efficiency and tolerance of a given medicine in real conditions, by comparing the reaction of those patients who have received the given treatment to those who have not. Beyond the broadening of its boundaries, clinical research effects its own transformation, particularly with the use of connected sensors, which linked with Cloud Computing, will both allow patient monitoring during patients daily lives and generate the collection of gigantic data volumes. With the proliferation of Quantified Self mechanisms, nowadays it is possible to complete these tests without requiring the person tested to spend three days in a hospital; measurements of heart rate, sleep, body temperature, and other such tests may be completed remotely. This is a plus for patients and even makes the study more realistic since patients can continue their respective life routines. Hence, large biomedical datasets may exist in numerous forms, as is the case with aggregated clinical trials [COS 14], in genome sequencing, and in microbiology [MCG 08, MAT 13], or in bio-banks and cyber-banks [MAJ 05, CUR 13, COS 14].

It is within this context that Big Data technologies play a predominant role in transforming not only the organization of clinical research, but even its territory by bringing it out of the hospital silo so as to involve it in everyday life. Big Data has allowed science to make considerable advances, particularly through the cross-referencing of complex medical imaging data. Clinical research is based upon important hopes, in particular, in targeting specific drugs. Besides, it may be noted that genetics is the original testing ground for Big Data. According to a study by McKinsey, one of the principal advantages of "mega data" is illustrated by the analysis of more accessible and relevant data, such as the integration of R&D data.

A health user who is equipped with connected probes, either through being affected with a chronic illness and subject to constant monitoring, because they were persuaded by the Quantified Self method or, more prosaically, because their insurance company has promised them lower premiums in exchange for their data, becomes a player involved in clinical research.

The emergence of these NICTs around enormous volumes of data encourages us to reflect on clinical research. Classical clinical research has undergone a complex chain of events, which has taken a long time to complete involving regulatory procedures, logistical organization of phases I to IV, patient recruitment and monitoring, study observation, safety and protection of individuals and quality of care. These complex links depend upon each other, so as ultimately to produce data. This clinical research cycle has always been achieved in the same way over several years with a relative level of efficiency. The average time lag between the idea and its publication, is not compatible with the expectations of patients and decision-makers, being 10 years according to the NIH[39] study. A recent article in the review *Science* recommends that for each issue or drug we must to stop creating a new specific organization solely intended to respond to such an issue. Other articles encourage the improvement of this process. This is, indeed, achieved by significant multi-centric placebo-controlled clinical trials, which in the end respond to a single issue only after surmounting problems they can have a wide clinical application. This digital transformation of clinical research may have a positive effect on the necessary time lag to place treatment innovations on the market while introducing better safety measures, particularly by implementing observation and monitoring programs for patients in real life conditions.

These developments, of course, will necessitate a profound redevelopment of the current research framework and will frame both ethical and governance questions clearly, which are raised by personal data processing particularly. Previously, we were saying that health data was personal data and that, by contrast, the reverse was not true. Henceforth, with the digitization of clinical research, it is noticeable that we are moving towards validation of this reciprocity increasingly.

This is why clinical research has therefore completed its own transformation, particularly with the use of connected probes, which, linked to "Cloud Computing", will allow for the monitoring of patients in their "real lives" and generate the collection of real data streams.

---

39 This is US National Institute of Health – an organization specializing in grants and funding and research and training.

In this context, Big Data may contribute to shortening the time span of the clinical research process and make it more efficient. It is the conversion of clinical trials from *in vitro* to so-called *in silico*. Indeed, data sources increase, as for example registers, HIS, cohorts of all natures, e-cohorts, social networks, *SNIIRAM* medico-administrative databases (*Système National d'Information Inter Régimes de l'Assurance Maladie*)[40] and diverse information networks. Both the convergence in all its forms and the nature of data must serve to improve the shaping of future clinical studies.

The codification of both procedures and personal medical files opens the way to extensive studies of the best treatment combinations without, for all that, necessitating the implementation of full-scale long and costly test protocols. For example, Canadian researchers have perfected a means to localize infections in premature babies before visible symptoms appear.

Moreover, at the time patients were recruited for clinical trials, one of the major concerns was around the risks of overlapping, having two clinical trials for the same treatment indication but with slightly different subpopulations. Big Data may cater an insight into the extent of this overlapping and allows researchers to know whether two trials are in direct competition. When appropriate, the site and/or the sample might be modified for the two clinical trials.

This data collection development which researchers are able to complete may be micro-, meso- or macro- level data, which suggests the possibility of a scientific paradigm moving towards calculus. Beyond that, from the volume of data, it is necessary to take into account the variety, velocity and value of the latter [RUS 11].

Furthermore, given that the health user depends upon complex interactions between biology, psychology and social issues, the doctor has to be able to digitize an evolutionary and complex medicine by digitizing these parameters. This is why, thanks to information technology, medical imaging and Big Data, we are able to understand how the human body works, quantify a disease and predict its development, better simulate the action of a given therapy to optimize its effects precisely, such as some of the major issues of tomorrow's digital medicine.

---

40 These are health-related databases including insurance-related information.

The study of data, as well as medical image computer simulations, make it possible for us to build a personalized digital representation by adjusting geometric, statistical, physical or physiological models of the human body to the individual's anatomical and functional images. The digitization of the patient going from *in vivo* to *in silico* allow us to optimize the study of medical imaging content and to simulate both the likely disease development and treatment effects in the most realistic manner using virtual organs.

The principle of virtualization of a patient is to take specific measures for an illness so as to make an accurate patient-orientated digital model. Nicholas Ayache has stated:

"As soon as we have a specific model, we might project it back to:

– establish a diagnosis (diagnosis support tool);

– simulate disease development (prevention);

– simulate and plan treatment" [AYA 09].

This comes from articulating different levels of modeling whether geometric, statistical, physiological, chemical and physical.

Finally, we may emphasize that in the medium term, the creation of a digital patient in form of a hologram, which will be as real as a living person. The doctor will be able to carry out all simulations and tests on this avatar before making his actual medical decision or performing the relevant medical procedure. This point of view is not actually as utopic as it seems when products such as Microsoft HoloLens, which corresponds to the creation of three-dimensional transparent holograms have appeared. Such products make possible the improvement of individuals' daily lives. This technology is envisaged to improve the means of communication, learning and creation through using holographic platforms. Through holograms it will be possible to create, learn and exchange work and ideas more easily, but also to communicate in another way by virtualizing our actions. By using a virtual reality helmet, users may see fictitious and digital data superimposed upon real life. The relevance of this is to be able to integrate more easily the various elements of our environments, and also to be able to superimpose holograms upon reality.

1.2.4.1. Clinical data management

In France, the Clinical Data Manager (CDM) involved in the management of data gathered during a clinical study, that is to say an applied medical research project the purpose of which is to improve patient health by testing following pre-established protocol methods. This may relate to a drug, a diagnosis method, a medical device, a care protocol, or another medical issue. The Data Manager's mission is to structure database research data, to check that they are both relevant and meaningful and to prepare them for a statistical study so as to respond to questions, such as:

– do drugs contribute to improving patient health?

– is the diagnosis method studied more efficient? is the care protocol more appropriate?

– is this new medical device successful? (see Figure 1.3).

Initially, the CDM completes or assists in the production of a case report form which will make possible the availability of all medical information necessary for clinical research. The nature and extent of this data is fairly large. It may include medical history, demography, clinical events, medical images, treatments, biology, genetics, quality of life and other issues. Following this the CDM organizes data capture by means of the case study report form in the clinical database dedicated to this data software management. Subsequently, the latter checks the data captured in the database (specifically through the intermediary of Clinical Research Assistants (CRAs)). To do this, they plan controls to test both the presence and relevance of data, carry them out and ask for them. When appropriate, the patient completes doctor-recommended adjustments. Finally, the ultimate stage is the production of a report of actions taken, so as to check the database and evaluate its quality before sending it to the statistician for result analysis and interpretation. In summary, we may affirm that the CDM represents the person responsible for the database reliability and constitutes the interface between the different actors involved in clinical research, namely:

– the clinical study project lead;

– the programmers, who guarantee both the structure and architecture of the database and the computer checks to verify the relevance and the logic of the data; the patients and doctors, as a result of whom the data is able to be collected;

– the clinical operatives (particularly the CRAs) who will ensure the successful implementation of the study on the given site;

– the doctors and those working in pharmaco-vigilance, respectively in charge of drafting the clinical study protocol and the monitoring of undesirable side effects; and

– the statisticians who both analyze and interpret the results obtained.

Finally, it may be observed that throughout the process, the Clinical Data Manager always ensures that the methods anticipated for the study, the directives of the *Commission Nationale de l'Informatique et des Libertés (CNIL)*[41] upon the management of personal data, regulations and other national and international recommendations for medical research projects are followed. The latter is likely to work in any academic environment[42] which initiates clinical research projects.

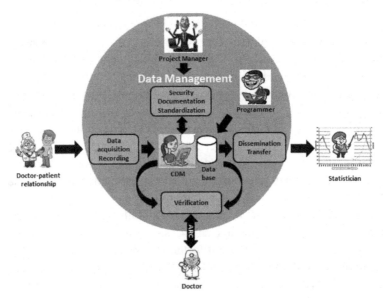

Figure 1.3. *Data management within clinical research*

---

41 This is the statutory body which protects the rights of individuals with regard to personal data.

42 This may be a hospital, a university, an academic association, not-for-profit study organization, a health authority or other organization.

Thus, the era of Big Data has created new possibilities for researchers in achieving a high relevance and impact among changes and transformations to the way in which we study biological, clinical and medical phenomena. With the emergence of the new data collection, technologies such as Data Mining[43] and advanced support analysis, it seems that major transformations are produced by research issues. For example, risk plays a major role in innocuous studies and the more data we have relating to such studies, the more the innocuousness of clinical trials may be guaranteed. Currently Big Data make the following possible:

– controlling risks relating to populations treated for particular diseases or with certain compounds with the aim of evaluating potential effects;

– relying upon ethical decisions taken according to the principles known about the drug studied;

– constructing Benefit-Risk profiles which enrich risk management plans.

Researchers may rely upon the "Data Management Platform" (DMP) to reconcile data coming from digital channels and Internet navigation and mobile data. They may make these data available to research laboratory reference systems or the pharmaceutical industry. These DMPs which are a comprehensive long-term platform that are customizable, extensible and flexible are in the process of becoming the laboratory of the future and Big Data innovation. All solutions must look to the future and respond to the numerous issues to which it gives rise (see Appendix 2).

It is preferable to opt for a unique product, which supplies all required services on one platform. There are many benefits, which issue from the DMP. They make it possible to:

– take into consideration the progress of its target: origin/destination;

– study the results of marketing campaigns;

– analyze data linked to prospective customer behavior, with due regard for individuals' private lives (anonymization);

---

43 Data Mining is a generic term, which encompasses an entire family of tools which both facilitate the exploration and analysis of data held within a reporting program such as Data Warehouse or DataMart. Techniques implemented whilst using this analytical and marketing tool are particularly effective in extracting significant information from large quantities of data.

– save time so as to reflect more upon the appropriate strategy to implement;

– acquire both client data and prospective client data which feed into each other (and not in an isolated and fragmented way);

– deciding the best future strategy in a dynamic way;

– centralizing and converging a multitude of data within the same technological space (through the use of a single provider).

Technological developments, which allow a data access facility, provide solutions. Moreover, the scientific interest in this observational data has increased, in particular for patient-reported data. Nowadays, from the "Patient-Reported Outcome" (PRO) to real-life patient data both with or without drugs, and with or without medical devices, this data is extremely interesting.

Thus, we go from using raw data to "usable" data. These significant volumes of data feed the self-learning algorithms that are integrated within the DMP. These algorithms are the functions, which determine the process which must be linked to each batch of incoming data. They save marketing specialists time, allowing them to reflect more upon the strategy which they wish to implement.

Furthermore, combining clinical trial data with that from another source relating to a given patient situation may reveal a specific treatment regime or allow for the identification of a new strategy offering the best chances of success.

Consequently Big Data is, above all, a tool that researchers manipulated to detect intelligently from among vast data sets linked to live significant data which such researchers can analyze and model. We can take the example of genetics with human genome sequencing based upon the analysis of the large volumes of data or 26 billion characters of the human genetic code, in a few seconds. In the medium term with the multiplication of Big Data" linked to the development of sensors of all types we will all be some day, whether while healthy or ill, occasionally or permanently involved in clinical research.

To conclude, we can say that Big Data has already changed the clinical trials sector completely by allowing for a reduction in development costs by increasing the chances of success of new discoveries, optimizing patient safety and in reducing marketing and commercialization delays.

1.2.4.2. The research project VICToria and the company Keosys

According to a study made by Parexel in 2012, the projections for R&D expenses within the health sphere of health (122 billion dollars in 2013 and 147 billion dollars in 2018), anticipate a growing outsourcing of clinical trials (27% in 2013 and 38.6% in 2018) for which a substantial portion (16%) necessitate medical imaging procedures. By way of illustration, from an investment in R&D of 127 billion dollars in 2014, clinical trials cost 65 billion dollars of which 19 billion dollars for research necessitate imagery for a total amount of 3 billion dollars.

The costs of imaging may be divided between software solutions (CTMS: Clinical Trial Management System) for actual clinical trial management (632 million dollars in 2014) and medical expertise for image interpretation, the design of treatment protocols and the management of clinical trials (2.3 billion dollars in 2014). It is worth noting that the Web and Cloud systems have a 73% market share of CTMSs with a predicted annual growth of 14.5% between 2010 and 2016[44].

Phase III clinical trials are the most expensive, taking account of there being a significant number of patients to diagnose. The principal objective of a phase III clinical trial is to confirm the observed treatment efficiency in phase II from a smaller patient sample, the probability of a strong correlation between the expected imaging results in phase III and those observed in phase II is high. From this viewpoint, a model of data imagery generated in phase II allows us to simulate the imaging results expected in phase III, a notable cost reduction in medical imaging in clinical trials in phase III as a consequence and the possibility of envisaging prompter marketing of certain drugs or medicines allowing correspondingly for swifter treatment of the patients concerned.

Modeling requires characterized images (information concerning the patient, targeted indications, therapy administered, therapeutic methods and other such information) and obtained in a homogenous format. Medical imaging data is standardized to the DICOM (Digital Imaging and

---

44 Markets and markets: CTMS Market: Global Trends, Opportunities, Challenge and Forecasts (2011–2016).

Communications in Medicine) which makes the distribution and visualization of an image possible, whatever its origin. The DICOM standard does not integrate characterization parameters which, when they exist, are stored in other supports and mainly RIS (Radiology Information System), which is detrimental to all modeling approaches.

The purpose of the *VICToria* project (medical imaging Big Data & Virtual Imaging Clinical Trials) is to constitute a medical imaging database characterized by the DICOM data fusion, characterization and exploiting this database so as to create modeling algorithms of the imaging results and developing a virtual platform allowing for the prediction of imaging results of within the framework of clinical trials phase III (see Figure 1.4).

This same "database" may serve to address the sales market for such characterized medical imaging data. Indeed, nowadays, no public commercial offer allows us to respond to the multiple user needs for characterized medical imaging for statistical, research or testing ends and for medical device authentication.

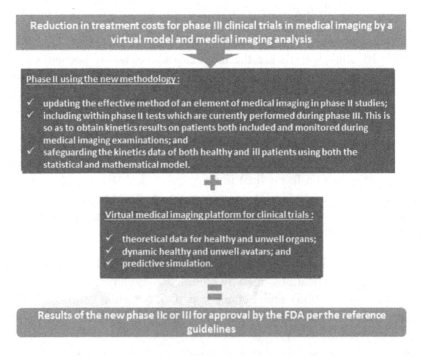

Figure 1.4. *Objectives and processes of the VICToria project*

This project has been initiated and run by the company Keosys[45] (based in St Herblain) which is capitalizing on more than ten years of experience in the development and distribution of medical imaging software solutions, in particular in clinical trials. To this end, Keosys has collaborated with more than 1,200 clinical trial management centers in Europe, in the USA and in Asia, and relies upon a network of radiology and nuclear medicine (radiologists and nuclear medicine doctors). Lastly, Keosys is the owner of the software platform IMAGYS for the management of clinical trials, of which 55 are currently in progress.

To complete the project, the following stages should be carried out:

– conformity with the legislation in force upon the use of health data for an international collaborative project;

– respect for ethics engendered by using health data;

– creation of an "unstructured" medical imaging database from "structured" data;

– mathematical and statistical data imaging modeling to both optimize and revolutionize authentication methods through phase III clinical trial imaging;

– predictive simulation from a database of avatars of organs and kinetic therapy responses (efficiency) to a drug or medicine at the time of a phase II study;

– economic and social model which is both necessary and adapted to the sale of the public of medical data imaging;

– invention, conception and experimental deployment of an *ad hoc* solution allows for gathering and characterization of clinical routine medical imaging data, without impacting upon productivity;

– identification of imaging files responding to specific criteria within an existing database; and

– any additional stages required.

All R&D projects achieved within the VICToria project framework will be re-written in research reports and held within a scientific database to allow both a scientific and possibly public development. This is a strategic

45 http://www.keosys.com/fr/.

point. The short-, medium- and long-term objective is to centralize and co-opt regulatory authorities and more specifically the FDA, around concepts devised by Keosys through the VICToria project. These research findings will also be subject to a scientific, targeted, planned and organized publication strategy.

The innovative character of the project in relation to the state-of-the-art sits in a medical imaging approach component of phase III clinical trials with the aim of cutting short their duration which allows more rapid availability of drugs to all of the targeted population. Furthermore, this will make cost reduction possible (by reducing the number of patients to be included) from relevant clinical trials.

In addition, the make-up of the so-called "characterized" medical imaging database may involve usable generic tools for other clinical routines (personalized medicine) and data exploration (Data Mining).

Finally, it is essential to state that the VICToria project takes into account both everything we have considered and our ethical evaluations that we have detailed throughout this book upon conception, creation and use of medical Big Data. Thus, Big Data must make it possible for researchers to concentrate on the moral obligation to maximize the value of data gathered by research participants, without, for all that, pursuing this data collection if that leads to major potential risks for the patient [CUR 13, MEL 13]. Consequently, it is acknowledged that Big Data analysis should be approached both fearlessly but without being excessively reckless either. Firstly, because by becoming a constitutive element of treatment, digital medical systems necessitate, being tested and evaluated, as does a medicine which not only extends the field but further increases the complexity of clinical research. Nowadays, by controlling drug evaluation, the difficulty is quite different when it is a question of evaluating the latter when linked to a smartphone, online services or an observation program.

If correctly integrated these mega-data may generate an encouraging analysis in the field of health research. This integration must be progressive and incorporate existing data, so that the analysis may be available for consultation in the context of research. An approach which manages the entire data analysis process, the integration of the data being explored and the data visualization by undergoing predictive analysis, as well as protecting against the risks linked to a constantly evolving market is advised.

Scientists and researchers must become proficient in a framework for systems of data reference, which adhere to international norms for data storage. For this, actors define joint metadata storage protocols, protecting the integrity of all data, establishing rules for different levels of access and defining collective rules that facilitate the combination of data sets while improving interoperability [OST 10]. Finally, these evolutions around Big Data within the clinical research sector will necessitate a profound redevelopment of the current framework and will clearly require ethical questioning, in particular with respect to issues raised by the data exploitation, which moreover will not all be about health data but what will become of it once exploited.

1.2.4.3. The research project by the French Grands Écoles

French public research around Big Data does not stop increasing in scale, particularly thanks to the dynamism of France's schools and prestigious universities. Such is the case with:

– the *École Polytechnique* (known as X) and the *CNAMTS* which joined forces, at the end of 2014, through a three-year research partnership, to develop new fields of data processing as a result of *SNIIRAM*. This database, which is one of the most voluminous in the world, is made up of more than 65 million individuals or several hundreds of terabytes. These Big Data represent health paths (reimbursements and hospitalization) of all compulsory health insurance beneficiaries in France. The objective of this research project is to favor Big Data health sector technological development. This partnership processes a program of algorithmic development around public health issues such as the detection of missed signals or anomalies in pharmaco-epidemiology, the identification of factors, which is useful for care pathway analysis and the fight against abuse and fraud. X signed a scientific partnership agreement with the department of clinical research and development at the *Assistance Publique – Hôpitaux de Paris* (AP–HP – see above) so as to promote the medical applications within its research programs and to strengthen its collaboration with health professionals;

– the *Centre Virchow-Villermé de Santé Publique Paris-Berlin*[46] developed research from Big Data upon computer-aided pharmaco-vigilance, electronic disease monitoring and massive Open Data processing

---

46 This is the Virchow–Villermé Paris-Berlin Public Health Center.

in large health institutions. The major issue is optimizing the use of existing resources (whether databases or cohorts) and to integrate a variety of sources (cancer registers, health insurance, and similar sources). In response to this challenge constituted by Open Data constitutes, the *Centre Virchow–Villermé* is participating in the development of an endowed university chair between *Université Paris Descartes* and *Centrale-Supélec* in partnership with AP–HP, and industrial partnerships. The study of "massive data" might assist in improving result and procedures within the health sector while cohort analysis contributes to identifying risk factors in public health and epidemiology;

– Télécom ParisTech has a Big Data pathway which is developing a strategic pluri-disciplinary research upon themes such as financial mathematics, so-called Graph-Mining and the exploration of social networks, ranking and collaborative filtering, attack detection, Internet publicity, indexing/research of multimedia documents and legal, political, economic, ethical and philosophical aspects relating to the use of personal data. Télécom ParisTech, in partnership with businesses and with the support of the *Fondation Télécom*, hosts three research and teaching chairs around Big Data within its group the *Institut Mines-Télécom*[47]. Subjects include Machine Learning for Big Data, Big Data and Market Insights and the Values and Politics of Personal Information. The field of pluridisciplinary research in the school is made up of four departments. Signal processing (Machine Learning, Distributed Optimization, Massive Multimedia), Electronic communication (Distributed Storage, Distributed Optimization), I.T. and Networks (Web Data Mining/Semantics, Parsimonious and Distributed Protection, Data Distribution) and Economic and Social Sciences (visualization, economics and business models, personal data law, Big Data public policy and Big Data sociology).

1.3. Issues surrounding the medical info-sphere

The French health system has faced many challenges one of which is a chronic deficit. Its complexity, the explosion of knowledge and its fragmentation, the need for each health player to succeed in working together at a time when the care pathway consists of too many silos, "medical deserts" and an aging population. Other challenges are an outbreak

---

47 This provides services such as start-up support, training, research and innovation programs.

of chronic illnesses, patients with multiple illnesses, new personalized treatment, ensuring that patients are made well or their condition improved, and that patients benefit from the digital revolution in a systematic way, as illustrated, in particular, by the use of Big Data. Henceforth, NICTs are investing in different medical and health fields and should thus make an optimization, possible which is as much qualitative as economic of all care and prevention processes, while adapting to the regulatory and legislative framework or by making it evolve.

This digital policy change is built as much around collaborative networks of scientific researchers or clinicians as around Cloud Computing, which allows each health actor to have patient information available. However, actors also have significant computer memories and algorithmic processing available which make possible the manufacture of decision-making tools. Finally, this digital revolution is also based on connected objects and so-called "bio-sensors" which are able to contribute to optimize pharmacology, epidemiological research and even prevention campaigns.

As a result of Big Data, there is always data on something somewhere that may be collected, analyzed and cross-referenced with the purpose of saying something, particularly data, which may harm an individual directly or indirectly. Man tends to change the use of technology by endlessly redefining his needs. Inventiveness seems to precede uses, "…when humans have a tool they excel at finding new uses for it. Often tools exist before there is even a problem to resolve and each one has the potential for unpredictable changes" [NYE 08]. Finally, under pressure from economic, ethical and legal issues, this concentration of information will, out of necessity engender a certain suspicion and fear, as well as a loss of confidence by individuals who may suffer significant detriment in the near future. A much greater dependence upon patient medical data from the adoption of Big Data practices, so as to better understand the patient's condition, might produce gaps and repercussions upon medical care, even in the doctor-patient relationship [MAC 07, BEA 09] and the relationship of trust between players [TER 14].

1.3.1. *The economic market for Big Data*

The transition from unconnected to fully-connected to technology represents a technical and economic reality which is vital for everyone. The service economy linked to the pooling of both infrastructure and Internet software develops to allow businesses to optimize both their cost and time while controlling their risks and reinventing their "business model". Economically, as well as technologically, Big Data provide a big step forward in business decision-making systems from registering data at the center of the decision and have a variety of necessary uses so as to make it possible for the firm to increase its margins through a better knowledge of its customers, adjustments in physical flows or the detection of errors. Through the detailed knowledge of behaviors and customer consumer habits, businesses are in a position to tender new offers and products, improve those, which exist already, build stronger links with customers and improve their commercial results [UMH 14]. Since the 2000s, recorded data has acquired a market value. Data has gained an economic value [CAT 83, GAL 94, SAV 58] conferring a wealth upon those who are able to appropriate it [CAT 85, MAL 97]. The value of these immense data volumes is in the quality, wealth and granularity of the "data" processed. It is from this mass of data, which is studied that algorithms are making it possible to identity personalized consumer profiles, that allow us to obtain a highly detailed and sharp appreciation in real-time of both behavioral developments and consumer habits. Equipped with the best technological and analytical tools, the firm is thus in a position to plan for and even anticipate both purchase decisions and customer behavior.

In these cases, data has definitely nowadays become an "economic good", with a value. On a daily basis, it is the target of transactions, even if in practice the latter rarely relate to a single piece of data. In the majority of cases, individuals only ever benefit from the financial increase in value that they generate from their own data. It is from this observation that the New York start-up Datacoup, offers to pay Internet users in exchange for a consented access to their bank details and the social networks that they use. This firm also offers the option of recovering the navigation history or data taken from connected objects such as watches or intelligent bracelets. Thereafter, the start-up sells data collected to professional organizations, after this has been anonymized. In exchange, Internet users earn eight dollars a month. The significance of such a system is to compare subscribers Web habits to their bank details. It may be noted that this new approach does not, for all that, allow Internet users to have total control of their data. Subscribers to Datacoup are not able to trace their data and know to whom their personal information has been sold.

From a civil law viewpoint, fraudulent re-use of data is, in theory, penalized as unfair competition law, this legal action having the *aim of protecting those who have no exclusive rights around* economic value. As for the European Union, it has only established data as *"a commodity"*[48] to both explain and legitimize its jurisdiction as regards protection of personal data.

The value of this Big Data may be realized by three types of the following functions, namely: predictive marketing, Web analytics, multi-channel relational marketing (see Table 1.1).

Predictive marketing:

– analysis of weak signals and guide to trends;

– looking after and management of one's online reputation;

– creation of "new business models";

– comprehension and anticipation of behavior and complex client pathways.

Web analytics:

– optimization of web traffic creation;

– personalization of navigation without identification

– personalization of adverts;

– optimization of web client pathways;

– KPI indicators: traffic costs, conversion rates, click rates, purchase frequency, rates of recovery, turnover generated and ROI for market share per segment and similar issues;

– calculation of customer value and arbitration of means.

Multi-channel relational marketing:

– customer knowledge;

---

48 Directive number 95/46 of 24th October 1995 thus devotes its first line to ratifying article 100A of Treaty of the European Community, which is the provision relating to the free movement of goods.

– segmentation and precise customer targeting (the most profitable, the highest risks, etc.);

– choice of the most successful channels on a per individual basis;

– optimization of cross-channel client pathways;

– automation of additional sales;

– personalization of navigation & content after identification;

– calculation of customer value and media arbitrations.

Table 1.1. *The functions of Big Data*

Subsequently, "Business Intelligence" (BI) is a business which, for a long time, has been devoted to data study for management and reporting purposes enriches the supply of Big Data. Indeed, the collection of multiple data as much from internal as external sources, provides a new clarity upon activities backed up by figures and indeed favors more the examination of statistical behaviors.

In this context, the monetization of Big Data is completed from the following four perspectives:

– offering free access to a service and in return collecting behavioral data relating to users;

– offering the basic big Data service functions free and charging for advanced functions;

– reselling data in an "aggregated" or "anonymous" way to third parties within a B2B rationale;

– encouraging users to maximize the use of their available data platform by offering third party firms access and/or to inject data through APIs (Application Programming Interfaces).

It may be noted that this platform system offers, on the one hand, the creation of operational relations and traditional BI dashboards, and on the other hand, new technologies such as visualization and predictive analysis. These solutions cover the entire analysis from obtaining data to the supply of analyses.

Finally, the exploitation of Big Data depends upon both the strategy and the needs of the firm. We may take the case of health with:

– so-called "personalized" medicine, where data is cross-referenced so as to personalize services and offers according to the health user. ("profiling");

– so-called "predictive" medicine where we recover external data so as to optimize care provision (using "predictions").

Thus, personal data are an essential resource for the digital economy [COL 13] a study by Boston Consulting Group established that the estimated total value of personal data by European consumers went from 315 billion Euros in 2011 to nearly 1000 billion Euros in 2015. The value of personal data from European citizens could even reach one trillion Euros by 2020 [BON 14]. As a result of personal data, firms are learning to understand their customers better, better target their prospective clients and can adapt their offers of products and services. According to the IDC[49] the global turnover generated by the Big Data Market was 3.2 billion dollars in 2010 and 8.9 billion dollars in 2014. With a growth of nearly 40% per year, the market should represent approximately 24 billion dollars in 2016 according to the firm Transparency Market Research[50]. According to AFDEL[51] and Lauvergeon Report (2014)[52], the benefits of the creation of a Big Data pathway in France may generate 2.8 billion euros in 2020 with an annual rate of growth of 7% and more than 100,000 directly related jobs within 5 years. The share of Big Data will reach 8% of European GDP in 2020. This trend is exemplified by the American firm Acxiom that specializes in the collection of data. It earned an income of 1.15 billion dollars in 2012 and which has approximately 1,500 pieces of data upon 700 million people worldwide. According to IDC, the French market around Big Data is divided up in the following way, that is to say 24% for software, 33% for services and 43% for infrastructure.

Concerning, the health sector the consultancy firm McKinsey estimates that for the American health system the annual economic potential of Big Data is 300 billion dollars, or 1000 dollars per inhabitant per year [MON 13] and, according to the IDC in 2014 annual productivity growth of +0.7%. This may be achieved by improvements in economic performance. Big Data analysis makes possible the optimization of existing processes on the basis of better knowledge. The same report by McKinsey indicates large-scale

49 International Data Corporation.
50 This is a US-Canadian firm conducting market research across sectors.
51 This is a business providing software editing and Internet solutions.
52 This was a report upon innovation head by Anne Lauvergeon.

implementation of Big Data technology, which would lead to more 17% potential savings for the American health system. Such savings will be possible if Big Data processing is applied across the following five sectors:

– cost control by automated repayments;

– prevention together with patient monitoring;

– innovation for better exploitation and dissemination of knowledge;

– diagnosis by helping health professionals to choose the most suitable therapeutic treatments;

– the so-called "distribution" of medical personnel with the availability of appropriately-trained professionals for the patient's particular circumstances (a GP or a specialist).

According to the French magazine *Les Echos*, health data represent approximately 27% of overall data right across the spectrum, growing at a similar rate to that of the overall market (4.6 billion dollars in 2015 and predicted to be 11.2 billion dollars in 2018), as is the branch of medical imaging (0.28 billion dollars in 2010 and predicted to be 3.7 billion dollars in 2018) which represents 30% of the health data market. Furthermore, it is considered that medical imaging data represents a third of all health data. From these estimates, we may obtain a projection for the global data market, within the health sector and within medical imaging for 2018 respectively of 1.5 billion dollars, 11.2 billion dollars and 3.7 billion dollars (see Table 1.2 below).

Year	2010	2015	2016	2018
World market in global data (in billions of dollars)	3.2	16.9	24	41.5
World market in health data (in billions of dollars)	0.864	4.6	7.29	11.2
World market in health imaging data (in billions of dollars)	0.285	1.5	2.4	3.7

Table 1.2. *The development of the world market in global data (in billions of dollars)*

Moreover, according to a study by Xerfi Precepta, the e-health global market, which was worth 2.4 billion Euros in 2012, is likely to increase by an average of 4% to 7% per year until 2017. The incubator Rock Health, which is dedicated to start-ups involved in the digital health-sphere affirms that investment in this sphere reached a record figure in 2014. The latter assessed

Big Data-linked investment as close to 381 million Euros over the first quarter of 2014. Total investment within digital health over the first nine months of 2014 was three billion dollars. At the mid-year point, such investments had already exceeded those made in digital health in 2013, which over the entire 2013 year only reached 1.5 billion dollars. On comparing this to 2013, the difference is noteworthy: the average total investments increased by 31% in 2014. However, the report seems to demonstrate growth within the DNA sequencing sector and the study of "data" stemming from the human genome. This trend was confirmed by a recent classification of the "50 Smartest Companies" produced by the MIT Technology Review in which the company Illumina came top, ahead of Elon Musk's Tesla and Google [VIL 14].

Consequently, this trend for the "commodification of data" grew with the mass consumption crisis. Henceforth, supply is acquiring its own identity through the use of "One To One" or CRM (Customer relationship management). Companies seek better knowledge of the consumer, of his tastes and routines, so as to make it possible to target more precisely the commercial action to undertake. This trend becomes fully apparent in the Web, which constitutes an endless pool around our behavior and our areas of interest with new, sophisticated and available tools which make it possible to collect, sort, classify and exploit data.

It may be noted that it is not data itself that is the market, but the knowledge that we can draw from it. We may take the example of RunKeeper, which is used by around 20 million joggers to measure their running. The application editor of the application is paid by major sporting brands or sport coaches who are wondering where to locate their sports equipment shops or in the case of sports coaches their studios. Thus, RunKeeper produces very accurate information (for example, distances run, actual runner objectives or similar data) for these sport professionals to then decide where to set up their business. We might develop the same reasoning for measuring an individual's weight for professionals working in food-processing and dietetics.

Here we anticipate here the full economic potential of these Big Data. However we must also be aware of the consequences of the personal data commodification, which calls for considerable caution. This is why nowadays the exploitation of Big Data is an essential issue for our society having significant prospects in both the economic and technological spheres. However, as the saying goes, "with great power comes great responsibility".

Ill-conceived from a procedural, social and ethical point of view, Big Data management might have disastrous consequences for Man.

1.3.2. *The ethical risks of using data*

It is always faster and constantly more appropriate. Information has exponential growth. Creation, maintenance, dissemination and use of Big Data is a major issue. This is so, whether it is a question of medical or personal data, sensor read-outs, documents, specialist term dictionaries or ontologies. These databases are essential for research, but also for creation and maintenance of new care services. However, the use and re-use of data all too often acts as a constraint, which prevents optimal exploitation. Reasons might include data sometimes being of unclear origin, of doubtful ethics, having non-existent traceability, uncertainty around intellectual property ownership, which is at first sight a difficult quality to ascertain. Consequently, securing data creation is both a competitiveness factor and a duty. This is not entirely without its problems. With the abundance of available data there are difficulties in its exploitation. Indeed the amount of available data increases considerably faster than Man's capacity to analyze and process it. The problem is thus overabundance of data.

In a general way, the behavior of certain number of public and private actors who have little respect for data protection rules is the source of a growing loss of confidence as regards Internet users and NICTs. For example, sub-contractors processing unsecure data might lead to data re-identification or result in data transfer to a third party country outside of the European Union. It is possible to imagine a certain number of practices around data manipulation such as the sale of the latter data without the explicit consent of its owner, the purchase of data by other organizations, aggregation or non-aggregation of data or targeted advertising starting from Big Data and other practices. For Dr Laurent Alexandre[53], the major issue is not the data as such but rather the externalization of data volumes through data management platforms, the majority of which are controlled by GAFA. The problem therefore is mainly focused around the control of processing algorithms. The necessary framework of expert systems cannot be completed

---

53 A panel discussion titled "Entre secret et transparence, quel espace?", *CHAM: Convention on Health Analysis and Management*, 26 September 2015.

without strict regulators in place. This leads to us towards prospective thinking in wondering about

– how do we exist when faced with GAFA?

– how will we avoid digital vassalage in the health sphere?

– how would we integrate the set of expert systems?

– what is the balance between the rationale of the American platform producers (GAFA) and the European CNILs?

This is why citizens are naturally led to ponder the following

– how is their data used by businesses? What organizations hold their data and what particular data do they have?

– how is their data analyzed and how do the results of these analyses direct the business in its activities?

– who has access to their data?

– do businesses resell their data to external third parties?

– to whom does responsibility for data exploitation belong?

The question around the data quality also contributes to reinforce this fear. The users of Big Data observed that voluminous data exploitation could increase the number of errors if data was not initially integrated. Consequently, numerous dysfunctions could blemish the data accuracy and the processing; for example, the data stemming from inaccurate sources, being duplicated, obsolete or no longer current or similar dysfunctions.

This phenomenon is further reinforced by the fact that increasingly data comes from sources external to the business, which uses it. It may be noted that to counter this situation, integrators have produced new solutions which make it possible to better trace and visualize data sources and reduce the error rate. Specialist suppliers in the study and cleansing of external data have also emerged. However, human analysis remains, in any event, fundamental, and the increase in specific skills linked to Big Data as such offers a strategic interest for the business. Through that, we show both the potential dangers and the reliability of mobile health [BUI 13, CUM 13] particularly within diagnosis and patient management [VIS 12], diabetes self-management [DEM 12] and asthma [MCK 13], and other such patient issues.

This sentiment of both fear and defiance is exaggerated immediately it concerns health data, from the fact that its nature is directly linked to personal intimacy. In France, Europe and also in the United States[54], health data is considered as being particularly sensitive. Henceforth, individuals are both suspicious regarding the use that organizations make of their personal data and they feel the effects of the quality of the data that organizations share. According to the study the "Future of Digital Trust" by Orange Healthcare which was published in February 2014, upon consumer concerns regarding personal data processing by businesses. The exploitation of personal data represents an essential element for the maintenance of consumer confidence in a firm, an organization or an institution, virtually in the same way as service quality. This is why ethical and social risks from the disclosure of medical data comprise a remarkably wide range of potentially harmful consequences for the data owner, such as:

– the exploitation of data against the person in a contentious case (inheritance, divorce, child custody or against an employer or other contentious case);

– the loss of opportunity linked to disclosing an illness (for example, AIDS, multiple sclerosis or cancer) to a third party (employer, insurer or lender) who refuses to employ the individual or to act in the latter two cases, as a result of this disease [REY 12];

– exclusion from society, rejection, marginalization, loss of job or depression which may lead to an employee's suicide; and

– reputation and brand image damage, harassment linked to knowledge of an illness, gibes and deficiencies or other damage.

At the same time, individuals are increasingly becoming sensitive not only to the risks linked to the illegal use of their data, but also the intrinsic value of data that industries have about them and as to the benefits which they might also justifiably derive.

The risks linked to the use of Big Data belong to the so-called operational risk category, such as informational risks linked to applications, developments, maintenance, infrastructure, servers, projects and suppliers. From this observation, we may set out the criteria taken into account for the

54 Since 1996, in the United States, the notion of sensitive data has been linked to health data by the Health Insurance Portability and Accountability Act.

analysis of NICT risks. The main ones are continuity, availability, traceability, integrity, confidentiality, proof and auditability. In these circumstances, firms that are involved in the treatment of and the Big Data market are faced with the following issues:

– data security (fraud, theft[55] and loss);

– data accuracy;

– the degree of data transparency;

– the reputation and the control of data on the "data" owner's behalf;

– the respect for private life and individual freedoms;

– the passage from "data" to information;

– the control and regulation;

– predictive analysis through algorithms;

– internal organizational models;

– free will during algorithmic operation.

[MIT 15] include five main identified spheres of ethical concerns being:

– free and informed consent;

– data ownership;

– private life (including anonymization and data protection);

– the digital gap between those with and without access to digital; epistemology and objectivity[56].

-

55 In February 2015, the largest health data theft took place in the US when hackers stole documents relating to 80 million patient members of Anthem (the second biggest health insurer in the US). Fortunately, this data only pertained to ID information such as names and addresses, and not that of illnesses and treatments linked to the insureds.
56 The idea of an objective discovery from Big Data reinforces the role of interpretative frameworks giving this data meaning so as to be able to interact with individuals and the world around us [GAD 76, HAB 84, SCH 00].

Moreover there are six sectors which break down as follows:

– the importance of epistemology[57] within Big Data evaluation;

– the dangers of ignoring damaging ethical effects at group level;

– the need to make the distinction between Big Data academic and commercial practices, in terms of potential harm;

– the changing nature of relationships of trust between individuals and the organizations using their personal data;

– the difficulty of providing significant rights of access to individuals who lack the necessary resources; and

– future problems owing to intellectual property stemming from Big Data analysis.

For both authors, these eleven themes constitute an in-depth critical approach in ethical guidance for the evaluation and governance of emerging Big Data practices.

Moreover, the principal of solidarity upon which the French health system in particular rests, could be challenged by certain practices favored by the advent of both mobile and connected health. Big Data risks accentuating discrimination, categorization and customization within society. Data is increasingly connected to us, much like a second skin, so as to better classify and discriminate us with abuses, which are linked to it. This is why we must not under-estimate the risk of a "digital fracture" corresponding to several dividing lines (social, economic and even geographical) which conceal highly diverse realities. In France, the *Conseil National de l'Ordre des Médecins* (CNOM) states that "an individual who is at ease with digital today in his familial and social surroundings may find himself lost tomorrow when it is necessary to reinvent his digital skills or care for his disease using a dematerialized mechanism. Those unconnected, having become the minority, are also those who are, above all, victims of social, cultural, and economic marginalization, which is all the more reason for specific actions favoring these communities. Considering inclusion in a digital society imposes the development of inclusive policies without losing

---

57 Literature upon ethics states that numerous articles have revealed a direct link between ethics and Big Data epistemology. The connections are the result of the perceived complexity of "massive data" and the processing algorithms used in analyzing them [CAL 12], which are beyond human comprehension.

sight of those who are the most fragile and who must remain a priority" [CNO 15]. Technological advances and data processing are a real asset but also pose risks for the security services. These services have three main strategies to ensure the protection of private life: namely anonymization, prior free and informed consent and opt-out[58], all of which we have gone beyond. In this light, we should agree to rethink our way of approaching the digital world and the use of our data. Protecting our private lives requires Big Data users to become more responsible for their deeds and actions. Individuals must be have control over of their data. In these conditions "empowerment" of the individual over his so called "essential data" becomes one of the challenges of developing connected medical devices and Big Data within health. To achieve this, it appears essential that personal data management is facilitated, lacking any operational, ideological or commercial bias. One of the responses with the emergence of user "empowerment" might be "Self Data", that is to say the production, processing and sharing of personal data by individuals, which is both under their control and used for their own ends. It is then a matter of making purposes compatible with each other by aligning the interests of the user and the firm. The notion of loyalty must reconcile Big Data and the regulation of personal data. We may use the example of the "Mes Infos" project[59] which experimented with "Self Data". This puts the individual at the heart of both the production and use of the data, which he or she produces.

At the same time, society must redefine the notion both of justice and of data ownership of data guarantee Man's freedom to act. Thus, resistance to data-linked data monitoring is not about those who having something to hide; "Everyone is resistant to monitoring, as it not a question of our private lives, it is a question of control, self-determination and autonomy" [EUB 12]. In interpreting this quotation we have to distinguish three dimensions of the private life concept:

---

58 This word designates a marketing or legal term describing an electronic address. Opt-out is authorized in France in the domain of "e-mailing" concerning commercial activities between B2B businesses. Opt-out is the means which makes it possible for the Internet user to stop a Web operation which they consider to be either intrusive or a hindrance to his private life, such as blocking cookies so as not to receive advertising materials.

59 "Experiment 'Mes Infos', Synthèse, Conclusions et Défis Pour le Futur du 'Self Data'", *Fondation Internet Nouvelle Génération*, Octobre 2013 – Juin 2014. (This translates as "'My Data' experiment, Synthesis, Conclusions and Challenges for the Future of 'Self Data'", *New Generation Internet Foundation*, October 2013 – June 2014').

– the secret, which implies the capacity to control, use and share one's data and the right to privacy which is linked to it;

– tranquility, the right to be left alone and not to be disturbed by unwanted solicitations, which assumes control of the access to one's private property;

– individual autonomy, a form of personal sovereignty which individuals will want to keep control over, without this necessarily being kept a secret.

Having a private life is the "human desire for independence in comparison to control by others" [CNI 12]. Big Data make a quasi-intimate knowledge of the individual possible through profiling. Moreover, the citizen may be opposed to such a substantial knowledge of him as an individual, as well as all consequent commercial solicitations. The individual demands the right to remain worry-free when faced with the multiple intrusions, which NICTs may represent for his private life. Consequently, how can we resolve this conflict between the individual's desire for knowledge through an economic actor as a result of "Data Mining" and the Law?

Furthermore, the processing of "massive data" must imperatively respect the individual. One of the risks of Big Data also hinges not upon judging individuals by their actual behavior but upon their propensity to behave as their data ascribes to them. The digital world is not able to reduce the human potential for probability and statistics plotted by algorithms. There is a risk of judging a person according to his relationships, his propensities and his habits rather than according to his actions.

Reflecting the nature of personal data that personal data represents being, on the one hand, a cultural issue for the citizen, having become a genuine DNA for his digital identity and a strategic advantage for businesses integrating an increasingly pronounced "data culture" within their economic ecosystem. The use of data constitutes a major value creation lever as much for citizens as for businesses.

The question of trust becomes vital for the individual who is worried about his fundamental freedoms, and for businesses as much in terms of reputation and brand image as building a lasting relationship with stakeholders.

One of the digital ethical issues might be removing existing discrepancies between the initial human intention linked to openness, sociability and value co-production for NICTs and their possible abuses and directional changes that we see in practice. From this observation, ethical approaches around Big Data must, in conjunction with extrinsic usage value focus upon the intrinsic value of these data. By "the intrinsic value of Big Data", we denote three main characteristics:

– whether these data are of good quality by means of both their content and nature;

– whether they are developed from human will and intention;

– whether they lead to specific behaviors and arouse appropriate behaviors for a person or a group of people.

Hence, where uses are unpredictable, data considerations allow for the opening up of the prospects for possible uses, and thereby favoring the prevention of certain use abuses.

In this context, the current development of Big Data poses a wide range of ethical questions around the protection of consumers and citizens against the spread of their personal data and around a potential global "over-mathematization", namely an increasingly large number of decisions taken by technological machines. The issue is to return control of personal data to the consumer and the citizen. The entire question lies in the positioning of the cursor, raising the following:

– who uses which data?

– for what purpose?

– what free will do data users have with the advent of algorithms?

– where is it stored?

– how can I retain control of my personal data?

The user often loses all control regarding potential data dissemination as numerous studies have shown. Information asymmetry between users and suppliers of services tends to develop through new forms of production, new types of production and new processing methods. It is the era of Big Data, being a world, which is ruled by data the issues and aims of which we must understand:

– what is its role?

– who will process and control it?

– how will they do this?

Data production may involve a relatively complex mechanism being a mix of human activity, sensors, one or several data processes and various types of data enrichment by different actors. Contributors may claim involvement in the value created by data exploitation leading to us asking the following:

– how might we link different sources of data?

– what value should be linked with them?

– what are the different changes that are achieved?

– what intermediate data are produced?

– is the integrity of the data both produced and received guaranteed (particularly with the use of an electronic signature mechanism)?

– who will have responsibility for ensuring that specific digital rules are properly observed?

– what is the ownership regime for this data?

– what licenses are applicable?

– how will we make sure that the data that we transmit, or which comes via our connected objects and us, does not allow for formal identification or interpretation, which is outside of our control?

– what degree of transparency is there?

Big Data accentuates the transparency as a result of both the digitalization and digitization of human activity. How should I separate who I am from where I am? What extent does the advent of Big Data afford one a private life? Why are too many ISs recording data that they do not need to retain? Moreover, the aims of the report, "Electronic Frontier Foundation", on the subject of location confidentiality which is concerned to knowing whether we can always move around without our basic movements being systemically and secretly recorded by a third-party for a later use.

Moreover, the implementation of all personal data processing is subordinate to consent by the individual concerned. This imposes upon the individual responsible for data processing a data obligation with regard to this individual. The protection and safety of data hold a threefold challenge of trust, reputation and reliability. Patrick O'Sullivan, Professor of Ethics at *Grenoble École de Management*[60] said that Big Data is here to stay for the simple reason that information technology and the Internet are here to stay. Nowadays, we must outline the boundaries around what is acceptable. The ethical dialog begins by questioning the limits of confidentiality. Does anyone have the right to gather data about another individual without their permission? When individuals give their consent, are they aware of the implications of what they are doing?

As a large mass of unstructured raw data, Big Data is not self-explanatory. Furthermore, the specific methodologies, which make it possible to interpret data are subject to all kinds of philosophical debates. Can data represent a "true objective", or is all interpretation even biased, out of necessity, by a form of subjective filtering, or still more, by the manner in which the data are "cleansed" [BOL 10]?

To this must be added the problem of actual data errors. Large volumes of data collected on the Web are often unreliable, falling prey to losses or outages and these errors and lacunae are multiplied as we cross-reference multiple data sets [CAI 81]. Clinical Big Data are subject to availability biases and are only in themselves a digital representation of an anatomical, physiological or other reality.

Doctors, researchers and other scientists should therefore, know to treat with caution interpretations deduced from the analysis of this data. The data available to us, as abundant as they are, only make it possible for us to instigate beliefs and not entirely valid theories. The accumulation of patient data in real life care situations must not substitute a scientific approach and the conclusion of theories which are capable of explaining both disease development and therapeutic care.

As a consequence, it appears essential to better understand both the properties and limits of Big Data whatever their extent. The latter carry an almost infinite quantity of small incomplete heterogeneous information. However, that does not signify that they are either random or representative. Interpretation is at the heart of analysis of this data. Whatever the size of the data volume, it is subject to limitations and biases. If these limits are not understood and stressed, biases and interpretation problems may be

---

60 Grenoble School of Management.

expected. This is why, so as to make statistical claims when faced with a significant volume of data, we need to know where the data comes from. It is also essential to know the weaknesses of these data and to take account of them. Such an approach involves acknowledging both the individual's identity and his viewpoint informing the analyses which it might produce [BEH 96]. We must not lose sight of the principle that "correlation is not causality", and that a probability is directed at a significant group of individuals but not one individual. Consequently, we must not neglect the influence of the environment and epigenetics. Thus, a predictive power may be completely transformed according to the way in which the individual will react to a piece of data (see retroaction).

Finally, monitoring and coaching capacities offered by connected solutions open the way to new economic opportunities, particularly for insurers and mutual insurance companies in the health-sphere. The temptation to package the total contributions or those of reimbursements through a "no-claims bonus" system, in relation to the insured's conduct, is important. This practice has already been applied in the United States, South Africa and recently in France.

Eventually, the main ethical concerns linked to data, which stem from NICTs, correspond to private lives and monitoring, trust, individual freedoms, social exclusion, security and data protection, the user or the disgruntled citizen, use and exploitation.

Consequently, the dividing line between data that poses no problem of intimacy and data which is potentially personal and/or sensitive is quite difficult to anticipate. By cross-checking, we may sense that the majority of data comprising Big Data is potentially personal. Moreover, what are we to think of predictive behavioral data? These are, without doubt, new sensitive data for which a new management method must be envisaged. *In the light of these observations, we must establish regulations through actual, precise and well-founded objectives so as to make good use of Big Data.*

These objectives are, in part, linked to the following data protection policy:

– defining general trends and priorities (proportionality);

– protecting the intangible business assets (security and confidentiality);

– sensitizing and educating both management and employees at all levels;

– developing, implementing and maintaining a system of data protection (this should include policies, roles, responsibilities, processes and standards);

– assuring conformity and checking;

– respecting the rights of parties interested in the data being fairness and transparency (the right to information, consent, the right to object, the rights of access and rectification);

– identifying and processing priority weaknesses;

These regulations around Big Data integrate common challenges with existing data, such as:

– the relevance of data processed;

– the responsibility for data examination;

– combining data which stems from distinct sources;

– structuring combined data sets intended for more comprehensive analysis;

– avoiding both the accentuation of social discrimination and categorization;

– controlling processing interconnections;

– creating a unique and re-usable reality format;

– working out advanced analytical environments;

– the development of data usage;

– controlling data access;

– the responsibility for applications;

– data process compliance;

– management of the lifecycle of the analytical tool (*complete data tracking and traceability*);

– limited data storage;

– the purposes of data collection and use;

– respecting consumer data expectations (obtaining the right to privacy; unsubscribing, controlling data usage and limiting intrusion into their private lives;

– consent of the "data" owner.

Finally, dematerialization assumes a framework of clear and coherent legal rules, relating to the body of common law rules with which they interact so as to institute trust and safety, which users expect of this "datafication" of objects.

1.3.3. *The law and regulation around personal health data*

Big Data is in a position to constitute a vast field of business development and value creation. These gigantic data volumes which are available to businesses create new perspectives and make it possible for them to reinvent their activities through new offers and products, the improvement of pre-existing ones, the establishment of stronger links with their customer bases and the improvement of commercial results. Henceforth, "data is increasingly subject to obligations. Coveted as it is, it also becomes a criminal target". [DAR 98], leading to still more important legal issues [GAL 94]. As we saw in the preceding section, this technological turning point raises a whole series of questions such as:

– to what extent and under what circumstances might we acknowledge that data from the human body might be subject to monetization?

– who is the true owner of the data?

– does the user have effective control over the data?

– have they been informed of the possible resale of his data? How can they monitor and control the data that is sent out?

– should one classify and categorize it?

– should we fear personal data use?

– what can be done with this data?

– where are they actually stored?

– how can the legal framework prevent abuses and fight against the harmful use of personal data without paralyzing digital economic growth?

– how might we prevent the exploitation of "lucrative anomalies" amongst individuals without checking progress linked to NICTs?

Thus, the need for a clear and precise legislative framework on metadata use appears necessary so as not to slide into hysteria around Big Data.

1.3.3.1. *The legal nature of personal health data*

Personal health data are a sensitive subject for every individual. Data protection is ensured by complex, comprehensive and constantly evolving legal texts, which can possess significant differences, between the United States where regulatory application operates upon a sectorial basis, and the European Union and France which have imposed their own regulatory frameworks.

The issue of data's legal nature and its appropriable nature has concerned lawyers for a long time. Nowadays, one thing is certain: data is a value, indeed an "economic good". On a daily basis, Big Data are the subject of economic and financial transactions. However, the status of "legally-protected interests", and therefore their appropriation is much more vague and ambiguous. The concept of "data theft" does not really exist in legal texts. Lawyers have established that theft though use of a data medium or a breach of confidentiality in order to constitute an offence. In the civil law sphere, the fraudulent re-use of data is in principle penalized as unfair competition.

The European Union has only established data as a commodity[61] to justify its competence regarding personal data protection. This directive is limited to according an individual the right to scrutiny and control around his data. Personal data is also subject to a hybrid regime between non-appropriation and rights benefiting the individual whom it concerns. We find bioethics and legal principles where "everyone has rights over their body but nobody owns it". It therefore appears impossible to claim to retract biological samples on the grounds that we should own them. On the economic front, this makes possible the free circulation of data without the individual involved being able to impede it for unjustified reasons. Indeed, let us take, for example, the hypothetical case of a legislative framework resulting in a public appropriation of personal data. The simple recovery of an individual's surname and forename would inevitably lead to the obligation to obtain a user license. This example illustrates the reason why

---

61 Directive 95/46 of 24 October 1995 thus devotes line 1 to the ratification of article 100A of the European Community Treaty, the provision relating to the free movement of goods.

lawyers do not wish to link a piece of data to an appropriable legally-protected interest.

Moreover, according to [EYN 12] "personal data seems to have changed its nature. Henceforth, it captures intrinsic elements of the individual". The individual will be reduced to a mass of data. The author explains that data escape the individual's control. "Firstly, the individual does not succeed in grasping it intellectually. Secondly, the individual seems to be legally unable to protect it". Moreover, such control assumes the exercise of moral and tangible control over data. The author notes a relaxed relationship between the individual and the newly received data. With the explosion of technology, the collection of personal "massive data" used to discern civil status, as well as aspects of both an individual's private life and public life. Today, we have gone from collecting data, which characterize parts of an individual's life influencing the public arena, to data collection, which transcribes the essential elements of the human being. Jessica Eynard states:

"Unlike first generation data, second generation data appreciates the constitutive elements of the individual, those which make him a human being. That being said, the individual finds third party data collectors managing to read him as if reading an open book without his needing to speak".

Thus, exploiting "mega-data" may often expose the business to legal risks linked to non-compliance with the laws in force, which are often underestimated or little known. Non-compliance with the legislative framework contributes to increasing customer suspicion as to the fair use of their personal data by the business and the loss of control of such data. Moreover, trust is at the heart of the relationship between a business and its customer. It is therefore necessary to discern with clarity the legal issues of Big Data, so as to not threaten the bond of trust [BAL 14].

Moreover, certain uses of "mega-data" put individual freedom at risk. Numerous American states use software programs which make it possible to be in a better position to predict moments or geographical locations for the crime commission. Such an application leads us to ask questions like "How should we capitalize upon this data without endangering individual freedoms?". In permitting the identification of individuals who are essentially "at risk" of committing a crime, by better understanding human behavior, but also better anticipating how this is linked to genetic profiles, these NICTs may be used by health services, insurance companies, and even health mutual organizations to refuse treatment or customers, and manage the behaviors of the insured party, or other uses [REY 12]. Do such situations and perspectives encourage us to reflect upon the nature of the safeguards to put in place?

This is why the law constitutes the cornerstone of the "Big Data" issue. Far from only providing constraints, it appears as a compass serving as a guide to the understanding of issues of an ethical nature (trust, principles of governance, transparency, confidentiality and doctor-patient confidentiality), and of a legal nature (responsibilities, insurance cover framework and contractual and intellectual property issues). Too often designated as a parameter of increasing complexity and of constraints, the law allows us to identify the need for transparency, governance and regulation which stem from big data. Legal constraints have the purpose of reconciling the actors of NICTs. For this, legal issues which intervene at the management level of a business wishing to monetize Big Data relate to several levels of the business, such as:

– what is the civil liability regime in relation to a technological solution which takes control of business stock?

– what contractual obligation is associated with a form of predictive analysis?

– is this a contractual performance obligation or a duty of care?

Consequently, the decision-maker should question the insurance cover proposed as many of the consequences may be considerable. Significant attention should be paid to the drafting and negotiations governing the "Big Data" service contract. We can take the example of using a solution exploiting Big Data which is mainly based upon a licensing model. We may then consider the following:

– what will be the legal regime for databases created within the business due to this solution?

– will these significant volumes of data allow the business to justify the status of a database producer?

– will it be possible to develop this data from an economic point of view, and if so, according to what parameters and from what activity scopes?

1.3.3.2. *The legal framework around Big Data*

In France, so that a business may acquire legal protection as a database producer, it must be in a position to justify substantial investments whether these are at the tangible, human or financial level[62]. However, in order that these investments do not prove to be entirely wasted, it is still necessary that the technological mechanisms for both collection and analysis of Big Data are put in place in accordance with the applicable legal principles. For example French businesses exploiting personal data must conform to the specific rights instigated by the *Commission Nationale de l'informatique et des libertés* (CNIL), with respect to the opt-in[63], specific data particulars and security and confidentiality mechanisms, and all other legal requirements.

Moreover, during a Scientific Congress organized by the university Panthéon-Assas-Paris II and the CNIL at the Senate on 7 and 8 November 2005, Robert Gellman, an attorney with the Supreme Court of Pennsylvania and a privacy and information policy consultant, indicated that the American approach for personal, data regulation was very far removed from the European approach, which was based upon the presence of an independent data protection authority and around comprehensive protection standards.

Thus, the United States does not have an independent authority dedicated to data protection and has no general framework for data protection in the private sector, but rather sectorial legislation. The regulation of the American market favors state intervention. The means of regulation operates either by a business voluntarily implementing internal codes of best practice or in a contractual way, through agreements between economic operators and their customers.

It may be observed that some countries' infrastructures include national public authorities which are very strict with industrial espionage and anti-terrorism laws, or more generally, public order rules that force Cloud Computing service providers to disseminate customer data to their clients

---

62 Under French law L. 341-1 and supra of the *Code de la Propriété Intellectuelle* (the Intellectual Property Code).
63 This is when the Internet user authorizes sending email messages for business purposes to his inbox.

which they hold in these countries' territories. This is the case in the United States with the Patriot Act and the Foreign Intelligence Surveillance Act.

Thus, being the opposite of the United States, which has different rules for different states, and where there is no such authority specifically dedicated to personal data protection, nor any obligation to declare data processing, France is equipped with a regulatory and legislative system which is relatively constraining. This is particularly so under the *Informatique et Libertés*[64] Law, which transposes the 95/46/CE directive into French Law.

It is the reference text as regards personal data protection within European Union countries. It is worth noting that a new European regulation is in the course of being drafted, which is more restrictive for Big Data actors.

The *Informatique et Libertés* Law of 6 April 1978, amended by the Law of 6 August 2004, transposes the 1995 directive into French Law. It lays down the principles to be respected during collection, processing, storage and maintenance of personal data. It reinforces the right of individuals over their data and states the CNIL's powers of inspection and sanction. As soon as the CNIL is made aware of legal breaches, the organization may send a warning to the business at fault (such a warning being likely to be made public).

If this action has no effect, the CNIL may impose financial penalties (these being a maximum total of 150,000 Euros, which is doubled if it is a repeat offence) and may send victim complaints to the Public Prosecutor to request the imposition of criminal penalties.

Moreover, it is the entity or individual (although, it tends to be a legal entity) with the requisite legal obligations. The individual or entity responsible for processing is defined as the individual or entity (generally, an entity) that either alone or with another individual or entity should state both the purposes and the means of data exploitation. The European Directive applies to businesses who exploit Big Data on French territory, or if they are established outside of the European Union resort to data processing facilities which are located in France.

---

64 The Data Protection Act.

For example, an American start-up which is not located in France will be subject to the French *Informatique et Libertés* Law in the event that it has servers on French soil. Likewise, a company located in France but using, for example, data processing facilities located in the United States, will also be subject to French Law.

In addition, the obligation for fair data collection falls within the principle of transparency which comes from the 1995 directive and which has thus been transposed into French law. Consequently, the fact that certain data are accessible directly upon the Internet does not prevent the French *Informatique et Libertés* Law from applying. We may take the example of Google Cars who received a fine of 100,000 Euros from the CNIL[65], which considered unfair their collection of Mac addresses[66] so as to compare SSID log-ins for Wi-Fi network users, without the knowledge of the individuals concerned. The company DirectAnnonces was also fined by the CNIL for storing individual property adverts with the aim of suggesting specific alerts to businesses by particular activity sectors. For the CNIL, the absence of information given by DirectAnnonces did not make it possible for individuals to have clear information available as to the business's collection of their data, or to exercise their right to object to the use of their data within a reasonable time limit[67].

Moreover, French legislation regulates the action of cross-referencing data from different files so as to obtain both more detailed and better quality data. Thus the French *Informatique et Libertés* Law (Article 25) limits interconnections from files from other individuals and entities whose goals differ significantly. We consider interconnections as soon as there are at least two files or personal data with different purposes being used which are linked in an automated way. This interconnection enforces prior authorization of the *CNIL*.

The *Informatique et Libertés* Law imposes an obligation upon the data controller to keep personal data only for a limited period according to data categories and treatments. For example, Big Data collected for purposes

---

65 Decision number 2011-035 in a restricted format of the CNIL setting out details of a fine against the company Google Inc.
66 This is the unique address taken from a computer network card.
67 Decision number 2009-148 in a restricted format of the CNIL setting out details of a fine against the company DirectAnnonces.

associated with marketing must not be kept for a time period longer than three years from the date of collection or the last contact from the prospective customer. Only "mega data" relevant to explicit, legitimate and specific uses may be exploited. It is important to note that in examining Big Data, anticipating the use which will be made of it is always a complicated issue. The principles of suppression and targeted collection go against the need for the largest possible volume of data. The length of time that data should be kept should not exceed the time necessary to achieve the aims for which they are collected.

Moreover, any data collection is only lawful if it is both legal and not contrary to public order. Nevertheless, within the framework of Big Data processing, the verification of the legality of collection is a very delicate undertaking, owing to the multiplicity of data sources, and, as a consequence, the relevant legislation, which fall within different legal regimes according to the state and/or the sphere of activity concerned. We see that legality of data collection also assumes upholding contracts, standard terms and conditions and intellectual property rights linked to databases, because they are not contrary to public order legislation.

Finally, the recent cyber-attacks by Big Data hackers of which eBay[68] and Orange[69] were victims conveyed the importance of intensifying efforts around personal data security. The *loi Godfrain* (Godfrain Law) of 5 January 1988 penalizes any individual wishing to infiltrate an automated data processing system (ADPS), particularly in an espionage file through an intermediary. The purpose of this intrusion is to distort or hinder the operation of the ADPS, or to falsify or even destroy fraudulently obtained data. The *Informatique et Libertés* Law forces controllers or sub-contractors exploiting Big Data to fulfill all necessary conditions to guarantee the protection, security and confidentiality of personal data used. Thus the integrity of this data must remain intact, without being damaged and denatured or indeed the target for controlled access.

1.3.3.3. *The purpose of data exploitation*

According to French legislation, the purpose of Big Data processing necessitates the data being determined to be made explicit and legitimate and

---

68 This was the compromise of a database of 145 million users in May 2014.
69 This was the personal data theft of 18 April 2014 reported by Orange. It potentially impacted on 1.3 million existing and prospective customers.

it is laid down that the individual about whom the data is collected knows beforehand. This is why the return of informed consent of individuals around the dissemination of personal data represents a significant legal issue.

However, there is an exception to this rule as soon as data has not been directly recovered by the individuals concerned. In this case, the data controllers do not have to produce this information if it proves impossible to give or demand, for dissemination, the efforts being disproportionate in relation to the interest of the approach. The purpose of the processing and its communication to individuals, as well as obtaining the consent of individuals who are the subject of this personal data processing, therefore constitutes a significant legal issue.

According to the 1978 Law as amended (Articles 6 and 38), the so-called "future" data processing parameters must be agreed in respect to any data processing following its collection, and if its purpose differs from the main and ancillary purposes declared or recorded. Subsequent processing which is incompatible with the initial purpose for data collection is illegal. On the other hand, a subsequent exploitation is authorized and does not need a new legal basis within the meaning of Article 7 of the law, such that its purpose is not incompatible with the initial purpose or purposes. As an exception to this rule, processing data for statistical, historical or for research aims is not incompatible with the initial purpose or purposes. This may concern processes as varied as analysis tools for Internet sites or Big Data applications used for research ends.

It is likely that the European Big Data regulatory proposals may impose upon data controllers the obligation to supply more precise data for the intended use (such as "improvements in practices", "marketing purposes", "computer security" or "future research") by individuals involved, by identifying, if the need arises, the clauses and the standard contractual terms and conditions justifying the processing or even the legitimate interests pursued by the data controller. A departure from the original purpose is, therefore, forbidden. The data controller must submit this information when the data is collected and gathered, and if need be, the consent of those concerned required. Businesses processing Big Data are, therefore, limited to the purposes which are disclosed at the outset.

In France, the obligation to declare the processing purpose is carried out at the CNIL. There is no real equivalent of this approach in other European Union countries.

1.3.3.4. *Free and informed consent of the individual linked with the data*

Consent, when it is requested by Law, is in any case assumed to be given to the person or entity in authority. It designates all expression of specific, free or informed will. French Law demands that any exploitation of personal data is achieved with the consent of the individual concerned, except for the preceding exception. This thus leaves a particular vagueness as to the expression and the means of obtaining this consent. Indeed, the *Informatique et Libertés* Law only indicates that "personal data processing must have received the consent of the individual concerned", leaving open the possibility of implied consent. French law has not retained the wording provided in the European directive of 24 October 1995, which states that the individual concerned must have "indubitably given his consent" ("unambiguous consent"). This must be free and informed consent which imposes upon the businesses responsible that the data exploitation be transparent as to processing procedures such as the purposes, nature and data recipients, information linked to possible data transfer to a non-European Union country, the identity of the data controller and the rights relating to the person concerned (such as the right to privacy, rectification, access and opposition to processing).

The notion of consent implies both the individual's right and the capacity to control his own information, and to impose limits upon use and re-use of the latter through research structures, health organizations or third parties [ROS 14]. However, to exploit the potential of these large volumes of data, consent may need to develop from strict regulation for each potential data use towards equilibrium between control and personal sharing, particularly when serving public health and/or environmental protection ends [DAV 12].

In 2013, an enquiry led by the CNIL and nineteen of its global counterparts proved that information given to Internet users is insufficient. The study sets out that 20% of the most influential global sites, and 50% of Smartphone and tablet applications do not provide any information on actual data uses, thus preventing users from having the option to provide their free and informed consent for the use of their data.

In December 2013, in these circumstances CNIL gave Google a symbolic fine of 150,000 Euros for the associated use of personal data stemming from all of its devices and services, which was insufficiently described in its confidentiality policy with Internet users. According to the CNIL, the Internet giant did not inform its users in enough detail of the circumstances and purposes for the exploitation of their personal data. The corporation was criticized for a lack of transparency and user information concerning the use of such data and control over it [CNI 13]. Following this fine, on 31 March 2014 the search engine finalized modifications to its confidentiality rules.

In addition, the European Court of Justice declared on 13 May 2014 that Google was responsible for the exploitation of personal data appearing on its pages. On this basis, the Web giant was obliged to destroy existing personal data in the search results of an Internet user who had made such a request. Since 29 May 2014, Google has offered Internet users the opportunity to request deletion of their data which the business considers "irrelevant, obsolete or inappropriate" through a questionnaire, because of a real risk of loss of user confidence.

Moreover, for Brent Daniel Mittelstadt and Luciano Floridi [MIT 15], it is preferable to redefine the relationship between organizations using personal data (calling them bio-banks) and the individuals concerned, by placing more emphasis upon the notion of data sharing, or support for research and innovation, than upon consent as such. Thus, bio-banks could establish a contract based around solidarity and data sharing, and not around individual autonomy through the individual's free and informed consent. The individual should be kept up-to-date upon the details of the research its potential applications, the risks, future uses, procedures, the benefits, and the potential commercial value of the data processed [PRA 13]. Finally, even if it is explicitly asked for, the consent may be manipulated or biased, due to the fact that the Internet user could be pressured into giving it. This scope of consent might be broadened in the case of a faster detection of epidemics for public interest reasons. It should be underlined that the legislation is relaxed for given data sets as soon as the data collected is anonymized very quickly.

1.3.3.5. Anonymity of personal data

According to the French *Informatique et Libertés* Law, personal data correspond to "all information which relates to an individual who is either identified or directly identifiable, due to an identification number or one or several elements which are particular to him". In these circumstances, if the data exploitation concerns anonymized data then this law does not apply. This is why we see that a large number of Big Data applications imply that anonymized personal data will, thus, make it possible for us to avoid the legislative framework of the Law.

It should be observed that the European directive defines anonymized data as being: "the entire means likely to be reasonably implemented, either by the data controller, or by another person so as to identify the aforesaid person" so as to determine whether the data is anonymized.

In France, the Law requires consideration of the process of discerning whether an individual "might be directly or indirectly identified". For the CNIL, irreversible anonymization is the only loophole in the *Informatique et Libertés* Law. Moreover, with triangulation techniques, cross-referencing and cross-checking linked to Big Data, such an anonymization appears almost impossible to attain! If "massive data" technologies are neutral in themselves, data processing which when taken in isolation is not an identifier, might lead to a form of "re-identification" of an individual. This thus poses the question of whether it is necessary to apply regulations either before or according to the result obtained.

Three cumulative indicators make it possible to know whether an anonymization solution will provide satisfactory guarantees in this sector:

– the correlation and the option to link together data which is associated with an individual;

– personalization and its potential to isolate an individual;

– the possibility of acquiring data about an individual by inference.

Finally, private lives and anonymization have often been linked in literature, by the fact that one's private life as raised by Big Data uses may be addressed by straightforward deletion of identification information [JOL 12]. Anonymization has often been considered to be the minimal requirement to protect both user private life and the confidentiality of an individual concerned by the personal data processed [CHO 14].

1.3.3.6. *Data Mining and individual profiling*

Generally, the designers of Big Data-linked NICTs (such as Cloud Computing) put in place a system of backdoors[70] giving them access to all data stored. This system provides a means for the service provider to access all stored data. Furthermore, the American authorities, through the Patriot Act, have the right to directly access Cloud data which is stored on American corporate servers (or by foreign businesses with economic interests in the country) wherever such servers are installed.

It appears fundamental to protect data through IS security and the management of risks relating to personal data exploitation.[71] For this, it is recommended that data protection is considered from the moment of system design (so-called "privacy by design"[72]). It thus seems fundamental to pursue these different initiatives, whilst sensitizing private actors to the risks around freedoms and private lives [ACH 13]. The Data Mining technique [BRA 13] shows the interest in Big Data and data aggregation, and will provoke a change of scale. It will not be a fundamentally new activity. Henceforth, deposits tend to collect significant volumes of aggregated data with "unlimited possibilities for data matching and Data Mining" [PRA 13] owing to the huge volume of data [STE 13]. In this respect, it is in this sense that we must demystify the practice of Data Mining. It is a matter, above all, of an intellectual technology[73]. It is a tool which allows us to make certain mental processes both easier and automated. The extraction and synthesis of preexisting information has been a regular business activity for researchers for as long as scientific research has existed. For example, instead of recovering and tying up tens of thousands of pieces of data, it is possible to entrust this task to algorithms.

These Data Mining technologies offer, owing to the process of artificial intelligence (AI), the opportunity to process these monstrous masses of data so as to extract crucial information, which is a determining factor in a more effective decision-making process:

---

70 Backdoors are confidential access points to a processing device, a program or an online service installed by the designer.

71 Data intrusion, viruses or data damage.

72 "Privacy by design" involves accompanying members of industries during the development of their services so as to integrate problems linked to personal data beforehand.

73 It serves the same purpose as, for example, the abacus or double entry bookkeeping.

"Thanks to the process of AI which it uses, Data Mining makes possible the scope for time-saving, provides the means and allows for individuals to be able to understand this data". [OMA 02] Some writers in the field affirm that "The virtuous circle of Data Mining is to change data into information, information into decisions and decisions into profits" [BOU 98], while others indicate the dangers of Data Mining and profiling. [EYN 12] explains that this situation will end in an uncontrolled use of information with the aim to anticipate individual needs and behaviors of the individual. Profiling would imprison the individual "within a profile that does not correspond perfectly to him, but on the basis of which, however, decisions are made which relate to him".

Finally, the Big Data market can only flourish on one condition, which is by establishing of a climate of trust. To create it, business must guarantee the conditions in which data entrusted by a third party will be exploited and define the data uses, in order to guarantee customer protection. We, in a particular way, may observe a conflict between an individual's desire for knowledge through an economic actor, thanks to Data Mining technologies, and that individual's right to respect for their private life.

1.3.3.7. *The protection of databases*

The protection of personal data is ensured by a complex legal framework which is constantly evolving, revealing particular differences between the United States – where there is a regulatory sectoral approach – and France and the European Union, which have laid down their own regulatory frameworks. Processing this data may therefore expose the business to risks which are often underestimated or little known. The principal risks are of a legal nature, linked to non-compliance with the Law in force, while the other risks particularly concern the business's reputation with its clients. This is why trust is the cornerstone of the relationship between a business and its customer. It is therefore vital to clearly understand the legal issues around Big Data so that this bond of trust is not threatened.

Creators and producers of databases are protected by the *sui generis* right, as well as under copyright. This protection around the content databases occurs as soon as their creation, authentication or their conceptualization evidences "a substantial financial, tangible, human investment" according to Article L. 341–1 of the French *Code de la Propriéte Intellectuelle*. This notion is taken up by European Law in almost equivalent terms: "a substantial investment from the qualitative and/or quantitative point of view"[74]. In these circumstances, substantial database content extraction[75] or re-use[76] by a third party may be exposed by the creator of this database. It should be observed that such regulation lays down a requirement for database producers to justify the acquisition or the location of servers, data exploitation or storage platforms, investment in significant network capacities, as well as the recruitment of qualified individuals for the development and maintenance of databases.

It is possible to state several major principals as regards personal data protection, such as:

– limiting the removal of data to circumstances where it is strictly necessary;

– the need for a legal basis for all extraction and exploitation of data;

– balancing the public interest requiring extraction with the interests of a private citizen to protect his private life;

– the deletion of data as soon as it is no longer necessary to retain;

– the control of data processing by the individual concerned and by the data controller;

– sharing of powers by authorities regarding the data transfer.

Respect for confidentiality occurs when the relevant equipment and premises are secure, as well as when arrangements are made to safeguard files, users permit means of access to data, there are control systems for such access and the dissemination of data takes place by electronic means [BIR 13].

---

74 Article 7 of the directive 96/9/CE of the European Parliament and Council, of 11 March 1996, includes the legal protection of databases.

75 The substantial nature of infringement of property rights is assessed on a case by case basis but takes account of a range of indicators such as the nature of data extracted, whether or not there is competition, the availability of data extracted outside of the database, the reference to the contents of the database and other appropriate indicators.

76 The notion of reuse is quite broad, as it encompasses all unauthorized acts, with the objective of public dissemination of all or part of the contents of the database. This therefore forces Big Data actors to acquire prior authorization before the use and processing of all third party databases.

Furthermore, databases benefit from two independent legal regimes, being legal protection of copyright and the legal protection of the database creators.

The European Community directive of 11 March 1996 around the protection of databases, transposed into French Law by the Law of 1 July 1998, made a dual protection of databases possible; copyright protection (in accordance with the provisions of articles L. 112–3 and the subsequent provisions within the *Code de la Propriété Intellectuelle*[77], and protection by a right of *sui generis*, that is to say a right which is specific to database producers. To claim copyright protection, the database must constitute a genuine original intellectual creation. In the event of the content being original (page layout, presentation and a specific form of extraction) copyright protection applies. The rights of database creators belong to the family of rights related to copyright. This set of rights makes up a particular part of literary and artistic property.

Copyright protection is regulated by Articles L. 112–3 and the subsequent provisions of the *Code de la Propriété Intellectuelle*:

"Article L. 112–3 – Authors of translations, adaptations, modified versions, or arrangements of copyrighted works enjoy the protection instituted by the present code without prejudice to the rights of the author of the original work. It is likewise for authors of anthologies or collections of works or diverse data, such as databases, which, through the choice or the arrangement of subjects constitute intellectual creations. A database includes a collection of works, data or other independent elements, arranged in a systematic or methodical way and individually accessible both by electronic and other means."

Legal protection for database creators is governed by the provisions of articles 341–1, and the subsequent provisions:

"Article L. 341–1 – The creator of a database, by which is meant the person who takes the initiative and the corresponding investment, benefits from the protection of the database contents when its creation, authentication and presentation attest to a substantial financial, material or human investment. This protection is independent and applies without prejudice to

---

77 The Intellectual Property Code.

those resulting from copyright or another right with respect to the database or one of its constitutive elements."

It is appropriate here to observe the extent of the protection given which is defined in Article L.342–1 of the Code:

"The creator of the database has the right to prohibit:

1) the extraction by permanent or temporary transfer of all or part, whether substantially relating to quality or quantity, of the contents of the database onto another device by any means and in any form;

2) the re-use, through making available to the public of all or part, whether substantially relating to quality or quantity, of the contents of the database whatever its form.

These rights may be passed on or assigned to third-parties or be subject to a license. Public lending does not constitute extraction or re-use."

Finally, we are able to set out the specific case of Open Data; that is to say, information which the state, regional and local authorities and public law-enforcing institutions make available to all so as to achieve their public service goals. This data is generally exploitable under an open license which allows the reproduction, copying, publication and dissemination of public data and to process it on a commercial basis. This license generally requires the obligation to state both the data source and the date that it was last updated.

1.3.3.8. *Personal data confronted by the principles of free movement and accessibility*

Certainly Big Data is a particular category of data as a result of being associated with an individual's private life. It remains no less the case that it has an informative value and is, therefore, able to be transferred, particularly within the EU, where the principles of freedom of movement of people, goods and capital are a fundamental part of the foundation of the European Community. This movement of personal data is in a particular way "secondary" to that of people and goods, in the sense that it is by necessity linked. This is why restraining or limiting the transfer of data has the knock-on effect of limiting the free movement of people and goods [FED 08].

We can see that the development of French legislation has increasingly favored the movement of data through the concurrent requirement of the relaxing of data processing conditions. This principle is based on the premise that personal data may only be freely circulated insofar as interested parties have a certain level of trust in the use of their data (see the doctrine of legitimate expectations stemming from the general principles of European Community law). To achieve this, they need to be kept informed of all useful details regarding the exploitation of their data (see the principle of transparency).

This argument consists of guaranteeing the means of this transparency, which is necessary for the free movement of data, prior to processing, with the aim of optimizing the trust of individuals involved in the circulation of data which pertains to them.

In addition, member states of the European Community consider that the free movement of personal data should be subject to, on the one hand, a conventional approach to cross-border movements which is necessary for a single market to operate effectively, while to so-called "sovereign" activities linked to public order, and police and legal cooperation in the sphere of criminal offences, on the other [FED 08]. Thus, Articles 29 and 30 of the European Union Treaty present a space for "freedom, security and justice" making possible close cooperation between the judicial authorities and the police within member states.

In 2013, the American government implemented the "Blue Button", known as "Smart Disclosure", so that employees within the Department for Defense are able to upload their own health data. This makes it possible to limit considerably the misuses that might occur from the fact that the user is the only decision-maker. It is worth noting that epidemiological studies cannot be completed without full access to health users' digital files. In 2014, this system became more widespread with the implementation of a new site and a more successful program entitled "Blue Button +" being rolled out. In this version, health data are interoperable through particular standards and APIs. The aim is to make it possible for developers to create applications using this data, such as for example "iBlue Button" [BEC 13], which reorganizes Medicare information (the health insurance system implemented in the United States) in an ergonomic way.

1.3.3.9. *The ownership of personal data*

Ownership is a complex subject as it may refer to rights concerning the data redistribution and modification, as well as the notion of intellectual property and to innovations developed from its analysis. The redistribution and modification of data may be limited to the data "owner" so as to maintain data integrity, while access to data analysis is open to "analysts" for the study of innovation and development (see intellectual property) [MIT 15]. In practice, we note that the majority of operators and manufacturers exploiting data often consider themselves as the data "owners". Moreover these matters are fluid, which therefore poses the question of their appropriation which is associated with their legal nature and connection to their "holder". French law remains vague around the notion of data ownership. The fact that data is collected by a natural person or an entity does not justify subsequent appropriation. Do these reasons call into question data ownership?

The issue of consent is closely akin to that of the holder of the piece of data. Who may have access to the data available on the Internet, such as public data from social networks? Although initially free, users must pay for the majority of such services, which make up the main asset of businesses like Facebook or Google, hence their opposition to the European legislation. While organizations and institutions were, up until now, both producing and using their own data, data brokers nowadays sell business data or even state-owned data to various others. This situation appears increasingly, often, particularly in the United States, and prompts us to wonder about how feasible data protection through intellectual property law actually is. As stated by the investigating magistrate [BRU 06], "intellectual property (which is the natural sphere of intangible assets) nowadays sees a continuous expansion within specializations (with computing technologies, biotechnologies, etc.)". We may then ask the following question: why has there been no growth in its development within the sphere of personal data?

One of the fundamental principles of intellectual property law is that "it does not protect data, but simply original expression". In France, we rather find it *in absentia*. The *Code de la Propriété Intellectuelle* revolves around original works. Databases are only affected inasmuch as "through the choice or arrangement of subjects, (they) constitute intellectual creations". Personal data and information are clearly excluded from this definition.

Acknowledging the description of property rights to evoke the link between the individual and the data which relates to him poses a number of issues, as this ends up acknowledging the possibility of a complete arrangement of data.

Moreover, if the individual may negotiate the data which affects him or her, he or she cannot, on the other hand, completely dispose of it. It will always be associated with him. The approach which consists of acknowledging data appropriation "instigates an option for Man to arrange his own data when only the data possession is actually involved" [MAL 97]. As far as we are concerned, we think it is possible to envisage a possibility analogous to that of intellectual property.

The question of discerning whether intellectual property is a form of property in the traditional sense of the word certainly causes us to enter into a debate, albeit academic, but as an ongoing discourse leads to lively discussions. Moreover, this debate may have consequences for the hypothesis that we pursue, knowing whether personal data may enter into the civilian ownership mold.

Today, there are two schools of thought which are positively opposed. The first school, which is the majority view, takes the *communis opinion doctorum* approach, considering that arguments which favor the acceptance of intellectual property as an actual form of property prevail. The others, who consider this approach absolutely unnecessary, use the term intellectual property. They consider that it is not simply sufficient to place inverted commas before the word "property", but it is necessary purely and simply to delete this misused term. One of the major arguments of the critics of intellectual property is to discredit the temporary nature that is attributed to it. The inalienable nature of traditional property seems in this case to be lacking. Moreover, nowadays for the majority view, this is not a valid objection.

The intangibility of the matter in question challenges the level of control over economic usefulness which should be reserved to it. This control over of its economic use is an important criterion within property law. The issue of law and demanding an intellectual property right, in addition to reserving a moral right, is indeed a right of economic use over the item.

In such circumstances, the data owner will benefit, in part from the value which is generated by these uses. This will also bring about better regulation and control of personal data by encouraging individuals to invest fully in them. We may use the same logic with the possibility of creating an actual personal data right. The individual whom the data affects, in addition to reserving a moral right over the personal data, may wish to keep control over the economic uses of such an item.

It is in this sense that we therefore envisage ownership of the data: control and the reservation of the economic uses of data.

As we have seen previously, the concept of "knowledge is power" reigns supreme. It constitutes a form of wealth, as the person who has knowledge has a distinct advantage compared to he who does not. It is therefore highly coveted, which is why it is necessary to protect it and in particular through intellectual property rights. A solution would be to protect personal data through an intellectual property right. This has been suggested, particularly by [HUN 99]. Laure Marino and Romain Perray resume the issue: "…in this approach which flirts with intellectual property, everyone would become the owner of the commercial exploitation rights over information which concerned them" [ROC 10]. There would then be a system of "royalties" set up, which would be managed by a copyright management company.

However as [SAM 00] states, "the protection of works and that of data both pursue different ends". Intellectual property rights favor creation by instigating a regime which ensures protection of author works, so that they might derive a benefit from his creative activity, while no third party might appropriate his work or copy it. Intellectual property rights thus have the aim of encouraging creativity and the dissemination of copyrighted works.

When envisaging ownership of personal data, we observe that such a project pursues a diametrically opposed aim, protecting personal data which exists already and not encouraging individuals to produce even more personal data.

The concept of ownership emerged well before intellectual rights. In many aspects, its theoretical and philosophical foundations as well as its legal regime seem obliged to dismiss them from its sphere:

"The establishment, through incremental steps, of intellectual property by the French Parliament in the form of temporary rights does not accord with the concept of logical and clear ownership. They, indeed, are determined according to commercial and industrial policies and are only defined by the casuistry of both their purpose and content. Moreover, their intangible purpose deprives them of their physical basis from which property benefits under the general Law, based both around possession and physical exclusivity. Their moral dimension, in comparison with the general property regime, seems full of peculiarities. Their limited duration contrasts with the perpetuity of property ownership under civil law" [MAP 09]. Thus, personal data has in itself has become a form of "asset". It has an intrinsic value and processing makes it possible to benefit from particular services, often free of charge, owing to the value that these data create for businesses (see free access to Internet services). This is why it perhaps may necessary to envisage a dual protection with moral rights over data (for example, inaccessible data), and an economic right which would make it possible to reserve economic use rights in the item. This is in the same vein as copyright.

However, we must nuance our ideas around this notion of "data ownership", due to the fact that data is only a part of the information. Moreover, data is free of copyright, hence the principle of free movement of data. Besides, data exploitation achieved thereafter does not make possible the affirmation that data have, for all that, a new legal status.

Eventually, the Law appears a necessary vector for Big Data processing. By giving back command and control of these data to targeted individuals through better information transparency, by sensitizing each participant to the fundamental principles of managing data collection, conserving data and the analysis and use of personal data, legal standards aimed to frame the "Big Data" supply, manipulating it in an optimized and secure space. We are witnessing a race against time between the exponential development of NICTs and the law which is constantly obliged to redefine its range of actions, so as to respond to various problematic situations created by Big Data processing.

2

Ethical Development of the Medical Datasphere

As Lucy Suchmann observed in 2011, through Lévi-Strauss, "…we are our tools…" and our personal health data are an integral part of us. In these circumstances, it becomes necessary to question the value of Big Data in the health sphere.

At the beginning of the digital era, the value of data processing was demonstrated by the creation of tools intended to manipulate data, and then by working out the processes which were manipulating these tools. Nowadays we realize that the value is partly to be found in the information itself. It may be noted that the individual has an impact and a direct influence on the market value of his personal data, especially by prohibiting access to it and thus increasing its market price. In this context, we may imagine that an individual can manage his digital history as he pleases, by continually and automatically renewing it. Data has an "individual" value which may be manipulated. Furthermore, an individual with a sought-after, or even unique profile, will have data with a high product value at their disposal. This is why part of the internal increase in the data value comes from its profile, its relevance and characteristic features, and the individual themself. As the "data" is perishable, its monetization is being devalued constantly, as each split second constitutes a significant element of its value.

This intrinsic value of information depends upon the "why, how and within what limits it is used" [DUP 13]. The value is not simply in the data alone, but also when this data is collated with a multitude of other data.

Currently, NICTs are capable of studying and exploiting all available data with a very sharp granularity. This concerns relevant information, but also weak signals, which make it possible to identify new behaviors and new user types or segmentation criteria. Consequently, Big Data has become a means to enrich both thinking and action. Weak signals which are picked up only obtain their real qualitative value when they are cross-referenced with other data and other diverse sources. Hence, the necessity for multiplying and accelerating data cross-referencing since weak signals result in high volume processing. We may take the example of the handheld phone. What is the purpose of the mobile phone if you are the only person who owns one? As long as numerous other people own a mobile phone then the use of your own device takes on both significance and meaning, as you can communicate remotely with other individuals.

Moreover, Big Data is not uniquely synonymous with significant volumes, but may also concern the types of data and the processing complexities of such data. We can take the example of data resulting from an individual's DNA sequencing, which represents about 800 Mb. From the density angle, this may seem small on the scale of Big Data, and of course, this human genome comprises around four billion pieces of data and numerous data patterns.

From this observation, Big Data has an internal value which becomes more important and is demonstrated as soon as it is used within a process framework or occupational activity. The intrinsic value of "data" remains implied and of no significance if there are no algorithms to manipulate or exploit it. Both the action and expression of data lies within the processing algorithms which rule our world. Consequently, tomorrow's corporate culture will rely upon platforms which are based upon analytical and "data science" algorithms[1]. This data science has no need for hypotheses or ideas, but exclusively an army of automatic and statistical learning algorithms which process data to find its meaning.

---

1 "Data Science" may comprise various angles (Data Mining, predictive analytic processing, automatic learning, etc.) but its main objective is to find new information within "data", as well as predictive models which can reveal probabilities.

The "Why" poses a question around cultural issues, especially around the purpose of data. Both the processing and analysis of Big Data call into question traditional decision-making and predictive models on the basis of new inductive and no longer deductive processes. This marks a Copernican turning point for numerous generations of decision-makers who must now learn to use the commons which comprise the Internet in order to make use of a significant volume of multi-form structured or unstructured data. This digital revolution thus imposes upon businesses the need to fast-track the acquisition of a genuine "data" culture. The "How" expresses the repercussions of this culture upon what we refer to as the "real environment" of a business, namely the following factors; strategy and methodology, structural and technological issues, organizational and regulatory issues and relational and cultural issues. Hence, if businesses understand the actual value of "massive data", then they will force their environment to evolve by reconfiguring it from what they learn from such data. Increased data value occurs by a business organizational transformation. This is the price to pay for "data" monetization!

Data also forces us to wonder about the scope of "limits" linked to the risks of use around Big Data. It is not possible to have optimal, efficient, coherent and sustainable data usage without Big Data ethics. Data value offers a means to facilitate discussions relating to the organization of the alignment of policies, commercial practices and individual behaviors around Big Data processing.

Our ethical evaluation suggests options around how to align shared human values with initiatives proposed within an organization. This represents a work space for an efficient action plan which we can rely on to achieve an optimal alignment between human values and actions to implement.

This "algorithmic ethic" will be required in the years ahead as the cornerstone "of the relationship of trust to be established with the market" [DUP 13]. This increase in the ethical value of data will certainly become one of the components for legal responsibility and future regulations framing Big Data processing. Such a context contributes to both making users and public bodies more alert to the exploitation of "massive data", and forces us to wonder how far can we exchange our private lives for increased convenience?

This chapter will comprise three large sections which deal with ethical modeling, particularly based around the risks and ethical issues of the medical Datasphere, the selective ranking of health data centered on data structuring, and finally the ethical evaluation of Big Data, illustrated by a radar chart allowing us to visualize of the axes of "info-ethics management".

2.1. From the study of risks to the translation of ethical issues in the medical datasphere

The growing digitalization of medical data, the enhanced endless capacity to store digital data, the accumulation of types of information resulting from this thus contributes to the introduction of some fears and uncertainties because of its multiple and often complex uses, its impacts, which are both difficult to measure and affect very different populations, and its information, which is sometimes out of control. In 2001, the *Kennedy Report* stated that "all health care is dictated by information, to ensure that the threat linked to incorrect information is a direct risk for health service quality and governance within the NHS (National Health Service)" [2].

Consequently, the best way to approach new ethical issues posed by Big Data is to use an approach which treats all forms of existence and behavior as both authentic and real, even those based upon synthetic artifacts and stem from engineering. This "synthetic e-environmentalism" approach forces a change in our view around the relationship between the Greek terms *physis* (nature and reality) and *techne* (practical science and its applications). This is why it has become necessary to have a deeper knowledge and understanding of the use of NICTs within the medical sector, to protect the private life of every citizen. According to the philosophy of information by [FLO 09], the question of whether nature and technology may be reconcilable is not a question with a predetermined response, in waiting for it to be determined. This appears to be more of a practical problem, for which possible solutions should be implemented. This line of questioning does not revolve around a

---

2 http://webarchive.nationalarchives.gov.uk/20090811143745/, http://www.bristol-inquiry.org .uk.

possible amalgamation of these two spheres, but rather whether this association is successful.

In these circumstances it becomes fundamental to begin considering personal health data through a Neo-Platonic systemic ethical prism (Ψ, G, Φ) to remove doubts and control uncertainties surrounding devices and uses of medical data in this new dematerialized ecosystem. To do so, we have implemented a guidance-based approach allowing the transition from a risk-analysis to the expression of ethical objectives around personal health data, via links aligning these two ontologies.

It can be said regarding risks in business today that it is necessary to list these risks, rank them, link them to processes and to implement an appropriate governance model, so as to manage them as much from a financial performance, conformity, continuity and image point of view as from the angle of data protection. Consequently, it is necessary to have a conscious and clearly defined approach for risk evaluation and management. Next, it is necessary to include this approach within an information protection policy. Nowadays, it is the expression of needs which is difficult. What should be protected and to what extent? How should we lead ethical thinking regarding the current use of medical ISs and Big Data in the health sphere?

A pragmatic and progressive approach to common risk mapping is a prerequisite, both for the risk management approach, but also for a successful approach to data protection.

2.1.1. *The ethical systemic Neo-Platonic modeling (Ψ, G, Φ) of complex data*

The appearance of Big Data, essentially fed by raw data, has enabled the advent of algorithmic rule; through extra- and infra-confidential signals which are quantifiable, operating by the most proactive configuration possible, rather than by best practice standards. These are aimed at individuals exclusively through warning devices independent of human control. From this observation our thinking is oriented very quickly to both the working out and implementation of adaptive modeling so as to analyze, understand and process these large quantities of complex data.

The individual perceives "data", interprets "information", makes links with other "knowledge" that has been memorized and is then capable of acting based on such "knowledge". He thus acquires skills that he is then capable of repeatedly implementing, thus translating a "practical wisdom" [RIC 90]. Hence this approach, which is both epistemological and ethical, is part of the fundamental model to understand the human dimension for use of information and communication technologies (ICTs). Our transdisciplinary study naturally invites an epistemological critique revolving around "knowledge-processes" which integrates Leonardo da Vinci's neo-Platonic thinking of "doing to understand and understanding to do" [VAL 41, VAL 48].

To make this successful transition to simplification, we must use both the correct representation and modeling, which entails substituting a process description for a report. So as to be operative, the concept of information must be both understood and used in a more systemic framework which joins together action through knowledge. Thus, knowledge is finalized within action. It translates the passage from knowledge to know-how. Knowledge becomes information with respect to a function. It provides instruction both upon an aim and for a given action. It is a question of a real knowledge challenge both from a theoretical and a practical point of view. In this way, this process of working out info-ethics allows the passage from a state (A) of complex, disorganized and fluid knowledge towards a state (known as Ω) of simple, structured and teleological knowledge. In this way, this process of Big Data towards info-ethics is illustrated by the action of large-scale sense-making. The analysis and intelligent processing of these various data (Data Intelligence) must lead to decision-making.

We have chosen to represent the complex and simplified states of knowledge respectively by the Greek letters Alpha (A) and Omega (Ω), in relation to their symbolic aspect[3] (see Figure 2.1).

---

3 In the Christian tradition A and Ω symbolize Christ eternal. Alpha (the first letter of the Greek alphabet) which conveys the dawn of time (see the first chapter of the Gospel according to St. John) and Omega (the last letter of the Greek alphabet) illustrates the end of the world (see the Apocalypse according to St. John). This metaphor was taken up by the Jesuit Pierre Teilhard de Chardin so as to represent human evolution going from Alpha (A) to Omega (Ω.). Finally, physics and chemistry use the symbol Ω traditionally to indicate a state of equilibrium of a given system.

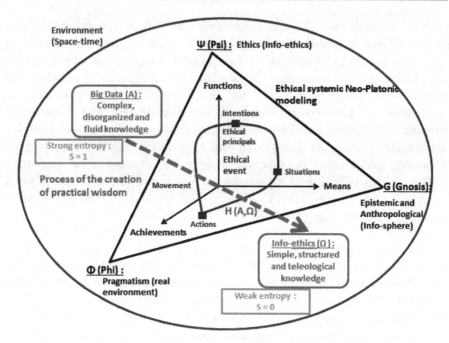

Figure 2.1. *The transformation from Alpha to Omega through the Neo-Platonic, ethical systemic prism*

This transformation takes effect through the intermediary of a neo-platonic ethical systemic neo-Platonic (Ψ, G, Φ) which integrates aspects of ethics (Ψ: Psi[4]), epistemology and anthropology (G: Gnosis[5]), and pragmatism (Φ: Phi[6]: the real environment[7]).

---

4 This Greek letter is often used to designate psychology, psychiatry, psychotherapy and psychiatry, globally known as the sciences of human thought. This symbol means the soul or psyche.

5 The term "gnosis" means "knowledge" in Latin.

6 This Greek letter determines the golden number which equals 1.618. Since antiquity, this symbol has represented harmonious divine proportions. This makes up the basis of structures within architecture, art, anatomy, music, literature and both tangible and practical aspects of science and the arts. Phi also means the term "pharmakon" (the science of human medicine) in the Hippocratic Oath.

7 The real environment is a favorable dimension which involves location (identification, localization, estimation, characterization, cartography and ranking) and protection (acquisition, formalization and preservation).

This research into info-ethics contributes to working towards an entropy (S: the degree of disorder)[8] which is very low, having, indeed, a degree of disorder which is practically zero . This process of recognition of info-sphere (or Datasphere) knowledge[9] linked to the pragmatism of the real environment makes it possible for us to simplify our knowledge, by approaching it both statically through our environment and dynamically through our interactions. For [MOR 04], ethics is inseparable from complex knowledge[10], being "a knowledge which connects together and is both expressed and created because we wish to be responsible or supportive citizens". This ethical thinking around the use of NICTs is fed by a triptych (action – skill–responsibility) which applies as much in medicine as in information technology.

The systemic approach is relevant in the health sphere where numerous decision-making elements, which stem from several sources, interact. The ethical decision corresponds to a delicate balance between those involved in a given situation. This decision is unique and cannot be replicated, according to a given environment and time. Although always subject to questioning, it is in perpetual motion. Ethics appears as soon as there is a conflict because it is then necessary to choose, prefer or opt for particular values, while sacrificing others.

Consequently, ethical decisions are complex by their very nature, and perspectives and opinions largely vary between individuals. These decisions vary even more when the organizational demands of management, investors or the market are included within the mix. This is why a precise and targeted exploration of a shared set of common values is necessary [DAV 12].

---

8 The word "entropy" was introduced by Clausius and is derived from a Greek word meaning "transformation". It has always represented complexity, and therefore, the possible disorder of a system, a structure or an organization.

9 The info-sphere (or data-sphere) leads to actions such as updating (data evaluation, updating and enrichment) and development (data access, dissemination, sharing, exploitation and integration).

10 Edgar Morin (1991) uses the term "self-ethics" so as to designate the need to "increase the complexity of the discernment" in the action. The word "self" for the author means "fundamental autonomy" (*Autos*).

Finally, this ethical modeling (Ψ, G, Φ) can be compared to what we termed "Ethical Data Mining", implementing algorithms with the aim to bring about new, "info-ethical" information, resulting from the analysis of a significant quantity of data. The reduction of the quantity of information is at the core of an ethical dilemma. Is it or is it not necessary to intentionally delete information so as to regulate, and make operational, this info-ethical information?

2.1.2. *The process of ethical-technical guidance*

To our knowledge, no formal approach which makes it possible to form interrelationships between risk analysis and the demands of personal digital data has been established by work in this field.

The object of this section is to set out an associative integration of these processes. In practical terms, we are proposing to devise a guidance system in which ethical "data" objectives stem from associated risks. This is made possible by coherent and semantic associations between the ontology[11] of these two processes.

The identification of ethical decision issues contributes to developing perspectives and politics which lead to the alignment of human values within Big Data processing. For this, it is necessary to know what the values are and how to enforce them, so as to improve innovation and reduce the risks of use.

Furthermore, our guidance approach, which makes it possible to pass from the data owner-incurred risks to the expression of the ethical demands of data, proposes an enhanced tool for better controlled and managed personal health data (see Figure 2.2).

This approach of concept alignment from a risk-based ontology to a demand-based ontology of ethical objectives is set to change.

---

11 The ontology represents a data model with a set of concepts in a given sphere, as well as the relationships between these two concepts. It is used to reason regarding the objects within the sphere concerned.

We may envisage policies such as:

– enriching both ontologies by introducing associative links between concepts, which make it possible to reveal potential conflicts between risks and/or ethical issues. In turn, this would make it possible to offer better governance in risk-specification, to suggest several scenarios related to ethical issues to achieve;

– automating the risk characterization stage.

These alignments make it possible to reduce tensions stemming from the legislation through a better understanding of constraints and demands, improving consumer adoption by reducing disinformation around the use of consumers' digital data, reducing the risk of unintentional and unanticipated consequences of Big Data exploitation and favoring collaboration from values which are explicitly shared between actors.

The act of bringing together the two systems of reference (risks and operational objectives) to confirm the relevance of scenarios, lead to the rethinking of risk monitoring indicators.

Alignment methodology consists of four stages which form a continuous loop [DAV 12]:

– *questioning*: discussions around fundamental structural values after their identification. A good understanding of the human values around Big Data processing is fundamental;

– *investigation*: the examination of processing practices for actual and real data and an evaluation of the alignment of fundamental organizational values;

– *enumeration*: the explicit written expression of the alignment and gaps between simple and clear values and practices;

– *action*: tactical plans to fill any alignment gaps which have been identified and to both encourage and train around how to maintain the alignment within a dynamic environment.

The first objective is to model a body of knowledge in a given sphere, which may be real or imaginary. In our case the field is real and corresponds to the info-sphere which is characterized by the Real Environmental Parameters (REPs) which frame Big Data.

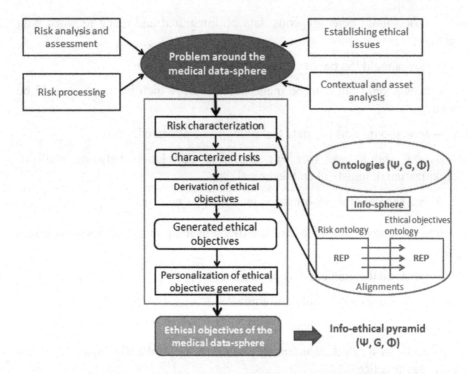

Figure 2.2. *System architecture of the translation of the ethical objectives of the medical Datasphere*

From bibliographical research around the subject [DHE 07, PON 09, ABB 01, BRE 02, GAR 97], we were able to split the REPs into four particular spheres: structural and technical (ST), strategic and methodological (SM), organizational and regulatory (OR) and relationship-based and cultural (RC). These multi-sectoral "key reality elements" interact with each other, making it possible to give both an application and a real value to the ethical framework.

Analysis around the context of medical ISs and Big Data contributes to us asking a series of questions that may be classified into two families of a different nature.

On the one hand, questions within the sphere of data processing:

– which computing and mathematical models should be chosen?

– how should they be implemented?

– how should heterogeneous data be integrated and made to work with us?

– how should ISs be set up?

– how should big data be made accessible? Which interfaces should be used?

– how should new big data technologies be allocated?

– how should we sort out and find correlation between medical, organizational, logistical and technical data?

– and several other information technology questions.

On the other hand, there are questions in the human and social sciences fields:

– what are the medical decision criteria?

– what are society's rules and limits?

– what are the professional rules?

– how can we find a consensus around the use of the Big Data tool within everyday practice?

– is this technological tool usable "in situ"?

– how might NICTs gain acceptance morally both with health professionals and health users?

– and many other human and social science questions.

Our governance approach may be completed in three steps:

– potential risks, recorded on the basis of the definition of the problem of the medical Datasphere, characterized on the basis of risk ontology;

– deriving ethical issues associated with the recorded and characterized risks;

– deriving the list of ethical needs which is personalized according to the context of the medical Datasphere.

The approach used for the development of ontologies is based on organization of concepts starting with the more general concepts, which are then followed by the more specific ones. Each concept must have a unique and independent meaning, but each sub-concept represents a corresponding specific concept. For example, organizational risks associated with decisions owing to dysfunction [LAM 11, ALB 02, ISO 03], "business" risks, accident or malicious intent–related risks, associated with the internal or external business dynamics (see Figure 2.3) [VAS 12].

Risk
- *Business risk*
- *Error risk*
-Execution error risk
-Error use risk
- Error handling risk
- Information loss risk in data processing
- Error transcription risk
- Incomplete information risk
- Destruction information file risk
- Transmission error risk
- Information management error risk
- *Vulnerability risk*
- *Residual risk*
- *Malicious acts risk*
- Information disclosure risk
- Network intervention risk
- Unauthorized system access risk
- Unauthorized privilege use risk
- Unauthorized tools use risk
- Intentional loss information risk
- Theft risk/unauthorized use information risk
- Information handling risk
- False information entry risk
- *Organizational risk*
- *Accident risk*
- *Threat risk*
- *Operation failure risk*

Figure 2.3. *Risk ontology list*

Moreover, we have developed the ethical objectives ontology, taking our inspiration in part from the analytical method of the codes of ethics when using information and communication technologies (ICTs) proposed by D. Johnson in 1985 [JOH 85]. In his book *Computer Ethics*, Johnson suggests that professional codes of ethics should be considered through four types of obligation, namely regarding society and the employer, customers, colleagues and other professional organizations. We associate two levels of action with this:

– recalling Beauchamp and Childress's four bio-ethical principles [BEA 01], namely the principles of: charity[12], autonomy[13], non-maleficence,[14] and justice[15], which should provide a framework for personal data so as to avoid carelessness, lack of foresight or professional negligence;

– a reference to which it is necessary to refer so as to clarify the issues and duties of the citizen and professionals in respect of personal medical data.

Thus by relying upon numerous field surveys, targeted interviews with around one hundred participants (information system managers, IS editors, health organization managers, health professionals, patients associations, health users, public institutions, and other organizations), as well as research upon the subject, we have been able to work out an

---

12 This contributes to the well-being of others. It must respond to two very precise rules: the action undertaken must be both beneficial and useful, that is to say it must have a positive cost-benefit relationship.

13 This indicates the fact that an individual gives himself his own rule of conduct, since the Greek terms *autos* and *nomos* respectively mean "himself" and "laws or rules". The aim of this principle is to involve the patient in the decision-making process.

14 This has the objective of avoiding harm to the one to whom we owe responsibility (the patient) and saving him from prejudices and harm which would not benefit him. Its purpose is, therefore, to do good and abstain from doing harm. This principle appears in the Hippocratic maxim *primum non nocere* (first, do no harm), the consequence of which is to do good to patients and to keep them away from harm and injustice.

15 This has the aim of sharing all available resources between patients (in terms of time, money and energy). This principle is linked closely to the concepts of equality and equity which directly intervene in the process of a court decision. All actions should, ideally, tend towards perfect equality, however according to the circumstances and the nature of the individuals involved, fairness is often essential, to establish priorities and a particular hierarchy in the actions being completed.

ethical analytical model for personal health data. Our ethical goal is made up of:

– the intrinsic value (conception) relative to data: organizational training perspectives (1);

– the management value (implementation) linked to the data and processing algorithms: the perspectives for internal processes (2); and

– the value of exploitation (usage) relative to data: client perspectives (3); (see Figure 2.4).

Our study tool draws its inspiration from the *"balanced scorecard"* (BSC) by [KAP 96] incorporating the perspectives of their dashboard (DB), excluding the financial angle on account of our dealing with an ethical valuation.

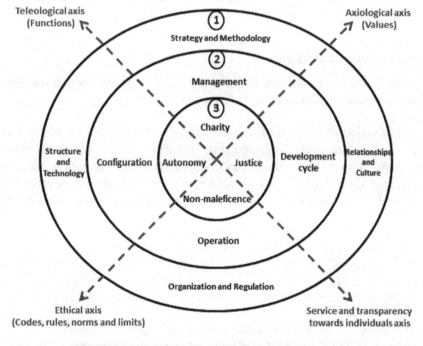

Figure 2.4. *The ethical target of personal health data*

This model is observed according to three interacting sides [BER 15]:

– the first point of view, so-called ontological (or structural aspect) considers IS within its structure. It embodies the idea of "the existence" of the system;

– the second point of view, the functional aspect, considers the role fulfilled by the IS. It embodies the view of "the operation" of the system;

– the third point of view, which is so-called genetic (or the dynamic aspect), considers the IS within the context of its evolution through time. It embodies the idea of "the evolution" of the system.

Our reasoning around our ethical modeling is structured according to four main axes, which both complement and interact with one another:

– the axiological axis, which comprises human values;

– the teleological axis[16], which describes the purposes of either an action or a fact;

– the ethical axis, which explains the rules, norms, laws, codes of conduct, standards and limits; and

– the service and transparency towards individuals axis, which translates human relationships between those involved.

The division of this ethical target highlights twelve sectors which form what we call "info-ethics management" (charity, justice, non-maleficence, autonomy, strategy & methodology, organization and regulation, structure and technology, relationships and culture, management, design, development cycle and operations) necessary for optimization and better control of Big

---

16 The concept of acting teleologically is largely developed by Habermas in his work "Communicative Action" [HAB 87] in which he achieves an aim or provokes the arrival of a desired state by choosing and using in an appropriate manner the means which, in a given situation, appear to assure him success. "This model for action is often interpreted in a utilitarian sense; we then assume that the actor both chooses and calculates both the ends and the means from the point of view of the maximum use or the expected use".

Data within the health sphere. These twelve parameters are successively described in Tables 2.1, 2.2 and 2.3.

Consequently, we have listed 26 justifications representing the principle objectives which should surround the conception, development and use of personal health data. These 26 recommendations integrate the four universal ethical principles which are connected to social values. Amongst these actions, nine are linked to the principle of charity, six to the principle of justice and non-maleficence and five to the principle of autonomy. We may also classify these items according to the nature of the following linked social values (see Table 2.1).

– seven belong to the "preservation of social links";

– two belong to "efficiency";

– four belong to "concern for one's neighbor";

– four belong to "caution";

– three belong to "universality";

– five belong to "responsibility"; one belongs to "social justice".

Following this, we have been able to establish our own division of ethical criteria around the conception, implementation and use of personal health data (see Table 2.1).

We have been inspired in part by the analytical methods for the codes of ethics for the use of ICT, as proposed by D. Johnson in 1985 [JOH 85]. Thus, we have classified these ethical indicators, according to two aspects:

– "society and human-based" which constitute obligations with regard to society and patients; "medico-legal" which constitutes obligations regarding colleagues, profession and legal institutions.

Justification surrounding personal health data	Fundamental ethical principles	Associated social values	Obligations regarding
1) Assistance in medical decision-making instituted by the health professional (HP)	Charity	Concern for one's neighbor	Colleagues, organization and profession
2) Promoting the quality, organization, management and planning of patient care			Patients
3) Working for the good of the patient			
4) Sharing transparent and accessible information between the patient and the HP		Preservation of social links	Colleagues, organization and profession
5) Ensuring that the patient receives both quality care and is able to make informed choices			Patients
6) Improved continuity of care			Colleagues, organization and profession
7) Assisting the minister of health to respond to waiting times and health care for the health user	Justice	Responsibility	Patients
8) Instituting legitimate patient rights and information processing			
9) Establishing a duty of security, integrity, traceability and medical data protection			Legal and regulatory institutions
10) Evaluating performance and establishing the fields where action is essential by listing dysfunctional aspects.		Efficiency	Colleagues, organization and profession
11) Enabling an epidemiological or statistical analysis (ESA)			Society
12) Improving and reinforcing interaction with those external to the care structure.		Preservation of social links	Colleagues, organization and profession
13) Strengthening the availability of HPs			
14) Sharing out in a fair way both the disadvantages and the advantages of such a tool within the workload of an HP		Social justice	Colleagues, organization and profession
15) Developing and sharing information which is both accurate and adaptable to the whole population		Universality	Society

Ethical objective	Detailed principle	Principle	Stakeholder
16) Following legislative regulations for medical data	Universality	Non-maleficence	Legal and regulatory institutions
17) Respecting the rules for data storage, hosting and dissemination instituted by the CNIL			
18) Both minimizing and eliminating harm to patients owing to incorrect information	Precaution		Patients
19) Reducing unnecessary or miscalculated risks			
20) Ensuring the accuracy medical data collection and its permanence			
21) Ensuring both technical relevance and the human validity of the tool			Society
22) Putting the patient at the center of the decision by supplying him with more complete information more quickly to ensure, better patient autonomy	Preservation of social links	Autonomy	Patients
23) Respecting the patient's private life and medical and general confidentiality			
24) Adapting a technology to the knowledge and know-how of the HP	Caring for one's neighbor		Colleagues, organization and profession
25) Ensuring the consent and commitment of the data owner	Responsibility		Patient
26) Respecting the right to prior information, rectification and detailed objections by the data owner			

Table 2.1. *The list of ethical objectives surrounding conception, implementation and use of personal health data*

In addition, as Gilles Duhamel[17] maintains, information issued to patients which is contrary to communication, must be objective, adapted to the patient, based on scientific proof, up-to-date, reliable, easily understood, accessible, transparently sourced, relevant, and in accordance with the legislation. The data must be of operational and strategic relevance, as well as having a cognitive effectiveness as to the knowledge which it provides. It makes it possible to categorize, calculate, collect, measure and gather information. Thus, data enables the clarification of various decisions of a strategic and methodological, structural and technological, organizational and regulatory, and relational and cultural type, concerning the information to exploit [BER 15]. We may classify data according to different categories according to their nature. We may distinguish, on the one hand, *operational data*[18] (or *transactional* or *flow data*) from *systems of reference* data[19] (or *master data*), as well as *primary data*[20] (that actually observed) from *secondary data*[21] (which is calculated).

Moreover, from a number of studies upon the property of the *information quality* (IQ) [WAN 98, BAT 06], we can highlight:

– IQ dimensions such as precision, objectivity, credibility, reliability, speed, access, availability, security, relevance, added value, completeness, exhaustiveness, data quantity, redundancy, data interpretation, ease of understanding, concise representation, and coherent representation;

– IQ categories such as the intrinsic and extrinsic aspects, the context, the environment and the representation are relevant (see Table 2.2) [FLO 13].

For [FLO 13], digital IQ study relies upon a bi-categorical analysis (being e-mail delivered and navigational) comprising eight main dimensions:

---

17 General Inspector for Social Affairs. The French Government department *Inspection Générale des Affaires Sociales* controls, audits and evaluates structures and policies, advises local authorities and provides help with projects in the health and other infrastructural sectors.

18 These data are linked to daily business activity. They are highly volatile and develop quickly. They concern particular events.

19 These data develop slowly and are stable over a given period of time.

20 These data are captured by an effective system. They are instantly of high quality provided that they are correctly captured and disseminated.

21 These data result from a recalculation of primary data. If the calculation is robust and tested, the quality of this data depends exclusively upon the quality of the primary data.

precision, objectivity, accessibility, security, relevance, speed, interpretation, and comprehension (see Figure 2.5).

IQ categories	IQ dimensions
Intrinsic	Precision, Objectivity, Credibility
Accessibility	Access, Security
Context	Relevance, Added value, Completeness, Exhaustiveness, Data quantity
Representation	Interpretation, Ease of understanding, Concise representation, Coherent representation

Table 2.2. *Examples of IQ categories and dimensions*

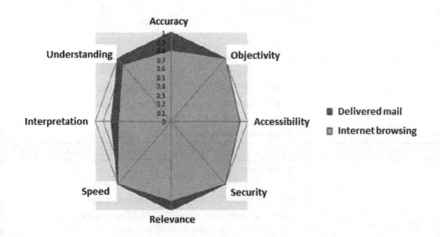

Figure 2.5. *A radar chart of IQ bi-categorical analysis*

In these circumstances, using available information which includes literature and a field survey (questionnaires and target interviews) with around fifty people involved in the data-lifecycle, we have been able to elaborate a list of criteria around "data" quality, so that information users may form their own opinions and views (see Table 2.3).

Data quality is directly linked to need for a common lexicon for systems of reference, models and data mapping[22]. It represents the aptitude for all of the

22 Data geolocalization, defining roles and responsibilities and a few basic parameters: May I disseminate? If yes, to whom? Who decides? What regulatory constraints apply to the data which I am managing? There are many related questions.

intrinsic data criteria (data availability, freshness, traceability, technical and/or functional coherence, exhaustiveness and making data secure). This satisfies internal demands (decision-making, operation and management, and other similar factors) and external demands (standardization, regulation and other factors) for setting up a structure. It should be noted that these characteristics are applied in standardized approaches, also known by the term "CAVAR" (completeness, accuracy, validity, availability, restricted Access).

Sphere of study	Info-sphere	
Sphere of study	Strategic and methodological	Structural and technological
Epistemology: Piece of data/Information	27) applicability 28) richness 29) adaptability 30) well-ordered 31) flexibility 32) ability to develop 33) performance 34) re-usability 35) pragmatism 36) consolidation 37) functionality/efficiency	49) coherence/meaning 50) accuracy 51) integrity 52) comprehensive 53) authenticity 54) reliability 55) robustness 56) legitimacy 57) nominal/Database
Sphere of study	Organizational and regulatory	Relationship-based and cultural
Epistemology: Piece of data/Information	38) relevance 39) stability/Continuity 40) assurance 41) pluri-disciplinary nature 42) systematic operation 43) reference 44) normativity 45) maintainability 46) regulation 47) auditability 48) coordination	58) security 59) confidentiality 60) federation 61) dissemination 62) accessibility 63) social interaction 64) universality 65) availability 66) cooperation

Table 2.3. *Criteria around data quality in the info-sphere*

Having all of this information makes it possible for us to respond to value issues during the lifecycle. This is why the question of data quality is at the core of the issues relating to data value for such occupations. How might the value of data, the quality of which cannot be guaranteed, be enhanced? Individuals should be able to judge for themselves the quality of the data within the digital info-sphere[23] which they have in their possession. Finally, we might also benchmark data by evaluating the extent of its digitalization, the multiplicity of sources, variety of formats, data volume and privacy.

Consequently, apart from storage and data accessibility, the value created by Big Data lies in both the interpretation and exploitation of this data. The establishment of this list of questions upon the management value of health data was, in part, developed from various working parties and interviews with people in the field. This was completed by CIGREF (a network of large businesses) whose aim is to "promote digital culture both as a source of innovation and performance".

Ultimately, our data development model may respond to various expectations, such as, for example:

– identifying the strategic potential of data and the impact on the firm's business model (creating new products and services);

– improving knowledge (of the customer, of the ecosystem, and other actors);

– defining the potential for value-sharing with partners (the issue of profitability);

– checking the "horizontality" of a given piece of data (a piece of data will be more highly valued if it can be used in a relevant manner within different contexts. What is the scope for internal efficiencies? How might external efficiency be integrated?);

– improving decision-taking and management in real time: reactivity, anticipation, assimilation, and value propositions;

– differentiating the organization from others through the ethics of given uses and CSR (by differentiating such uses, ethics could be a source of value creation) [CIG 14].

---

23 This word was coined by [SIM 89] in his science-fiction novel entitled "Hyperion". Subsequently, this term was taken up by [FLO 98] designating the environment in which information develops. This info-sphere leads to actions such as updating (encompassing evaluation, updating, enriching) and data development (access, dissemination, exploitation and integration).

Info-sphere	
	67) is there a policy and strategy for management of this health data?
	68) are both the responsibilities and tasks of each actor clearly defined as regards health data management?
Management	69) has an organization which is specifically dedicated to health data management been set up?
	70) is there a forward-looking management with the required health data user skills in place?
	71) is there a specific and sufficiently developed baseline health data management team in place?
	72) has a classification and ranking by level of importance been compiled?
	73) have so-called essential health data been modeled?
Configuration	74) is there a means in place for sharing data?
	75) is there a directory of essential health data?
	76) have heath data flows and locations been mapped?
	77) has the same piece of data only been collected once?
	78) are unstructured data stored in an organized way?
	79) is there an identifier system for useful sources of unstructured data?
	80) has a policy for monitoring the health data life cycle been implemented?
	81) have all data collected been subject to specific monitoring?
Development cycle	82) have all data, which have been altered been subject to specific monitoring?
	83) have all health data quality dysfunctions been managed until properly corrected?
	84) is there a proposed system for "reporting" health data in place?
	85) are there systems for health data preparation so as to develop coherent data sets?
	86) is there a system for health data processing and examination in place?
	87) are the databases properly managed?
	88) are the appropriate access authorization modules for the databases developed (connectors, web services, APIs, and other such modules)?
Operations	89) have the Big Data applications been set up?
	90) has the health data been archived, potentially replicated, and is it subject to backups?
	91) is there a quality control system for health data backups in place?
	92) can the health data be restored on demand?
	93) are business continuity tests around health data regularly carried out?

Table 2.4. *Questions around info-sphere data management*

2.1.3. *Identifying relationships between the two ontologies*

Connecting the concepts of these two ontologies makes the reduction of direct user involvement in matching the risks and ethical issues in the system possible. This approach is achieved in five stages:

– the recovery of all databases supplied by risk evaluation methods;

– the identification of potential scenarios with their accurate description, as well as the list of associated actions;

– the study of each scenario listed, which is linked to the risk ontology so as to connect associated risks with the given scenario;

– at the same time, the actions of each scenario connected with the ontology of ethical objectives are examined;

– relating the risk/scenario links with the scenarios/ethical actions links so as to produce alignment links between the concepts of both ontologies (see Figure 2.6).

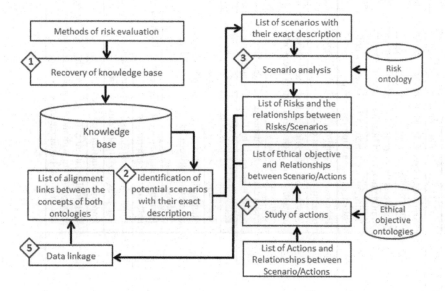

Figure 2.6. *System for identifying alignment links*

It can be seen that the list of risks obtained by using the guidance system is more accurate. This accuracy is due to the fact that through customary links we may work out all of the sub-types of risk. This precision makes it possible for us to identify ethical issues accurately. Table 2.5 follows and sets out the alignment links between risks and ethical objectives surrounding conception, and the setting up and use of personal health data obtained from using our method.

Risk ontology	Ethical purpose ontologies	Datasphere characteristics
Business risks	Assisting medical decision-taking instituted by the health professional	Strategic and methodological
	Assisting the minister for health to respond to both waiting times and health care for the health user	Strategic and methodological
	Instituting legitimacy with the patient both in terms of patient rights and information processing	Relationship-based and cultural
Organizational risks	Promoting quality, organization, management and planning of patient care	Organizational and regulatory
	Sharing out in a fair way both the disadvantages and the advantages of such a tool within the workload of a health professional	Organizational and regulatory
	Evaluating performance and establishing the fields where action is essential by listing dysfunctional aspects.	
	Following legislative regulations for medical data	Organizational and regulatory
Threat risk	Working for the good of the patient	Relationship-based and cultural
	Sharing information which is both transparent and accessible between the patient and the health professional.	
Error risks (management information)	Ensuring that the patient receives both quality care and is able to make informed choices	Structural and technological
	Improving and reinforcing the interactivity with actors that is external to the care structure	Relationship-based and cultural
Error risk (use-transmission)	Improved continuity of care	
	Putting the patient at the center of the decision by supplying him with more complete and prompt information. Better patient autonomy	Structural and technological

Risk ontology	Datasphere ethical purposes	Alignment
Error Risk (use-manipulation)	Developing and sharing information which is both accurate and adapted to the entire population	Strategy and methodology
	Both minimizing and eliminating harm to patients as a result of mistakes	Structural and technological
	Adapting a particular technology to the knowledge and know-how of the health professional	
Maleficence (risks of information disclosure – risks of intentional information loss – risks of theft/unauthorized use of information – risks of information manipulation)	Establishing a duty of security, integrity, traceability and medical data protection	Relationship-based and cultural
	Ensuring both technical relevance and the human validity of the tool	Strategy and methodology
	Enabling an epidemiological or statistical analysis (ESA)	
System failure risk	Reducing unnecessary or miscalculated risks	Strategy and methodology
	Strengthen the availability of health professionals	Organizational and regulatory
Vulnerability risk	Ensuring both consent and commitment of the data owner	
	Respecting the patient's private life and medical and general confidentiality	Relationship-based and cultural
	Respecting the right to prior information, to rectification and detailed objections by the data owner	Organizational and regulatory
Any other risk	Ensuring the reliability of medical data collection and its permanence	Structural and technological
Accident risks	Respecting the rules for storage, hosting and dissemination, instituted by the CNIL	Organizational and regulatory

Table 2.5. *Alignments between risk ontology and the ontology of Datasphere ethical purposes*

From these ontological alignments upon which we have previously elaborated surrounding the creation, implementation, and exploitation of personal medical data, there are several measures and recommendations which are vital to guarantee both the quality and protection of personal health data (see Table 2.6).

– indicate the origin of the data; whether it is raw data, consolidated through various data producers or developed from third party data;

– personal health data may only be collected and processed for a determined and legitimate use (see the purpose principle);

– only data which are relevant and necessary to the objectives for exploitation should be processed. The analysis should be justified by the business's legitimate interest (see the principle of proportionality and data relevance);

– medical data should be circulated upon assurances as to meeting confidentiality requirements and within a quality process;

– indicate clearly the date of data transfer or hosting so as to ensure that the information is both current and up to date;

– encode the piece of data to ensure traceability and the monitoring;

– the tools for information transmission should be valid;

– medical data is constantly developing and should be regularly updated;

– the data is able to be revalidated (there should be capacity for revalidation of the diagnosis, therapeutic strategies and other factors);

– providing consistent information based upon medical evidence issuing from medical sources and references (both internal or external validating bodies) to guarantee the credibility and the validity of data. Relevant aspects include the percentage of valid data, the means of selection of valid data, the method of validation (criteria), results (both qualitative and quantitative) of the validation and frequency of validation (see constantly developing data) [IMI 13];

– indicate clearly whether the information is based upon scientific studies, expert consensus or upon a given experience or a professional or personal opinion;

– ensure that medical opinion or advice is given by qualified practitioners;

– describe the recruitment process (contributor typology, contract with the supplier, the means of remuneration or individual consent);

– indicate the means of production, the make-up of or of the conversion of the data;

– describe the process of using and keeping of medical data by the supplier, as well as the conditions in which the user will be able to access his own "data", to guarantee the integrity, security and confidentiality of personal data;

– personal data should not be kept indefinitely and the length of time it should be kept should be assessed according to the purpose for which it is processed;

– assess the information both rigorously and fairly including that used to describe a product or a service;

– respect intellectual protection rights, whether it is a license to use a given source, the rights of the producer/supplier of the data or modification of the license due to data processing;

– ensure that suppliers respect general regulations and particular regulations linked to the processing of personal data;

– except for legal exceptions, the employer has a legal obligation to ensure the security of the personal data that he exploits, so that it is not divulged to unauthorized individuals (see the principle of security and confidentiality of data);

– data coherence necessitates a period for coordination [FOU 08];

– the information should be made more accessible to the patient or to the general health professional so that he can both understand and use it in the best possible conditions. To achieve this both products and services used should be described in a clear and easy to read language which is appropriate to target users.

Table 2.6. *Recommendations for the development, implementation and exploitation of personal health data*

In the light of these considerations, it seems necessary to provide at the core of Big Data implementation and exploitation, drawing upon sociology and ethical responsibility, a conceptual framework of good practice for this data. A good use of personal data based upon organizational intelligence therefore consists of eliminating, ranking and organizing accessible data in order to give it both meaning and coherence, rather than simply accumulating it. This is equivalent to saying that having technology without ethics and knowledge equates to having a body without soul or spirit.

Finally, this ethical charter and these recommendations should not be used as a rigid framework, but rather as a flexible structure to integrate the design, implementation and use of personal health data.

2.2. The selective ranking of health data

Big Data responds to a number of precise objectives, which include the extraction of useful information from stored data, the study of this data, the efficient return of results from analysis or even increased interaction and inter-relationships between the data and its users. Hence with the "massive data" in hand, it is conceivable that large volumes of data may be processed in real-time, which will make possible the monitoring of electronic data flows and analyzing service quality. Anticipating changes may be one of the keys to a brighter future, whether this is through multiple sensors on a system to detect a dysfunction or a fault, or by studying waiting times for users and health professionals within the medical sector. Big Data, in a broader sense, makes it possible for us to attach value to data which before could only be used unaltered, by completing statistics over prolonged periods or by cross-referencing data.

From this observation, we are led to pose four principle questions around the processing of data:

– what information do we need to be able to innovate and to be competitive?

– what data is available to us which is either under-exploited or unexploited?

– are we ready to "extract" useful information from our data?

– are we capable of managing the new security risks [COR 12]?

2.2.1. *The architecture of medical data*

Personal data is information which makes it possible to identify individually, in a direct or indirect way, an individual. [LAU 06] It is, therefore, a question of data comprising elements which characterize an individual, and are likely to affect, or have repercussions upon, their privacy. Consequently, we can understand the requirement for a measure of protection for such data. It therefore appears essential to have an accurate interpretation of the architecture of Big Data. There should be optimum visibility around the structuring of this data.

The document is a stable and long-term information medium that has value. This definition allows for regrouping under five functional data usage subsets:

– data content (information): relevance, legibility, coherence and accessibility;

– data form (structure and existence): authenticity, integrity and identification;

– data function (purpose): categorization, calculation, collection, measuring and gathering;

– data management (long-term and stable) involving considerations of preservation, storage, sustainability and lifespan;

– the framework (both the value and environment) in which it is used, considerations being ownership, rights of access, the license for exploitation, authorizations, management and monitoring.

Concurrent with this, we note that the usage and processing of Big Data may be characterized by four means of regulation:

– regulations (legal texts and codes and rules of ethics);

– architecture, structuring and technological tools;

– organizational or technical standards (founding aspects); current market practices.

Nowadays, these significant volumes of data constitute a real engine for competitiveness. Thus, in an increasingly competitive digitized environment, data is now perceived as an asset to value and monetize. "Data" is a digital asset which may be identified according to the three following types:

– a proprietary digital asset (the loyalty card);

– a jointly-owned digital asset (alliances and partnerships);

– a non-proprietary digital asset (external to the business) over which it has no control.

Potentially exploitable data types within Big Data may also be categorized by a three-way distribution:

– data known as *observed* data, stored within an IS;

– data known as *contributory* data, produced by users; data known as *deduced* data, all information available made through the processing of powerful algorithms.

Thus businesses perceive a major triple issue in Big Data processing:

– data is viewed as an operational performance vector. Hence, by making their processes more efficient, businesses tend to strengthen their position, particularly through better targeting of investments, the ranges that they offer and their sales efforts or the allocation of their resources.

– increased development occurs through service personalization. Indeed with Big Data, businesses have the opportunity to adjust their offerings (of both products and services) around the value perceived by the customer. To achieve this, businesses must acquire an excellent knowledge of their customers, so that their offerings match the needs and expectations of the latter. We are witnessing a real personalization of services offered.

– data is perceived as a direct or indirect source of revenue. This is why, henceforth, businesses are developing a commercial activity centered around data, based around its rarity and strategic value for third parties. This may translate into data monetization, but also into development of activities around data exchange, or of data in exchange for services (as is the case with B2B2C partnerships). Finally, to a lesser extent, businesses may practice data donation so as to improve their brand image.

Growth sectors for value creation mainly concern:

– improving research and development;

– the creation of new products based around data;

– optimizing production processes;

– the efficiency of targeted marketing;

– improving managerial approaches.

Having both identified and characterized the intrinsic value and then the management of personal health data, as well as the list of ethical issues which are linked to Big Data exploitation, we can cross-reference all data sets so as to make up a pyramid (Ψ, G, Φ) of info-ethics representing a tool for increased value of personal data, both through its ordering into a hierarchy and its ethical selection (see Figure 2.7).

The new term "info-ethics" only serves to symbolize this essential question of the meaning of a piece of information, that will come up in all societies integrating the digital world. Info-ethics is not a new form of ethics. On the contrary, it is based around social values and fundamental proven ethical principles of the Ancient Greeks, such as charity, autonomy, non-maleficence and justice tending towards human dignity, but seeking to practice them in the new context of the global information and communication society.

In forming this triangular representation, we were inspired by the pyramid of knowledge, with the DIKW facets (data, information, knowledge and wisdom). The objective of this pyramid is to formalize the way in which thought is structured, in order to proceed from unstructured factual data to possessing the capability to use it in the best possible way.

It begins with the collection and visualization of Big Data. According to [LEB 01], data represents "observing reality completed with the help of symbols which are likely to be understood by human beings. Data is the origin of information.

The passage from one to other results in a data interpretation mechanism by an individual or a group to add meaning to a piece of data. This is why data becomes information as soon as we interact with it, describe it, process it and connect it together. This is the "design" phase. Then, before converting into knowledge, information must both work out a concept and a reference point resulting from actual experience, practice and knowledge already acquired by those involved. In other words, knowledge is not exclusively produced from available information, without integrating both individuals' actual experience[24] and the capacity for abstract ideas necessitating both "intelligent design and conceptual designs" [NON 94]. As Albert Einstein stressed, "Learning is experience. Everything else is just information" [AVE 12].

---

24 With their socio-political values, norms, referents, cultures, acquired skills and other qualities.

Thus, information becomes knowledge when the two are linked, providing it with meaning and forming a whole. It is the "mapping" stage. Finally, the passage from information to knowledge happens through an information cognition mechanism, generated by the accumulation of prior knowledge, personal experience, and explanatory systems of reference. Knowledge becomes intelligence when we know how to use it to make good decisions. This last stage is known as "ethical data mining" or "algorithmic ethics" based around an ethical judgment and relationship evaluation approach.

The 93 items which make up our ethical modeling represent the various building blocks of the pyramidal structure (Ψ, G, Φ) making it possible to progress from Big Data (A) to info-ethics (Ω) and thus tending towards an informational entropy (degree of disorder) of virtually nil.

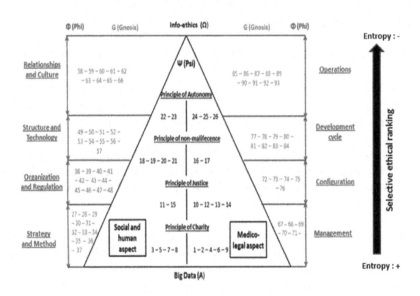

Figure 2.7. *The info-ethics pyramid (Ψ, G, Φ). For a color version of the figure, see www.iste.co.uk/beranger/data.zip*

Finally, we can also present data on a micro-, meso- and macro-spectrum [RAY 14]:

– *micro-data*: this is at the level of aggregated data resulting from technological capture by human intervention, social networks, machines and physical parameters. The data may take the form of Tweets, messages via a blog or Internet forum, information resulting from the "Internet of objects", or "clickstreams" in user Internet monitoring sessions, and other forms.

– *meso-data*: this is the stage of partial data aggregation with very large data sets, resulting from the collection of micro-data. Thus, the extensive analysis of Twiter user behavior and Retweets over a given period, and in response to specific questions, will produce different types of information.

– *macro-data*: this is the phase of data aggregation within many large data sets such as large geographical areas (regions), industrial or economic sectors, or national and international levels. These data may be linked to electrical grids or even public transport flows (subway, tramway or bus) within a city.

2.2.1.1. Ethics and the selection of data

As we have seen before, we can introduce the progress of Big Data towards info-ethics within a neo-Platonic ethic systemic modeling (or Ψ, G, Φ). By its very nature, a complex system is a dynamic process integrating many interactions and retrospective effects. Within this, mechanisms that are very difficult to predict and control develop, which the traditional models were unable to predict [MOR 05]. This open system develops a structure from an environment of functions, actions, teleology and transformations. In these circumstances, ethics must mobilize intelligence, so as to confront the complexity which frames the medical information communication process through NICTs. Thus, the intrinsic strengths of this modeling are a consequence of its nature which is at once interactive, multi-dimensional, and actively oriented towards the meaning, knowledge and the teleology of a given event. It is made up of three different dimensions which link and interact with other:

– informative dimension (G): info-sphere[25];

– environmental dimension (Φ): the real environment[26];

---

25 This word was coined by [SIM 89] in his science-fiction novel entitled *Hyperion*. Subsequently, this term was taken up again by [FLO 98] to denote the environment in which information develops. This info-sphere led to actions such as updating (comprising evaluation, updating, enrichment) and data development (access, dissemination, sharing, exploitation and combination).

26 The real environment is a favorable dimension both in terms of location (identification, localization, calculation, characterization, mapping and hierarchy) and preservation (acquisition, formalization and storage). An IS environment is made up of four distinct levels: structural and technological, strategic and methodological, organizational and regulatory and relationship-based and cultural.

– ethical dimension (Ψ): info-ethics [FES 01].

We see that G and Φ belong to an objective set known as "informational rationality", whilst Ψ results from a subjective set known as "cognitive rationality" [FRA 94, ROT 04]. Finally, taking into account the diverse aspects of informational ethics makes it possible to reveal the following three levels of ethics analysis [BER 15]:

– *descriptive ethics*: this study takes us back to *practice* and its aim is the application of rules and uses. It must give concrete expression to the purposes instituted by the teleological dimension. This is concerned with means, procedures, processes and pathways put into place to achieve the "completion" of objectives;

– *prescriptive ethics*: this sphere can be characterized by *pragmatism*. It shows objectives, which were already presupposed within the initial action plan, but without being clearly expressed in a so-called *prescriptive* way. This sphere also returns to codes of ethics, the function of which is to regulate practice.

– *reflexive ethics*: this analysis naturally involves *contemplation*. Its aim is to provide all practices and norms with their "legitimization", hence having a certain founding connotation. This sphere is oriented by values which serve as both prescriptive and critical examples simultaneously.

Thus, giving meaning is a fundamental human capacity which continuously occurs. The individual perceives *data*, interprets *information*, makes connections with other memorized *knowledge* and is then capable of acting upon his *knowledge*. He thus acquires skills which he is then capable of implementing repeatedly, translating into a *practical wisdom* or info-ethics [RIC 90]. This communicational knowledge mechanism [TOD 07] is illustrated the following by Table 2.7.

Big Data transmitted → simplified and relevant information is received
Value recognition → acquisition → assimilation   → modification
Information received → knowledge
Exploitation (fed by theory and experience) conveys knowledge
Knowledge → practical wisdom (info-ethics)
Adaptation/flexibility/innovation/performance through experience

Table 2.7. *The communicational knowledge process*

2.2.1.2. *The domain of ethical analysis*

Our approach, which is both ethical and epistemological, is an integral part of the fundamental model to understand the human dimension of Big Data processing in the health sphere. Indeed, as Paul Valéry stresses, "Without internal and epistemological analyses, all scientific methods are only fragments of thought" [MOI 95]. This is why our trans-disciplinary analysis necessitates an epistemological critique mainly concerning "knowledge and processes" which take account of the Neo-Platonic thinking of "doing to understand, and understanding to do" of Leonardo da Vinci. [VAL 41, VAL 48]. That aside, we also refer to "information dynamics" worked out by [FLO 09]. This perspective consists of:

– the construction and modeling of information environments, integrating systemic proprieties, internal developments, forms of interaction and applications;

– lifecycle information, the different forms which data takes and its functional activities;

– calculations stemming from algorithmic processing.

Furthermore, the communicational diagram involves specific control filters for each area of study:

– the perception filter, which questions the nature, authentication and circumstances for Big Data capture;

– the conception and configuration filter, concerning considerations focused around choice, form, clarity and information ranking;

– the use filter with questions centered around information use, storage, and hosting;

– the disclosure filter with considerations oriented around dissemination and framing of knowledge with the patient; and

– the decision filter questioning shared medical decision-making between the doctor and his patient.

These filtering processes are strengthened by the fact that the sender and receiver rarely have the same interests and concerns. What is said by one is not necessarily heard by the other. Research in cognitive psychology has shown that the human being is never neutral. He filters, decodes, selects, and reinterprets information that he receives.

These filters allow us to ask a series of questions throughout the Big Data lifecycle on issues such as informed consent of the individual at the time of data capture, access and selection of information, information confidentiality and security, ideal conditions to make medical statements, the nature of information to transmit to the health user and patient participation in medical decision-making and other factors [BER 15]. In these circumstances, epistemology makes it possible to conceive an anthropology which is a primary condition for ethics, integrated in a loop where each stage is necessary for the others. By applying our ethical analysis domain within the info-sphere, we can follow the conversion of Big Data into info-ethics (wisdom and practice – see Figure 2.8).

Consequently, our so-called Big Data "ethical analysis area" is made up of four study domains and five axes. Our raw unstructured ethical data model is anchored within this analytical framework Each of the four spheres have different natures and issues:

– the information sphere represents both the nature and form of information. It integrates statistical and epistemic aspects of knowledge;

– the organizational and technological sphere groups together aspects relating to structure, technology, organization and regulatory, as well as Mintzberg's models and the information theory, first created by [SHA 48] and taken up by [FLO 98] which we will go on to explain;

– the political and strategic domain is made up of strategic, methodological, relationship-based and cultural criteria, as well as laws, legal texts and codes of ethics;

– the ethical sphere representing the characteristics of the four fundamental ethical principles [BEA 01] as well as ethical issues which are specific to the nature of the structure studied. Ethics is therefore constantly obliged to "remain engaged within its mission for legitimization, led to mobilize its introspective capacity, with reference to values" [HOF 91].

It is noticeable that the first two domains represent REPs centered on human exchange and sharing. This anthropological vision concentrates on human relationships. To achieve this, the following five complementary axes are articulated around these themes:

– the axiological axis (values);

– the teleological axis (functions);

– the ethical axis (rules, norms, laws, codes, standards and limits);

– the statistical axis made up of recalled historical facts and statistics. This information feeds our databases for the study;

– the epistemic axis, which integrates representations and models from facts. It is this bank of knowledge which underpins the calculations. According to Jean Piaget, epistemology may be defined "by a first approximation as the study of the makeup of valid knowledge" [MOI 07].

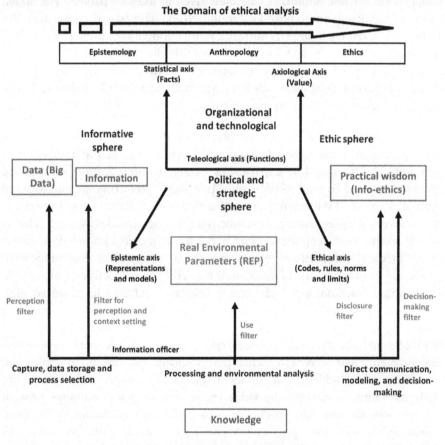

Figure 2.8. *Conversion of info-ethics Big Data within the sphere of ethical analysis of the info-sphere*

2.2.1.3. *The ethical ranking of Big Data*

With the advent of volume explosion, and the dawn of Big Data and Cloud Computing, the ranking and selection of medical data appears to be vital. This necessitates the application of a strategy for database production management by moving data between various storage categories, so as to improve operational performance achieved by the user. Consequently, such a mechanism allows the user to be relieved of the need to manage data location. Thus, beyond its information value, the aim of digitized medical communication is to restore the confidence of those involved in a given patient's care, while optimizing the care given to the said patient. The added value of medical communication through NICTs consists of taking this Big Data and then changing it into relevant information, giving it another dimension so as to alleviate, modify and amplify the perception that its receipt might lead to. If information groups together objective data, with the transition to medical communication which integrates both data ranking and selection of this data, then we return to the area of subjective knowledge.

This translates into a metamorphosis of data and information of an epistemological nature towards knowledge, which is linked to anthropology and individuals' real life experiences. Thus, communication of medical knowledge goes beyond simply objective data, preferring to put forward particular data and information rather than other such data. It may only occur at the level of dissemination of subjective and cognitive knowledge. This is why it seems more accurate to employ the term "medical knowledge" rather than "medical information" when we speak of medical communication [BER 15]. It is necessary to maintain the spirit of the objectives which make it possible to determine which data is relevant, and thus to avoid wasting time and resources in collecting information which is of no use. Our reasoning is inspired by the term "lean"[27], which describes a production management theory that concentrates upon the leanest waste-free management, and strives towards performance. Its aim is to strike out activities without added value, by identifying five main principles. These are defining value, identifying the value chain, obtaining a continuous flow of information, tapping into production and aiming for perfection. It is about centering on the value provided to both the user and the business, and delivering rapid results, seeking customer satisfaction rather than

---

27 "Lean" is a term coined at the end of the 1980s by a team of researchers from MIT to describe Toyota's production system.

technological excellence as well as eliminating actual problem causes as soon as they occur while encouraging those involves to improve their systems.

Furthermore, the informational process comes from the individual who is *the information user*, the central participant in the IS within an organization. Hence "...he will have to take into account the interests of his organization, interests which are defined by the company managers" [LEB 01]. By taking its source both from the real environment (Φ: Phi), in a given state and the sensitive world of the info-sphere (G: Gnosis) and within ethical thinking (Ψ: Psi), the informational mechanism ends up in creating practical wisdom (or info-ethics) through the ranking and selection of medical data. After an observation phase, actual activity is turned into data, the latter after interpretation, evaluation, ranking and selection become information, which, following a cognition process, in turn becomes new knowledge which serves as a learning aid to end up as practical wisdom. The passage of Big Data to information and then knowledge, as explained by our systemic Neo-Platonic modeling (Ψ, G, Φ), evidences that selective ranking of data contributes to diminishing entropy (a degree of disorder) of knowledge, so that it is put to optimum use. This methodology allows us to identify the hierarchical structure of data. In analyzing substantial databases, as a result of statistical power, the recourse to multi-level models becomes essential (see Figure 2.9).

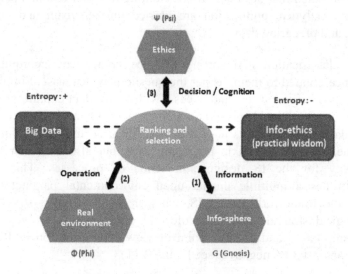

Figure 2.9. *Selective ranking of Big Data through the systemic Neo-Platonic prism*

Furthermore, the ranking mechanism followed by the selection of the initial data leads to an improvement in the qualitative value and the knowledge entropy, to the detriment of a quantitative loss both of data and information (see Figure 2.10).

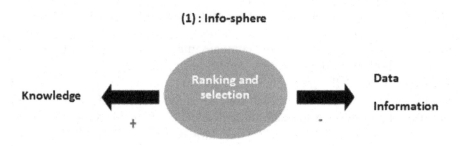

(1) : Info-sphere

Knowledge +

Ranking and selection

Data

Information -

Figure 2.10. *Selective ranking of data within the info-sphere*

An automatic selective data ranking system makes it possible for a storage unit to migrate the right category of data automatically according to each user's needs. It is worth noting that the ETL tools (extract transform load) integrate a cleaning stage for processed data.

It is estimated that 80% of activities aiming to either obtain a response or create an analytical application are carried out upstream and consist of cleaning and preparing data.

Data classification and sorting may be completed according to the importance granted to them, as per the questions which arise. Simplification leads to more efficient use and access, with better data capture and greater security. On the other hand, this results in a lower level of data integrity. Hence, data ranking results in greater simplification from the point of view of the health professional in practicing care, but also a greater technical complexity for the IS designer in terms of processes. This solution, therefore, has a multiple impact upon environmental parameters which provide the framework for an IS, whether this is from a structural and technological, strategic and methodological, organizational and regulatory or relationship-based and cultural point of view. The effect on REPs is 70% positive against 30% negative (see Figure 2.11).

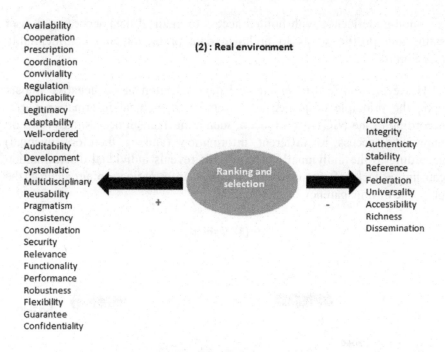

Figure 2.11. *Selective data ranking within the real environment*

Our ethical approach is mainly based around the four ethical principles of [BEA 01] which we described during our introduction; charity, autonomy, non-maleficence and justice. These elements are designed at the same time as the tools for resolution of human problems and the tabs to integrate the ethical dimension within medical practice. The study of the selective ranking solution viewed through this ethical prism makes it possible to better learn and understand the unstable equilibrium which exists between data availability and data protection. This counter-balance may tend from one side to the other according to the context and the nature of Big Data.

Thus, this ethical data approach demonstrates that medical data selection has a positive effect for the principle of:

– charity with an adapted and relevant dissemination of medical information to health professionals and health users;

– autonomy with prior information (which is clear, precise, adapted and understandable) guaranteeing free and informed patient consent; and

– non-maleficence with limited access to medical data according to user status and profile so as to optimize data protection and confidentiality (see Figure 2.12).

However, this system of medical data selection has a negative impact upon the principle of justice as disseminated medical information varies according to the NICT user. Indeed, such a mechanism necessitates rules on remit and access to different information (and is therefore unequal) according to the individual's profile. This reveals individual discrimination causing a lack of symmetry in medical information going against the principle of transparency of information.

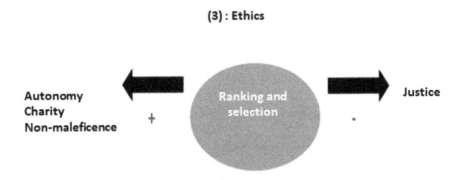

Figure 2.12. *Selective ranking of data within ethical thinking*

In this context, it does not seem obvious to maintain equilibrium between the availability of health data and its confidentiality. In our opinion, NICTs do not make it possible to respond entirely to this problem. This is why ethics and Big Data user behavior play a decisive role in guaranteeing confidentiality.

Finally, given that this selective ranking of medical Big Data plays a dominant role in the level of data complexity as well as user accessibility, we may assimilate a "medical organizational intelligence" Indeed, data accessibility leads inevitably to a series of questions such as:

– is the data presentation clear and understandable?

– are the database interrogation times sufficient?

– is the data classification both coherent and documented?

– does the organizational structure of the business make available to users both the technical tools and/or the necessary accompanying devices?

From these considerations we can integrate our practical wisdom creative process (info-ethics) through the concept of organizational intelligence[28] which makes possible this integrated transformation of operation, information and decisiveness/cognition.

By definition, a hierarchical database is a database whose management system links data recordings in a tree-like structure where each recording only has one owner. The individual processing the data must recognize its intrinsic value so as to acquire it and then assimilate it. This, out of necessity, requires a phase of data transformation. The exploitation of information is made possible by the integration of theory and experience dialectics so as to provide knowledge which may be adapted according to the situation. The application of this knowledge through an ethical framework translates into an individual's practical wisdom. A code of ethics has the function of mobilizing organizational intelligence so as to confront the complexity of not just life, but of the world and indeed the field of ethics itself.

All medical data, which is gathered and accumulated subsequently, will have a role and a particular place that is attributed to it according to a given analytical plan. Not all of this data will have the same place and some will completely disappear following both the communicational development of the data device and the nature of IS users. We therefore end up with a pyramidal representation, the basis of which constitutes raw health data with the maximum level of complexity and to which only the IS designer has access. All of the medical information is disseminated by every medical service involved in the patient's hospital care journey. According to Nonaka, [TOY 00], accumulated information and knowledge should be shared by all actors involved. Medical professionals (from the hospital) and the doctor caring for the patient must know where medical information is located, where medical data is stored and how to access it urgently. According to the

---

28 It is worth noting that we can make an analogy between "organizational intelligence" and the term "economic intelligence" designating the "control of strategic information which is useful to economic actors" [JUI 04]. Economic intelligence is more globally a skill to subtly and globally understand a complex environment and to take the right decision [ALM 01].

parties involved, when there is an information differential within an organization its members cannot interact on an equal basis, revealing the flaws in the ethical principle of justice. This then hinders the different interpretation of new information, putting at a disadvantage the creative process for medical knowledge, and therefore, endangering both the patient diagnosis and treatment by doctors.

Subsequently, information which is both organized and selected is turned into knowledge so as to be accessible by the invoicing service (concerning administrative information) and by paramedics, who intervene in patient care (for medical information). Finally, the applied knowledge, that is to say the definitive and simplified medical conclusions of treatment and diagnosis, are handed down to the patient so that he, in association with his doctors, may take a shared medical decision. The patient acquires much sought-after practical wisdom. We can debate and illustrate these thoughts by taking the example of the content of a medical consultation relating to a patient which consists of:

– relevant administrative data;

– the reason for the consultation[29];

– medical history[30];

– initial clinical symptoms[31];

– initial clinical examination;

– medical histories/allergies[32];

– treatment in progress[33];

– recent characteristics after commencing medical care[34];

– diagnosis and final treatment.

---

29 Initial symptoms and accompanying medical signs.
30 History of the signs of the illness.
31 Primary elements noticed by a health professional (whether or not they are a doctor).
32 This is part of the medical history.
33 This is part of the medical history.
34 This corresponds to data from complementary tests (biology, imagery, etc.) which in the end will allow the diagnosis to be made.

Potentially, the individual with overall responsibility for the IS is able to view all of this data (both administrative and medical). Only the initial clinical examination, the recent symptoms after which medical assistance commences diagnosis and final treatment, are within the doctor's domain. All of the remaining treatment may be undertaken by allied health workers (through task delegation) For his part, the patient has exclusive access to the reason for the consultation, the allergies, treatment in progress, diagnosis and the final treatment The invoicing department should only have access to administrative data relating to the patient. However, as Dr Loïc Etienne stressed[35], the fact that the patient considers the accessibility to his medical data for health professionals (doctors or allied health staff) as secondary, backs up the concept that the hospital report only accounts for part of the problem, ignoring some things which the patient might prefer to see either noted or investigated.

Moreover, it is not necessary to consider information retention as illustrating the doctor's discretionary authority, but more as simplifying and translating the information passed on and the expression of a form of kindness. Since information linked to medical activity evokes human emotions, communication and understanding of the perceived message is more important than the information itself [VIC 98]. What counts is the meaning of the words used. The IS designer should integrate a form of translation mechanism into his IS so that the patient can find information which is adapted to his level of ability, according to various criteria. This homogenization of simplified data through indexing, classification and sorting contributes to the ranking of this data.

Thus, data collected are not necessarily either compatible or coherent with the knowledge and ability of an individual who must be extremely conscientious in constructing, understanding and interpreting data so that medical information is both relevant and useful to him [KUH 99]. We should not forget that where health is concerned, the intrinsic value and weight of particular information counts more than the accumulation of non-targeted and disorganized information [FAV 98]. It appears essential to refrain from urge to want to use all data. It is necessary to accept the loss of certain

---

35 This is taken from an interview on the subject of medical data ranking, Paris, 16 December 2014.

data. This data selection happens as data is both processed and disseminated. It is therefore necessary to rank this data according to its explanatory importance and its intrinsic analytical weight [LAM 12]. This informational activity may be analyzed as the interaction of individuals with an information environment made up of aspects which are, by nature, social and organizational, cognitive, psychological, physical and dynamic (the evolutionary aspect).

In this context information asymmetry is sidelined when faced with dialog or shared decision-making as expressed by the patient.

Finally, such a system which is based upon organization and data sorting (both medical and administrative) forces a maximal complexity around the IS designer's tasks which should:

– control the conformity and/or the validity of data;

– manage and sort data (gathering, processing, prioritization, classification, dissemination, monitoring and other similar functions);

– organize and implement a mechanism and configuration of both data accessibility and information according to the nature of the IS user profile;

– restore databases;

– process and examine data and then medical information through data extraction, bringing together data and depictions;

– develop tools and/or approaches specific to its activity sector;

– achieve monitoring which is specific to its activity sphere.

Computing tools make it possible to manipulate all of these elements. Thus, *Text Mining* tools and interface modules both with users and with the individual responsible for IS at the health establishment allow for the sorting, classification and extraction of information contained in the database, while continuously feeding the database.

2.2.2. *Ethical Data Mining*

Faced with the problem of the overabundance of information as illustrated by the emergence of Big Data, Data Mining technologies offer, as a result of artificial intelligence devices (AI), the scope for processing these considerable masses of data to extract relevant and determining information required to take efficient decisions. Thus, the application of this intelligent NICT to personal data allows for the profiling of individuals, to predict their behavior and to act accordingly.

AI lies in the understanding of phenomena and their local adaptation. One of the criticisms of Big Data concerns the use of segmentation. The more logical a given volume of data, the easier it is to demonstrate any hypothesis by segmenting it "until obtaining a significant statistical correlation" [WLA 14]. Under these circumstances, intuition, which might wish us to draw more valid conclusions from a clinical trial including more patients or a greater mass of data, is therefore erroneous as it does not grant the means to monitor the entire mechanism for information discovery. However, the data does not deceive. It simply appears to be all the more significantly accommodating through being more numerous.

In light of this observation, we had the idea of working out an *Ethical Data Mining* approach that consists of integrating, throughout the stages of the Data Mining process, an ethical framework so as to provide greater meaning and a function based on the validity of the tool in question. This tool particularly relies upon two rules and precise concepts:

– not losing sight of the causality of the processes throughout the data lifecycle. Out of necessity, this undergoes a perfect traceability and knowledge of the system;

– maintaining both monitoring and control of the system at each stage of the data processing procedure and integrate.

Thus, as a result of the AI mechanisms that it uses, Data Mining makes it possible to save time, money and manpower so as to be able to both understand and tap into Big Data. The virtuous circle of our Data Mining is the conversion of massive unstructured data into info-ethics and then info-ethics into beneficial and coherent decisions. Data Mining therefore supports effective decision-making, which consists of all processes that make possible the mixing, sorting and analyzing terabytes of data in order to extract the right information. Very often data will come from diverse database sources; their number will necessitate gathering them together within the same architecture known as a *data warehouse* or data depot, before applying Data Mining technologies to them.

We consider AI as an integrated system of computer tools which automatically carries out data research and study, without the user having to enter or predetermine any hypothesis that the process will be assumed to have checked the accuracy of. Everything, including both the research and analysis, is automated. Consequently, Data Mining is based on the capacity of the machine to learn by itself, known as "the machine learning ability" [MAY 99]. Our *Ethical Data Mining* tool integrates our ethical neo-systemic modeling to both mix and sort data, to reveal hidden relationships and correlations between diverse data, thus allowing the discovery of a behavioral model. The reliability of our processing model mainly depends upon the validity and the "sourcing" of Big Data which are initially collected. The latter should not be biased or erroneous before collection. We may give the example of the software Google Flu Trends, responsible for assessing the global spread of the flu strain H1N1. This particular example demonstrates that the deployment of the possibilities offered by Big Data exploitation is intimately connected to the need to have at one's disposal both indicators and reliable data. According to a study by the magazine *Science* [LAZ 14], Google Flu Trends, for which the indicators were based upon key research terms, would have continually overestimated the spread of the flu strain H1N1 since its predictions would have exceeded by 50% the estimates of the Center for Disease Control and Prevention (CDC), which were based around reasons for medical visits [SAV 15]. Hence, the interest of businesses in information, particularly around customer behavior, is the practical use to businesses of detailed questionnaires on individuals from which machine reasoning will simulate not only their behavior but the assessment made by the decision-maker and produce effects. The intrinsic and qualitative values of these initial "mega-data", is therefore both essential and critical for optimum processing of the latter.

We can summarize the Data Mining process in six major stages (see Figure 2.13):

– knowledge of the sector and the occupation: all analytics respond to specific needs according to a given work environment and the sphere of activity. This is why, to ensure both the usefulness and meaning of the analytics, it is necessary to know very well the issues and ethical risks relating to the business sphere which will exploit this Big Data.

– knowledge of raw data: the next phase consists of evaluating the massive data available (or data that the business can procure) to determine what it might provide, then to understand how it applies to the business's customer needs. It might apply to the enterprise itself if it concerns internal use.

– preparation of raw data: during this stage, the data is prepared with a view to examination. Data sources are blended in a relevant and coherent way; integration constitutes an important part of this system.

– ethical modeling: this phase necessitates our ethical systemic neo-Platonic modeling (Ψ, G, Φ) so as to both monitor and frame it in the most rigorous and fair way possible for Big Data processing.

– evaluation: it is appropriate to assess the model so as to verify its efficient functioning and operational capability. This leads most often to adjustments and development, the potential addition of new data sources, data fusion and model modification, which has the advantage of being very flexible, and evaluation of a further hypothesis.

– deployment: when the modeling has been validated and is operational, the business may move to the final stage which is to deploy it.

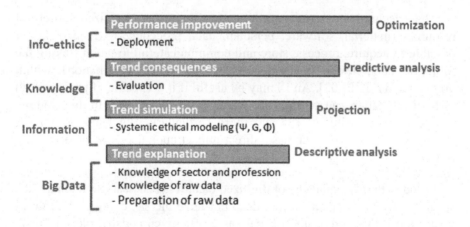

Figure 2.13. *The stages of Ethical Data Mining*

These stages constitute a complete cycle: once the ethical modeling works and the info-ethics are obtained, *Ethical Data Mining* supplies new occupation knowledge and new responses according to the given context. At this stage the cycle repeats itself, as soon as the business wishes to hone its strategy around Big Data, according to the evolution of the market environment.

It is essential to give data meaning. To do so, it is necessary to learn to "make the data speak", to know how to match them up, cross-reference them with other volumes of both internal and external data, by optimizing, whether in a qualitative or quantitative way, exploitation. Such an approach cannot be carried out without an evaluation tool which makes it possible to both measure and monitor the ethical value of raw data during its entire processing thus the three stages of conception (intrinsic value), implementation (management value) and use (exploitation value).

2.2.3. *Ethical evaluation of medical Big Data*

The evaluation of NICTs and the Big Data which they produce is a complex multi-dimensional task, involving different resources (data, devices, interfaces, artifacts and other resources) considering different characteristics (functionalities, usability and other features).

These technological tools are defined as being "an organized entirety of resources (material, software, personal, data, procedures) which makes it possible to acquire, process, store and communicate information (taking the form of data, texts, imaging sounds and other information) within organizations" [REI 02]. An IS may be useful if it is capable of providing all of the information and services for which it was conceived. In this context, evaluating the quality of ISs and more particularly Big Data becomes a major strategic issue, which has a direct impact upon the uses and adoptions of ISs.

Faced with this avalanche of digitized data, it is necessary to maintain the spirit of all of this "data" which does not have the same value. A scale of values must, therefore, establish the value of a given updated piece of data, according to what it reveals or not about the DNA of the digitized individual. Measuring the ethical value of "massive data" value now seems inescapable!

2.2.3.1. *The increase in value of intangible capital*

Nowadays intangible assets appear to be a determining element for our businesses and all of our economies and societies. The new socio-economic transformations, of our industrial production locates intangible assets within different sectors, (such as IS, research and development (R&D), organizational processes, reputation, broad-based innovation, and other such assets) at the heart of value creation mechanisms.

There is no universal definition to describe intangible capital as the co-existence of several terms as much in the field of research as in managerial practice: intellectual capital, immaterial asset, invisible asset, intangible asset, specific or immaterial assets and rare resources, are all expressions that are used equally in literature. Henceforth, NICTs and dematerialized data have become specific and important business assets.

Consequently, in a dematerialized society, immateriality is an invitation to us to relocate organizational performance in space and time. From this observation, [BOU 03] suggested studying immaterial capital management especially NICTs, from a dynamic and spiraling approach, around four themes which are organized and interact between each other:

– questioning around immaterial business assets;

– modeling so as to collectively understand and carry out activities;

– measurement so as to clarify collective visions and signaling; and

– transversal management (see Figure 2.14).

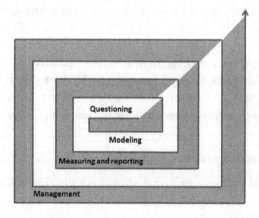

Figure 2.14. *Dynamic spiral for immaterial capital management*

– *Questioning*: By virtue of their dual nature, immaterial assets cause a measuring difficulty. This leads to a series of questions around the main immaterial capital characteristics, the various models to increase capital value, and linking ISs and immaterial capital at business level.

– *Modeling to understand better*: The organizational performance model becomes an analytical structure when faced with satisfying these twofold problems; on the one hand explaining the specific intrinsic criteria of each organization and business while, developing a common language, favoring both a dialog and a comparison between businesses, on the other. To do this, it is necessary to ask a number of questions. How should we approach Big Data in the new organizational framework? How might we assess them? How can we carry out both internal and external "reporting"?

– *Measurement to clarify collective approaches and promote "signaling"*: The notion of "measuring" includes means of recording transactions involving specific items such as investments in R&D or in software. This particularly involves a value judgment around business inputs.

– *The management of "immaterial capital"*: Immaterial assets represent an important management lever, and thus, in working out a common direction. "Mega data" make it possible to consolidate business organization, to provide it with distinctiveness and back its business organizational identity.

Moreover, by the end of the 1980s, various approaches around organization performance management emerged, which are confined exclusively to financial criteria. It is only with the emergence of the "Balanced Scorecard" (BSC) [NOR 96] that non-financial indicators developed. These researchers were interested in business strategy aspects through using BSC as a management tool, the objective of which is to make it possible for managers to implement strategies by using both financial and non-financial criteria. Norton and Kaplan (1996) based their research findings around performance indicators covering four main business perspectives:

– the customer perspective (what should we provide the clients with?);

– the financial perspective (what should we provide business shareholder with?);

– the organizational learning perspective (how should we manage organizational change?);

– the internal process perspective (what are the fundamental processes which both customers and shareholders expect?).

These criteria are determined according to strategic business objectives. The success of this method depends mainly on management quality and clearly defined perspectives.   Subsequently, this BSC approach was improved by integrating the issue of causality through a strategic map. This strategic map is a "cause and effect" chart, indicating the relationships between different strategic objectives, according to the four perspectives above (customer, financial, learning and process). This makes it possible to "realize" the passage from strategy expression to working out the actual value. According to [NOR 96], the strategic map is an essential tool for:

– clarifying strategy and facilitating communication with each employee;

– recording key features of the success of strategic implementation;

– "aligning" technological, organizational and human investments, so that they match strategy; revealing gaps in strategy implementation and thus facilitate the adjustment.

Finally, the study of immaterial capital positions Big Data as an immaterial and strategic resource for business value-building.

In this sense, the value of "massive data" is a design value, for both implementation and use relative to a multidimensional environment surrounding NICTs. Significant data volumes then become a value creation center for organizational business units and structures.

This, therefore, leads to the implementation of a common language and communication between general management, information management and business units so as to contribute in practical terms to the realization of this value. Thus, the governance of Big Data makes it possible to advance this value-building and to focus on issues linked to skill-management, strategy-management, risk-management and organizational performance of the business. Starting from these observations, we are led to ask a major question. How is it possible for Big Data governance to be approached using a BSC-type management tool, which allows us to assess the increased value of immaterial business capital particularly? In other words, what are the training and development conditions, and more generally, the conditions for the management of immaterial assets of "voluminous data"? How might these be approached from a governance perspective?

2.2.3.2. *The evaluation tool for personal health data*

When skimming through the material which deals with the various dimensions of Big Data quality, several concepts come to light such as accuracy, defining the part that data plays in the assessing how acceptable the proximity between the "data" value and the real value is, and their coherence, which designates the part data plays in maintaining a set of limits or business rules. There is also completeness that identifies the portion of information missing within the data or even how up-to-date the data is, which describes the portion of obsolete data.

Data quality is a notion which is both complex and multi-dimensional [RED 96] grouping together various semantics according to particular conditions. Numerous other approaches have been defined such as accuracy, accessibility, coherence and comprehensibility and others. [WAN 95] The classifications of these dimensions have even been described in certain scientific articles and works [BAT 06]. These dimensions interact between each other in an independent way [BAR 10]. They, generally, comprise of three components, namely individuals, tools and hardware and procedures used [CHR 03]. For [OLI 12], the quality dimensions of an IS are made up of the quality of artifacts which are produced during development (that is to say, the evaluation of models built), the quality of devices used in a given organization, the quality perceived by the NICT user (in other words, the quality of the IS's final interfaces), and the intrinsic quality of data. Each dimension groups together a set of measures and specific limits (see Table 2.8).

Limits for IS evaluation	
Processes	A large number of process measurements
	The difficulty of both collecting and interpreting measurements
	The difficulty of evaluating in advance whether a modification should be made
	The choice of modeling and the choice of formalities influencing the measurements (if developed using the model)
	Non-exhaustive evaluation

	Expensive evaluation
	Inter-dependent quality dimensions
Artifacts	Experimental protocols are generally complex and difficult to define
	Non-availability of professionals
	Difficulty of interpreting measurements
Man-machine interface	Insufficient account is taken of organizational characteristics
	The difficulty of evaluating the interactive part of adaptive information systems
	The non-existence of standardized user models and profiles for IS evaluation
	The inadequacy of evaluation tools adapted to IS evaluation
Data	A large number of available measures to evaluate data quality
	The difficulty of linking a given threshold to a given measurement
	Incomplete or approximate results
	The interpretation of results is often complicated

Table 2.8. *Limits involved in IS evaluation*

According to material around scaling data quality, we may both categorize and list three highly distinct types of approaches:

– empirical approaches, which use practical experiences. We may, for example, take [WAN 96], which directly questions the users of digitized data. The results of their interviews have made it possible for us to highlight four dimensions around qualitative data aspects: the intrinsic quality, representation and form, the contextual aspects and accessibility.

– theoretical approaches, which use "real world" and "IS" so as to confront one another. [WAN 96] applies to this method too, so as to examine gaps between reality and technology. These differences, translated as data quality "faults", particularly revealed three new categories of knowledge, viz. completeness, consistency (or relevance) and accuracy.

– intuitive approaches, which use a classification which is intuitively determined. Thus, [RED 96], data quality is categorized according to value, format and nature.

This innovative aspect of our ethical analysis model is that we have both compiled and collated these three approaches so as to create a neo-Platonic systemic method around Big Data. Under these circumstances, we have, therefore, decided to emphasize a study framework made up of three interpretation axes: actions, situations and intentions which make up an ethical event. This modeling may be observed according to the three aspects which interact between each other [BER 15]:

– the approach which is known as ontological one (or the structural aspect), considers Big Data within its structure and its form. It is the view of data "existence";

– the functional aspect approach considers "mega-data" as within its function. It is the view of "producing" the data;

– the approach, which is known as genetic (or the dynamic aspect), considers how Big Data changes over time. It is the view of "becoming" the data.

This modeling, thus, makes it possible to apprehend the simulation, accompaniment, forecasting and evaluation of Big Data, particularly within the medical sector. As we have seen previously, it is particularly inspired by the works of Shannon, Wiener, Morin and Floridi. The issue is being able to study at the same time epistemological, anthropological, philosophical and cultural elements relative to communicational and informational organization which Big Data processing imposes.

Finally, our model of study is neither an erudite instrument of applied ethics nor an empirical study aiming to draw up a picture of all of the ethical issues raised. It is more or less a question of a tool offering a precise answer to questions, which are, in other respects justifiable, than about professionals confronted every day with decision-making around the ethical function of Big Data. This "chiasmus" between the empirical survey and ideas suggested by ethicists and theorists makes it possible to equip actors involved within data usage so that they may take on a responsibility which is, henceforth, unavoidable. This is that of a justification which is structured around functions and means underlying significant volumes of data. Consequently, our vision divides into two parts: conceptual and methodological tools required to construct "algorithmic [data] ethics" and a description of ethical issues concerning a precise situation.

Using this intellectual approach, our model will be able to describe in detail in a static way, the Big Data environment, and in a dynamic way, activity flows and, in particular, existing interactions between this "massive data" [BEL 04]. Ethical evaluation comprises both an understanding of the way in which an organization uses personal data, which describes a wide variety of actions which are at the same time historical, typical, and behavioral, as well as an understanding of the values held by this organization [DAV 12]. Thus, what ethical approach is better adapted to equip professionals and decision-makers involved in the data market, so as to create healthy environments or behavioral modification strategies around NICTs?

It is in this context that we have sought to pave the way for ethics specific to Big Data within e-health; being Medicine 4.0 based around ethical analysis modeling and performance improvement through the best dissemination of health professional know-how. This study was made possible as result of working out our ethical analytical modeling of info-ethics illustrated by our pyramid (Ψ, G, Φ) seen earlier and which makes it possible to provide a weighting, backed up by figures, of all of these results.

From this ethical-technical guidance, the listing of ethical objectives around conception, implementation and use of personal health data as well criteria around quality and management of this "data" within the info-sphere, we have been able to construct an ethical data evaluation. This ethical development of personal data ends up by working out a radar chart which makes it possible to visualize the axes of "info-ethics management" (charity, justice, non-maleficence, autonomy, strategy and methodology, organization and regulatory issues, structure and technology, relationships and culture, management, layout, development cycle and operations) and identifying personal health data development zones. The objective is, therefore, to draw up an assessment of the ethical value of personal health data (see Figure 2.15).

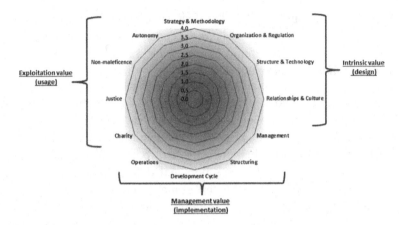

Figure 2.15. *Personal health data ethical increase in value. For a color version of the figure, see www.iste.co.uk/beranger/data.zip*

The radar chart produced at the end of the evaluation is located upon each of the 12 axes of "info-ethics management" to visualize and identify the areas of increased value to improve so as to use and control Big Data better in health and allied sectors. These 12 axes are distributed according to three value categories linked to the BSC perspectives of [KAP 96] which we have previously described:

– intrinsic (that of design): organizational learning perspective;

– management (that of implementation); internal process perspective;

– exploitation (that of use): client perspective (see Table 2.9).

	Synthesis of average scores by axis	
Intrinsic value (of design)	Strategy and Methodology	... / 4
	Organization and Regulation	... / 4
	Structure and Technology	... / 4
	Relationships and Culture	... / 4
Management value (implementation)	Management	... / 4
	Configuration	... / 4
	Development Cycle	... / 4
	Operations	... / 4
Exploitation value (usage)	Charity	... / 4
	Justice	... / 4
	Non-maleficence	... / 4
	Autonomy	... / 4

Table 2.9. *Evaluation criteria for valuing personal data*

We are applying the "scoring" scale following the 93 questions, which are linked to the intrinsic value, management and Big Data exploitation indicators (see Table 1.3).

This scale is constructed in the following way:

– a response: "yes totally" is worth 4 points/4;

– a response: "yes partially" is worth 3 points/4;

– a response: "neither yes, nor no" constitutes 2 points/4;

– a response: "no not really" equates to 1 point/4;

– a response: "no not at all" is worth 0 points/4;

– a response: "I do not know" represents x^{36}.

Consequently, from the results obtained we can both define and implement a "management ethics" system around conception, implementation and use of personal data stemming from NICTs. This ethic management integrates among other things the traditional stages of methodology, such as "the definition of data quality, measuring each of these measurements, the analysis of the evaluation results, quality improvement, and control of improvement effects" [FEO 05]. The techniques used for each of these phases varies according to the type of data processed (structured, semi-structured, or unstructured), the nature of the IS exploiting the data (peer-to-peer, distributed, or data depot) strategies for quantification and measuring, continuous improvement techniques and quality dimensions to consider.

"Info-ethics management", therefore, creates a common vision which makes it possible to guide an organization through aligning actions with human values. It is a tool to implement ethical decisions within a business. From all of the criteria which make up our radar chart, we can go back to each indicator, so as to monitor the ethical performance of Big Data processing by a business, through a dashboard system (DB), firstly through "tactical intervention"[37] and then "operational management"[38]. Such a

---

36 We do not take this question into account in the average score of the evaluation criteria.
37 The function of the "tactical intervention" dashboard is to establish concrete actions around the ethical performance of Big Data processing within an organization.
38 The "operational management" dashboard makes it possible to monitor whether or not actions are being carried out within a structure.

system may constitute a way ahead in the future as a Big Data continuous improvement tool. We may envisage that as soon as the 12 axes of our ethical evaluation tool have a score of less than 3/4, then the latter falls within the dashboard process. Each question with a score of less than 3/4 will be linked to a specific action on the ground. The correct application of this action will be checked within the business. Such an approach constitutes a useful map so as to inform the business around the how, when, who and where to apply these actions relating to the exploitation of digital data?

Finally, our tool to increase the ethical value of Big Data constitutes the cornerstone of our "algorithmic ethic".

2.3. Algorithmic ethics – the vital lead in personalized medicine

Nowadays, our environment and our digital uses are governed by various algorithms, functioning as a number of enclosures in an area which is increasingly closed and proprietary. The capacity to escape this algorithmic governance [ROU 13] appears increasingly complicated to implement, in so far as it is still possible. Concurrent with the public debate around the so-called "information commons", it is noted that this "algorithmic guidance" [CAR 14] issuing particularly from the Internet of Things, is bringing about new predictive regimes around a few spheres of our lives which had escaped it up until now [ERT 15]. In this context, on the basis of the works of, Elinor Ostrom, the winner of the Nobel Prize for Economics in 2012, around "the governance of commons", we may envisage institutional agreements so as to transform private digital data into "commons". The objective would be to target public health messages to at risk populations through the behavioral data of Internet users.

Ethical issues around "massive data", in particular within the health sphere, do not stop developing. Since the age of Antiquity, medicine has raised numerous ethical problems and has contributed to the development of bioethics so as to take decisions which are more humane and just. [TOU 53], "medicine saved the life of ethics". Nowadays, with the recent technological advances linked to Big Data we have noticed that it is now for ethics to save Medicine 4.0's life. Henceforth, it is the advent of what is known as "algorithmic ethics" of medicine.

Initially, with a simple statistical formula, algorithms nowadays make it possible from the exploitation of significant data volumes, to construct correlative models which anticipate and avert future events. This is why algorithms are located at the core of the Big Data, like ship captains navigating around oceans of digital data. These algorithms order, classify and rank into a logical order databases, making them intelligible by means of a correlative or predictive model. For the user, these algorithms convert gigantic volumes of data into personalized services in real time [IG 14]. By definition an algorithm is a series of instructions, which once carried out correctly leads to a given result. A logical series of operations makes it possible to attain a determined result.   The study of algorithms is the most researched discipline in data processing. It should be mentioned that its origins predate the birth of data processing in Persia in the seventeenth century B.C.E. (with the Babylonian algorithms to solve mathematical equations) and closer in time to us (in Baghdad, around 900 C.E.) with al-Khwârizmî who gave his name to the study of algorithms.

Thus, the study of algorithms is the art of describing with a very high degree of accuracy the actions to undertake a given task. For [MAK 13], "algorithms are functions which determine the action which must be attributed to each piece of data which is being entered. Advanced and self-taught machine algorithms, which are at the heart of intelligent data processing, are functions which are transformed through business actions into obtained results. This makes it possible with each new action or campaign to develop as closely as possible to the objectives which are set at the outset". We can take the example of a cooking recipe. This is why the description must be very detailed and precise so as to be able to be executed by the program.

In these circumstances, working out an algorithm involves the discovery of actions that is necessary to organize within the time, and to choose how to organize them to obtain the result desired by their cumulative effects. The algorithm may be represented as having voluminous ramifications in which binary decisions follow one another according to a series of predefined rules.

From this observation, we may naturally establish both a comparison and correlations around the nature and operation of an algorithm with ethics. Algorithms, as with ethics, find their definition and their formula within their purpose. They defined according to what they recommend, order or infer. They form a series of instructions and "a process" which is required to perform an action. Our systemic ethical neo-Platonic modeling (Ψ, G, Φ) relies upon, as with the algorithm, analytical bedrock comprised of three axes of interpretation: actions, situation, and intentions which make up the event. Intention[39] is linked to values. Hence, the subject of our work – to be specific the design, implementation and use of Big Data – which makes up the event within our analytical model is not a simple spontaneous action. It becomes integrated into a situation, into an intention which comprises values and into a specific social environment (see Figure 2.17) [BER 15]. Furthermore, following the example of ethics, an algorithm generally demonstrates the following stages:

– the declaration of variables: we able to precisely describe the indicators to be used within the algorithm. These elements may have different values. They are characterized by their name and their value. They constitute a piece of information;

– the initialization or data entry: we retrieve information and/ or initialize it;

– data processing: we complete necessary operations so as to respond to the problem posed;

– data output: we post the result and make a decision.

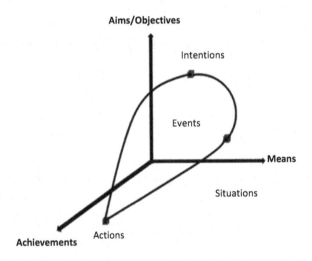

Figure 2.17. *Developing an event*

39 Intention constitutes the possibility of representing a state of affairs which is simply ideal, which is not present materially but which may be constructed because we often describe our "activity" as symbolic.

Consequently, the power and quality of our "algorithmic ethics" derives directly from the quality and data volume which we are able to collect. Indeed, the algorithm of ethical data management develops with the data sets which cut across them, attributing different weightings for each variable.

Furthermore, [DAV 12], an ethical decision must take into account notions such as:

– the intention of those who by direct or indirect means have access to the data in question;

– security: during the lifecycle of the data of each structure;

– probability: whether access to specific data will have beneficial or damaging consequences;

– clustering: correlation of available data brings about a mix of possibilities;

– responsibility: each stage of the lifecycle, provides different degrees of obligation for actors to deal with;

– identity: unique or multiple facets in the description of an individual's characteristics;

– ownership: for each stage of the data processing chain, there are rights of use based upon actor status;

– reputation: judgments and opinions are constructed according to available processed data;

– advantage: the added value which Big Data exploitation provides for the individual and the business;

– damage: negative and moral prejudicial repercussions stemming from access to sensitive personal data.

Finally, the above serves to emphasize that we must not forget that negotiating the use of customer data with business partners, out of necessity, provides a new set of values to take into consideration, which has the effect of complicating the use process.

Moreover, positioning algorithms at the heart of expert health systems, (such as IBM's Watson, Google's Qualico and others) which will soon replace the doctor, lead us to question both the fairness and loyalty of medical decision algorithms and filtering systems. Indeed, the "algorithmization" of medical decisions integrates important issues around both the processing and analysis of medical data.

The study of Big Data highlights correlations detected so that scientists may subsequently research causal explanations. This is why the designers of "data" usage models should demonstrate scientifically the interest of such an approach, the constraints associated with anonymizing data and the quantification of the risk which we are exposing ourselves to by sharing data [BLO 13].

We may take the case of a type algorithm used in medical imaging technology aiming to precisely represent both human and biological structures on a computer so as to improve disease diagnosis or treatment prospects. One of the numerous ethical interrogations revealed by these algorithms is expressed by the risk of creating false positives[40] and false negative implications[41]. These algorithms, therefore, have a value judgment determining element and as a consequence a code of ethics. The designer is thus led to make a trade-off between minimizing false positives or the number of erroneously negative results[42]. This compromise will inevitably be based around a value judgment. Generally, the designers choose a reasonable value for the threshold or the computer software parameters. The user will base his decisions on the release of software results that were completed according to the parameters based on ethical hypotheses set up by the software designer hence the necessity for these ethical hypotheses to be similar to those of the user arises. This is why the construction of an algorithm must make it possible for the user to choose their individual circumstances. It is, therefore, necessary that the designer of the IS leaves the user to specify the ethical parameters, and at the same time, the responsibility to specify the software default position, if required.

---

40 The algorithm activates a counting system (perhaps for example for cells or illness symptoms) in a digital environment; that is one which does not actually exist.

41 The algorithm does not succeed in identifying the image structure which actually exists.

42 The algorithm designer is confronted with a decision device which is similar to that encountered by individuals designing other technological artifacts. That then leads to value judgments integrated into an algorithm being similar to those appearing in the design systems.

Algorithms are constructed by Man. They use actual personal data and may make decisions on behalf of the business that created them; this applies even if the correlation between the two facts does not necessarily involve a causal link between the two. Under these circumstances, processing algorithms may be ethical so as to develop meaningful human value.

Moreover we, generally, neither know algorithmic rules nor the date when they are altered. This is why it seems essential to look deeply into the reasons, purposes and intentions of these algorithms with the aim of obtaining a better transparency, visibility and clarity of the latter. Hence, in place of considering algorithms as a natural element, as the objective picture of reality, we are led to study and take apart carefully each line of the code so as to make it more ethically acceptable. The ultimate goal is to create "processing algorithms which empower the data user rather than alienating him" [GUI 11]. The principle of our ethical algorithm applied to medical Big Data is to make possible a complete study of personal health data from the man-machine interface or even from the info-sphere, which reconciles both technology and medical ethics. Our modeling, therefore, corresponds to a technical language translation tool around ethical language, and vice versa. Our ethical Big Data model, out of necessity, undergoes this confrontation and exchange of genres for which we start from the universal, the general and the abstract moving towards the practical, the specific and the material. For Jean-François Mattei, "all theoretical reasoning is rational reasoning which aims for the universal" [MAT 05]. By its intrinsic nature the Italian terms *Homo Universale* (Universal Man) corresponds to Leonardo da Vinci's theoretical and abstract man. This conquest of the universal entails a rejection of immediately distinctive characteristics. The universal, thus, constitutes an ordered entirety according to laws of mathematics and physics which are represented by rules.

From this intellectual progression, we have sought the ideal representation which combines both the philosophy of thinking and mathematical precision so as to constitute an algorithm to resolve ethical problems. Data ethics is, nowadays, an element of the relationship of trust which must be built with the market.

Starting from this observation, we turned to the outline of Vitruvian Man (or *Homo Universalis*), around the study of the proportions of the human man completed around 1492 by Leonard da Vinci. This anatomical drawing, which integrates an important symbolic connotation, represents the synthesis of anatomical and scientific research. Wishing to express the unity of human proportions this image illustrates the twofold body movement. It does not represent the ideal man but the geometric model of a normal man. The latter is drawn within the geometric shapes of the square and the circle (see Figure 2.18).

The circle constitutes the symbol of nature (the macrocosm), infinity, the sky, the universal and spirituality. It represents Medicine 4.0 in our model. The square then illustrates the ancestral image of the earth (the microcosm) practical reality and reason. It corresponds to Big Data in our modeling.

The so-called "Temple" is the intermediary between one and the other, between the top and the bottom. Through the Temple we obtain the "square of the circle"[43] representing the indissoluble union of the spirit and physical matter. Vitruvian Man is in this Temple, having attained the square of the circle, he is, in fact, this temple. Thus, for Leonardo da Vinci, the man by himself is a direct link between the Holy Spirit and physical matter. If the outline is both in balanced proportions and mathematically perfect, the latter represents man as a pentagram inserted within a circle.

Thus the extremities of Vitruvian Man are in contact, with the circle five times, illustrating the five "Ps" of Medicine 4.0 (personalized, predictive, preventive, participative, and prognosis)[44]; and with the square on six occasions representing the six ""V" of Big Data (volume, variety, velocity, veracity, visualization, and value) which we described in our general introduction.

Finally, our ethical approach links up with the works on inductive algorithms at the core of Big Data technologies perfectly. The inductive algorithm should be combined with a reward (or convergence) function which evaluates the benefit of new inferences and, thus, limits their numbers. Like ethical development, with respect to a given problem, there is no unique and universal solution.

---

43 Squaring of the circle represents a traditional problem for existing mathematics in geometry. It is part of the three major problems of Antiquity with the trisection of the angle and duplication of the cube. The dilemma consists of constructing a square of the same area as a given circle with the aid of only a ruler and a compass. This impossible problem has given rise to the expression: "in attempting to square the circle one is trying to resolve an intractable problem".
44 See section 1.2.1 titled: "Medicine 4.0" in Chapter 1 of this book.

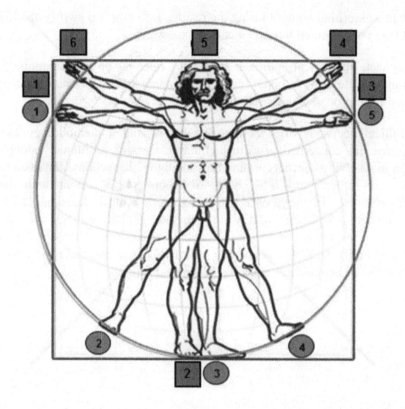

Figure 2.18. *Geometric representation of algorithmic ethics through Vitruvian Man*

However, it is typical for a reduced number of data processes to respond to a particular function. Following the example of an ethical process, the most optimum algorithms are evolutionary. They improve by adjusting their ways of data exploitation according to the most relevant usage which will be able to be made the particular item.

To work out fast inductive algorithms, the data processing should be both anticipatory and contributory. To achieve this, Big Data must convert this data into exploitable info-ethics as soon as possible for immediate use. Thus, our selective and inductive ranking transforms a large quantity of raw data (generally, unstructured) from a "growth" aspect towards a "clear" aspect, which is flexible and less voluminous. The speed of execution has a process at its disposal which makes it possible to focus on essential data which have meaning while at the same time being iterative. That implies it is possible to stop this algorithm without losing the results. Info-ethics is swiftly accessible and may be connected through a continuous system.

In fact, our ethical approach favors the opening up and examining the computer code so as to better monitor and understand the basis of decisions issued from processing algorithms.

Ethical decisions offer both a framework and a methodology to the organizations concerned so as to facilitate discussion on human values and assist in resolving conflicts around how to align risks, actions, and associated values. In other words, this helps to align tactical actions with moral considerations. This approach of recognizing ethical decisions and the development of the possibility to generate explicit ethical discussions provides businesses with an efficient operational capacity around conception, implementation and the use of Big Data processing algorithms, which will be increasingly essential in the near future.

3

Management and Governance
of Personal Health Data

Every company has its own culture, its organization, its governance mode and its project management models. Nevertheless, a number of significant and universal principles concerning governance can be identified, both at the approach level as well as that of actors and of responsibilities. Data governance is one of the key factors to success in the protection of information. It is one of the components that defines the rules, guides and charters of good practice, establishes references and policies (management, classification, storage, and conservation of personal data), and further describes the responsibilities and controls their application. Therefore, it becomes paramount to understand: how can the complexity around personal data management be apprehended and in particular in health fields? In addition, what are the possible mechanisms to process these data pools to turn them into consistent and relevant information? To this end, it is essential to have a detailed and an accurate understanding of algorithmic governance, of the environmental numerical ecosystem, of safety and protection, and of the lifecycle of Big Data.

3.1. Data governance and processing algorithms

Algorithms have made their way into our daily practices without our consent and modulate our relationship with the world without us being really aware of their existence, of the scope of their action, of their power and of the criteria they use to decide the fate of our lives on our behalf.

One of the aspects of the Big Data revolution relies on more powerful and accessible technologies, as well as on the mathematical power of the algorithms that make it possible to interrogate the data. The "mega data" raise a significant adaptation and upgrading challenge that requires a specific management and framework. The challenge is to avoid being overwhelmed by isolated initiatives from the business departments of a company seduced by Big Data, and that really do not bear in mind the 6 "Vs" (volume, variety, velocity, veracity, visualization, value) of these new forms of data, as well as their safety. The mission of this governance consists of optimizing the management of information risk and improving the structure usage behaviors, and the activity. It develops leverages that promote the strengthening and the fluidity of the devices related to the development of the activity or of the services offered by a company or a structure. The strength of the governance is, therefore, a transversal approach to an overview of the lifecycle of the "massive data" to master all the layers of the organization and to guarantee the efficiency of the process.

In effect, several examples indicate how a malicious or accidental usage of Big Data technologies can transform an algorithm into a silent and systemic tool that discriminates. Therefore, thoughtful and well-defined governance rules must aim at data and algorithms, such as:

– having a management policy centered on data based on a small number of principles. This supporting program of change must be enforced in the long term;

– applying governance methods to business priority data;

– analyzing the structure of a source and defining the modes of usage of this data according to its purpose (business) or its potential[1], in order to be correctly used;

– evaluating the reliability rate and the quality of the information[2], in order to optimize its use;

– implementing "information protection administrators";

1 This potential is complex to understand, since typically the value is revealed by coupling multiple types of information between them. It is, therefore, essential to evaluate this potential considering the other sources available.
2 The quality of the Big Data sources has direct impact on the usability of the information and on the complexity of the associated "cleansing" processes.

– establishing steering committees designated for the supervision and the data flow within the company;

– writing internal procedures and good practice guides on information protection and security;

– not to overlook the human (behaviors and education) and the organizational dimension;

– not to take decisions on outdated information;

– implementing a data reduction strategy where only the data that have a defined value are preserved;

– not to retain the information longer than necessary [CHA 14].

In summary, information governance promotes transparency in the management and in the utilization of the intangible capital by companies and organizations. The challenge is, therefore, to establish confidence and to better promote functional inputs within a structure.

This governance becomes a paramount strategy to the enterprise 2.0 that wishes to consider a model 4.0 that must respond to the following features:

– restore: the research and visualization functions, spontaneous and semantic research, data mining;

– understand: the evaluation, creation and the extraction of raw data, the contextualization and the securing, development lifecycle management;

– value: the selective data dissemination (or "push") to applications of the *mashup* type, or *ws*, exchanges of content through the Web and social networks, the collection of the information in its environment;

– master: the traceability of devices and of access (confidence), data de-duplication, the suppression of data and of non-relevant content;

– imagine: the personalization of the services, the socialization of the undertaking, the adaptation of such;

– win: speed, compliance, agility and efficiency;

– use: usage transparency, availability completely independent of the technical supports (tablet, computer, smartphone, etc.), integrity and content certification guarantee;

– coordinate: actors interaction modes in health care services;

– federate: structured and non-structured data, applications originating from NICTs, private and public Cloud Computing, the business value and the heritage value;

– coach: decision and action ("empowerment") capacity of users (consumers, citizens, patients or health professionals);

– anticipate: the interoperability of the solutions, the automation of exchanges between connected objects, the behaviors and habits developments;

– certify: the confidence from the use of the data.

In addition, govern also means to guide, to orientate, to set the path and to follow a suitable implementation. The data governance process must, therefore, organize all data-related decisions, according to research from [CIG 14]:

– heritage valuation;

– usage maximization of these data;

– quality optimization.

Moreover, information governance affects all the stakeholders in the market such as:

– solutions vendors and integrators who are obliged to develop their proposals to respond to changes in the market;

– businesses and individuals who achieve information flows for the entire organization;

– consultants involved in the digitization of enterprises.

Now, information and knowledge management has become a major issue for companies to:

– share and develop data and information flows that form the intellectual heritage and a part of the intangible capital of the organization;

– increase business performance (products and/or services), and marketing;

– promote and encourage innovation;

– improve administrative efficiency and reduce costs;

– ensure regulatory compliance.

It can be observed that the monetization of our data, or their layout in information sectors, can cause more suspicion and raise questions about which governance should be employed? In fact, this is what Antoinette Rouvroy supports, researcher in Law philosophy, at the Fonds National de la Recherche Scientifique (FNRS), interviewed for the investigation of the "Vie privée à l'horizon 2020" [CNI 14]: she defines Big Data as a new "algorithmic governmentality" which can be integrated "in the global context of capitalism", thereby promoting the individualization of services or consumption offers. Thus, the user is certainly placed at the heart of the device but "at the same time, no longer giving him, or her, the opportunity to express what his/her intentions, his/her desires, his/her motivations his/her preferences are, automatically inferred by digital devices".

As a result, assumptions that should be (re)clarified, and intrinsic evolutionary parameters that should be refined, which highlight the data collected under very specific conditions are associated to each model and algorithm.

In addition, in a world where the exploitation of data has become a major economic issue, companies are forced to integrate strong analytical models to extract the critical information and target their commercial offerings. Therefore, decision-making is primarily directed by data and no longer by the intuition of the actors on their market. Such a shift in commercial culture imposes rigorous and coherent management of Big Data and the NICTs that generate them, process them or store them. This data management concerns all the layers of the enterprise since this analytical modeling is present in all of the services[3] of the structure. The relevant management of these large data volumes is a prerequisite to allow companies to implement quick measures to improve their performance and their effectiveness [ROS 13]. This implies that organizations employ flexible analytical models that are scalable, and are easy to adjust and maintain. Consequently, it is essential to rely on management tools which allow a large number of people to quickly understand the NICTs and Big Data associated thereto within the company. This is the reason why tomorrow's challenge lays in the fact that anyone can understand the meaning of processed data.

---

3 The services notably comprise operational services, financial services, quality control, marketing and communication services and technical services.

Good data management must define the rules, devices, the boundaries and the organization that ensures the control of heritage data in line with the strategy and the imperatives of the company. All Big Data management actions serve different purposes but all are essential and must be distinguished among themselves:

– produce: define and deploy "process", services and equipment generating data, to respond to the programs of the company;

– collect: collect data available in a structured form or not, without necessarily having any *a priori* knowledge of their future use;

– store: retrieve and store a huge amount of data in perpetual growth, trying to order and streamline this stock in order to encourage the further processing of the data;

– study: carry out in-depth studies in order to value data internally or externally;

– value: make use of the data potential, in-house or by means of partnerships or through commercial relations.

After an emergence and discovery phase, Big Data-related technologies are today relatively accessible. The change required within a company is now cultural to reap all the potential benefits of these "mega data".

Furthermore, data management requires transparency and respect for the right of individuals with regard to their data. In particular, it involves informing the client about:

– the presence of a personal data collection process;

– the nature of the processed data: personal (name, address, employment status, etc.), sensitive (medical condition, religious, political, sexual orientation, etc.) and other types of information essential to the monitoring of navigation and customization (cookie, logs, etc.);

– the purpose covered by the usage of these data;

– the possibility of access to stored customer data and/or to refuse this collection or accompaniment mechanism.

The management of "massive data" contributes to assessing the value of the information that emerges thereof by facilitating its understanding and, therefore, its uses. The added value of this management is related to the time it saves in the quest for the "good" information, and to the ability for the company to save time in the search for the understanding of Big Data and for the meaning associated with consistent information.

Finally, the Big Data and processing algorithms manager is driven to consider a series of questions such as:

– what are the fundamental data to manage? What are their sources? Who are the producers? Is it necessary to reassess the history?

– how to remove the "noise" that disturbs the readability and the comprehension of the data?

– is it necessary to centralize the data?

– how is it possible to obtain a good traceability of the data? What is the lifecycle of the data? What are the various transformations carried out? what are the intermediate data being generated?

– what is the description level[4] where the data are located?

– what organization should be implemented to manage these big data?

– should data be open to the outside?

– how can data be connected with itself?

– what are the actors and producers of these processes?

– how can the effort/retribution balance be driven? Using what management tools? [CIG 14]

– would the neutrality of the algorithms be nothing but a myth and their manipulation a reality? [PAS 15] Should we not develop the control of the results produced by creating a profession of "algorithmists" composed of experts responsible for conducting controls to verify the reliability and the validity of the algorithms?

– were all the regulations specific to the nature of the processed data correctly taken into account?

– what is the ownership scheme of data? What is the applicable licensing?

---

4 Model level/flow level, enterprise model level/application model level, document level/ folder level, etc.).

Such questions cannot have answers without a thorough knowledge and understanding of the environmental digital ecosystem in which Big Data revolve.

3.2. The environmental digital ecosystem

The consumption and effective management of huge volumes of data represent two paramount requirements for any contemporary society. With the Big Data revolution, all companies have become aware of the potential that is offered to them. Now, they wish to bring forward the relevant information and take full advantage of it. But how can the available information be processed while ensuring the implementation of a performing ecosystem which is capable of storing them, of studying them and of developing them?

Due to its characteristics, Big Data leads irretrievably to a considerable conceptual change involving its digital ecosystem. Data warehouses are no longer at the center of the world. Many repositories and specialized tools are now responsible for applications or for new forms of analysis. Increasingly, data originate from sources external to the infrastructure through APIs. Consequently, the company that processes these data more closely resembles a distributed supply chain.

By its systemic dimension, the digital revolution induces important upheavals within companies. With the same force of disruption as the industrial revolution, it notably transforms the business model, the organization, the culture and the enterprise's strategy and management mode. Accordingly, companies making use of Big Data are thus facing a new ecosystem that can be broken into nine segments [KEP 12] (see Figure 3.1):

– network of partners: hosting providers, "data centers", HPC, manufacturers and Cloud Computing operators;

– key activities: consulting, calculation and storage;

– offer: collect, process logs, vertical applications, analyze, visualize, interpret, structure and store;

– client relationships: self-service, training and support.

– customer segments: administration, media, industries, banks, health, distribution, etc.

– key resources: flow rate, performance and space;

– distribution channels: B2B and A2B;

– cost structure: platform maintenance, membership, development, exploitation;

– revenue streams: data evaluation, sales/resales, lots/transactions, intellectual property, licenses, rents, etc.

The network of partners	Key activities	Offer	Relations with the client	The customer segments
Host Datacenter HPC Constructor Cloud Operator	Consulting Computation Storage	Collect Process logs Vertical applications	Self service Training Support	Administration Media Industry Bank Health Distribution ...
	The key resources	Analyze Visualize Interpret	Distribution channels	
	Debit Performance Space	Structure Store	B2B A2B	
Cost structure			Income flows	
Platform maintenance Subscription Development Utilization			Data evaluation Sales / resales Batch / transaction PI, Licenses, rentals	

Figure 3.1. *Big Data digital ecosystem*

In addition, this digital environment undergoes numerous developments of domestic nature, in particular:

– the explosion of dematerialized services and subsequent data volumes (mostly unstructured) originating from the activity of the Internet users and from the infrastructure;

– the decentralized ecosystem of companies and the heterogeneity of internal safety levels justifying the implementation of referential frames for the protection of data repositories.

As well as of an external nature, notably:

– the convergence of professional and domestic uses of SIs. In effect, social networks, discussion forums, Wi-Fi, blogs, instant messaging, Wikipedia, etc. often constitute usages incompatible with the applications and the requirements within a company. This is why more and more professional infrastructures establish codes of good practice, rules of use, and even ethical charters describing the value of these NICTs for the business;

– the complexity and the magnification of interrelations with the environment may cause a diversification and a danger of the threats. Furthermore, it becomes fundamental that structures reassess and develop their data protection policy;

– the strengthening of regulatory, contractual and legal constraints relative to the importance of transparency and of an increased Big Data "reporting". This situation integrates a certain balance between increased disclosure and control of the information, and the authenticity and the origin of the data upstream, as well as the recipients of the information downstream;

– the development of the extended enterprise, resulting in a transformation of the relationships with customers, business models, suppliers, employees and partners. This context requires businesses to expand their scope of data protection beyond the natural and the structural borders.

Although NICTs integrate new features facilitating access to data, their movements and their transformations, this is why Big Data reveal new needs, recommendations and requirements, such as:

– data integration tools must work both on-site and in Cloud Computing models;

– it is essential to define and describe a mechanism regarding the processes of accessibility to data via NoSQL and analytical databases, or through Hadoop;

– processing tools must keep evolving the ability to simplify the development and implementation of the transformations of the raw unstructured data into relevant and consistent information. These changes must be reused and exchanged;

– as the data supply chain becomes more complex, it becomes essential to perform a synchronization of the data between reference systems;

– the NICTs associated with Big Data must contain a flexible structure to facilitate a fast and accurate manipulation;

– it is paramount that these technologies incorporate transfer procedures with the ability to manage new volumes. Information originating from the study of huge volumes of data can be directed to applications so that a more accurate modeling of reality is effective. Thus, data may, for example, be synchronized through an analytical tool in memory, and not be reduced to SQL databases;

– a good assessment of integration technologies must involve present data and Big Data that are easily integrable and storable in canonical form. It is essential to build canonical forms for various types of information notably generated from smartphones applications, social networks, Web blogs, etc. Control of the changes brought to the conventional forms of data is facilitated by good management of the canonical identifications of the data in a lifecycle;

– these Big Data technologies must remain ergonomic and easy to use, to facilitate their access to a large number of people that may be directly related to the data, thereby promoting self-created solutions and discoveries;

– Big Data systems must be responsible for all processing at every stage of the data supply chain, and for presenting an automatic discovery and visualization of the models;

– it is essential that Big Data integration mechanisms be established to address several types of environments;

– an optimal Big Data solution must allow a guided experience in which an automatic learning process makes suggestions, before being directed in the right direction by analysts.

Finally, companies must take into account all the parameters and elements which contribute to the formation of an ecosystem for Big Data and ensure that they work together perfectly to make this digital environment suitable to all their requirements. Our environmental digital ecosystem can thus be shaped based on our PER, namely in the following domains:

– regulatory and organizational;

– relational and cultural;

– structural and technological;

– strategic and methodological.

3.2.1. *Regulatory and organizational aspects*

Professionals and industrialists are challenged to question themselves about the profile of the organizations that benefit from using Big Data, and about the influence of the Web giants in the redistribution of value. Specific skills appear critical to work on data: does this constitute a general acculturation to Data Mining? What specializations are required for the "new" professions, such as data scientists?

Therefore, companies are faced with many challenges and issues related to analytics and to the management of "mega data":

– how can maximum value be extracted from large volumes of data?

– what are the key functions for the creation of data value?

– which new management rules should be implemented?

– what will be the role of the Chief Information Officer (CIO)?

– how can the diagnosis phase be reconfigured to consider more autonomous uses?

– how can it be integrated into the existing data flows and referential frameworks?

– what actions should be carried out so these data make sense to the established organization?

– how to keep pace with the profound changes in marketing?

– how can large data volumes be managed?

– how can the role of the Chief Data Officer (CDO) be made more visible?

– how can existing and future analytics be seamlessly integrated to promote the adaptation of infrastructures to modifications?

– how can the complexity of NICTs required for data analysis be managed?

– what regulations govern the use of big data?

– how can open innovation be integrated so that it becomes the norm?

First of all, it is important to know what "data" must be stored and how they can be collected in real-time, then to process them correctly and quickly to achieve organizational changes. These modifications are at the heart of Big Data, because without the will to make adjustments, the study of data does not take place. However, the development of a vast data ecosystem should not be taken lightly, and not to imitate other companies. Instead, it is important to ensure in a pragmatic manner that this ecosystem will have a positive impact, whether at the level of the expectations of the customers or that of internal business processes.

Examining large amounts of data is not an easy task, but businesses must take care of it before implementing a management ecosystem. The data collected and the various interconnected data sets must reach a consensus within the organization. Therefore, understanding what should be compared and how to carry out the comparison is only one half of the whole process.

Our belief is that the concomitance of breakthroughs, particularly in terms of the evolution of the regulatory framework of the strategic model and technological breakthroughs concerning Big Data, leads to a significant transformation of the organization of companies. The challenges, the speed and the importance of future developments raise questions about the methodologies to be adopted by enterprises in order to accompany this change.

Moreover, the operation of a business today is still based on partitioned processes: client relationships, trade, production, finance, human resources management, etc. As a result, each direction has its own devices available, its IS, its "data". The organization of CIOs is mainly based on applications that consequently generate duplicate information.

It may be noted that an organization, with its multiple "in silo" interlocutors inhibits transverse initiatives, in particular the development of end-to-end use-cases, and limits the decision-making needed to launch Big Data projects. On the other hand, with the emergence of large data volumes, all these organizations tend to change. As a matter of fact, if any data has potential, it is only by cross-referencing the information that a significant value can finally be extracted. This underlines that it is important to break the compartmentalization to which administrations have confined themselves: the construction of "data lakes", "data hubs", or other equivalent concepts, corresponds to the first steps of this approach. These businesses are then referred to as "data-centric" enterprises. Accordingly, the data is recognized as a global asset of the company which supports all of the business functions. The purpose here is not to modify the structure of the company, but the way in which it operates. This necessarily results in impacts on the organization and on the functioning style of the company.

Thus, "data" is no longer appropriated by the management or the service which performs the collection: it now represents a transverse asset. To this end, it becomes crucial to separate data from usage. The datum is no longer an element inherently associated with a computer application, but must be accessible to all of the services that rely upon it. The final stage of decoupling is the principle of "data as a service", which allows the equitable access of information resources. However, such arrangements often require reappraisal of the IS architecture, which *a posteriori* is never an easy task. A background change occurs as soon as coordination between the various administrations becomes one of the major challenges of tomorrow's enterprise. This requires a robust and flexible architecture to harmoniously process new data types. The CIO ought to become a partner in the development of the business, and no longer as a simple provider of solutions.

Another impact is that data governance requires stakeholders to define a work and usage environment. Without this governance and willingness from the executive management, the company cannot succeed in its metamorphosis. This is why the transition to Big Data and the accompaniment of the strategy of data evaluation within an enterprise should mainly be conducted by a CDO.

Finally, the integration of analytical models in the company's systems is a milestone in processing Big Data. The availability of the implemented models is the last step of this device, both at the level of the enterprise and outside its borders. The production must not be a costly process and predictive models must be able to be deployed easily within others, especially ISs, by integrating themselves into proprietary applications or Web services. The development of centralized services, accessible by all, connected to various information resources, with a scalability capacity and with sufficient speed to meet demand, is an essential organizational step for a company. The applications and the services thus deployed in adapted computer infrastructures guarantee visibility to the company and an immediate reaction in the sector concerned. It has become essential that safeguard measures (such as data "minimization", pseudonyms, process proportionality, etc.) be applicable to prevent data from being employed in decision-making tasks or in measures that could be prejudicial with regard to people.

In addition, a series of actions must be carried out so that a company can properly address the advent of Big Data (see Table 3.1).

For example, the launch of a "data science" approach initially requires a double inventory: the inventory of the business objectives and goals being targeted, as well as the inventory of the data available or that can be mobilized[5].

Operational objectives	Actions to be taken
Carry out an inventory	– Identify the target business objectives – List the data available or that can be mobilized
Detect the possible limits and the improvements of the NICTs associated with Big Data	– Determine the useful external sources (for example Open Data) – Identify link gateways that do not permit enough interaction between end-users and information sources – Identify complex and inefficient analysis and processing tools – Detect the evolution ability of devices to identify those that block the organization of data processing to its full potential as its informational assets increase.
Re-evaluate the IT infrastructure	– Determine the restricting aspects of data management which provide an incomplete or obsolete vision – Be equipped with a flexible technology architecture for more substantial and varied collection, storage, and analysis of Big data – Anticipate the needs that would not express the business

5 These data comprise: data generated from operational processes (orders, invoices, activity reports, etc.) – data conventionally maintained and processed by the organization in addition to those collected without making any use of them (log data) – external data, open or not, which may usefully enrich the body of data available for analysis (emails, networks, forums, etc.).

Understand and converse with the market	– Conduct market research about the offers generated from Big Data – Think about use cases, build a pilot service, promote it to the business by describing its value-added – Decompartmentalize the data of various services by sharing the scattered "data" – Drive its ecosystems towards the digital revolution
Proceed to a digital transformation	– Integrate digital technologies into the strategic vision of the company, expanding the scope of its activities beyond development and marketing – Recruit new expertise in digital technology – Promote the transformation device in favor of restructuring. In an environment unstable by nature, the levers for the creation of value demand that new skills emerge – Modify organization and work habits by giving employees new spaces oriented towards creativity and innovation – Promote the transversality of teams – Overcome reluctance to the digital shift – Give significant autonomy to the subsidiaries of a company to implement these new organizational "designs" – Provide detailed information to collaborators about their new digital ecosystem, and implement permanent and broad monitoring to be able to apprehend it
Form one's own teams	– Consult Big Data experts – Draft a code of ethics for good practice about the usage of "massive data", and submit it to the teams that constitute the enterprise – Educate the employees of the company with respect to the regulatory framework surrounding data processing – Analyze Big Data-related innovative technological tools

Table 3.1. *Objectives and actions to be performed in order for a company to control Big Data*

In addition, for businesses, there are numerous legal and regulatory issues concerning their criminal and civil responsibility in the management of personal data that they collect and make use of. This requires compliance with regulatory and legislative texts destined to protect personal data, and thus the privacy of people concerned. It is possible to rely on the "principles of the guidelines of the OECD governing the security of systems and information networks[6] (see Appendix 4).

For businesses, this means it is imperative to be well acquainted with the texts, to take measures for securing adapted data, to be vigilant with signed contracts, particularly with foreign partners and involving potential impacts to personal data, to raise awareness, to educate and to train employees and others involved in the manipulation of this data, to implement evaluations and annual audits to ensure the compliance of the measures being adopted, and to anticipate the risks.

Finally, so that a code of ethics and/or an ethical charter be adopted by the members of an organization, it is imperative that the measures mentioned in these texts be implemented throughout the organization, and gradually within routine work activities. It should be noted that training is often used to improve and shape the approach and ethical behavior, both in the company and in the social parameters [CAN 08, LAU 97, MCK 08, REY 00, STE 08]. For this reason, it is essential that executives, organizational managers and higher levels of management be fully involved in the ethics of the enterprise [VAL 02]. This brings us to consider the cultural and relational aspects that constitute part of the Big Data digital ecosystem.

3.2.2. Relational and cultural aspects

Through the NICTs and the new storage and usage capabilities of "massive data", consumers were gradually able to discover offers and new services resulting in even more significant innovation needs. As an example of these new usages originating directly from the emergence of Big Data, one could mention price comparison engines, which naturally require huge processing capabilities of real-time data, and that enable millions of Internet users each month to make better and cheaper purchases, in particular in areas related to health (such as health insurance, mutual funds, pharmaceutical items, medical acts, paramedical accessories, etc.). Another area of high

6 The current "OECD guidelines for the security of systems and information networks: towards a culture of security" have been adopted in the form of a Recommendation of the OECD Council during its 1037th session, on July, 25 2002.

demand from consumers that has started to be addressed by Big Data technologies concerns direct communication between patients and physicians. Faced with the influx of messages, often untargeted and of no interest to their recipients, Internet users have used their "countervailing power": non-reactions, complaints, unsubscriptions, asking for more relevant and more accurate communication on behalf of brands. The consumer loudly claims his right to transparency and to its free and informed consent with regard to the ethical principle of autonomy.

Based on this context, this digital world requires us to build new reference systems. Everyone has the need to take ownership of the data that they have created, to understand what they produce. To this end, we need tools, experiments, and methodologies. We need spaces, places, physical or virtual, open, organized resources to interact, share and understand this new world that is presented to us. This requires a coherent organization of the cultural appropriation forms of this digital world in which we live. This digital culture can be characterized according to seven ethical and technical dimensions [AIM 13]:

– openness: connectivity, fluidity, and data;

– sustainability: safety, continuity and risk management;

– responsibility: societal responsibility, solidarity and well-being;

– interdependence: cooperation, partnership and alliance;

– confidence: coherence, meaning and cohesion;

– agility: innovation, flexibility and anticipation;

– knowledge: sharing, transversality and value creation.

Big Data projects are by their very nature transversal, whereas business organizations are generally structured in silos, thus making the digital transformation and decision-making more complex often due to fragmented resources and budgets. These companies need to establish a unified digital strategy to face competition, but also to optimally meet their customers' requests.

It is paramount to internally decompartementalize the data, and even with external partners, but also to collaborate together transversely. This concerns those from computing, data analysis and marketing, business, BIs or from CRMs. It is important nonetheless that enterprises avoid getting "intermediated" by more agile players that capture an increasing share of the value created.

It is desirable that the development of sophisticated, performing, and relevant algorithms brings meaning to collected data and simplifies the lives of people, by limiting the number of messages and by recreating value during each interaction. Through much more consistent and fairer communication and services, companies commit themselves to repay every consumer the value of the entrusted data.

However, we are entitled to ask whether openness and data sharing policies restore a form of dictatorship of transparency by claiming a "culture change" based on the rejection of the protection of personal data? The behaviors that users develop when faced with the processing of their data, as well as the regulations, the ethical recommendations and the controls that must be considered, must be studied.

In effect, the Big Data technological revolution, notably associated to the Hadoop ecosystem and to the principle of joint parallelism for data storage and usage, is primarily a cultural and a relational revolution. It is based on the increasingly shared observation that "mega data" is not merely a by-product of devices, services and applications, but can become a real vector of innovation for those who know how to value it, how to analyze it and how to process it in a scientific manner. It can be observed that beyond structural and technological aspects, this "analytical democratization" of data calls for cultural transformations. Generally, analytical expertise remains an area of expertise and supports a business or a service (risk, marketing, actuarial, fraud, finance, etc.) which inhibits the development of a genuine analytical business culture. Furthermore, it can be seen that the correlation between the lack of confidence and the use of NICTs in the client relationship is a real one.

Confidentiality and data security are as much matters relating to technology and to Law as to behavior. It is fundamental to train, inform and educate each of the actors present[7] in the production chain of health care, with respect to new purposes and points for vigilance [LES 13]. The human factor plays a key role in strengthening the security of digital ecosystems. It

---

7 Patients, heads of schools, health professionals, IS security administrators, hosts, manufacturers for the hospital sector.

appears paramount to reconsider the "ethics of the relationship" between individuals by means of digital technologies.

The question is, then, how can a degree of confidence and of relational and cultural harmony be regained? This requires that we question ourselves, on the one hand about the expectations of customers, and on the other hand, about the means for the implementation of technology tools in the customer relationship, and their relevance: do they facilitate the listening to and the understanding of the customers? Do they contribute or are they detrimental to the quality of the relationship? Do they provide more transparency? As a consequence, reflections on ethical issues – for example regarding personal data processing, as well as on moral behavior such as honesty, transparency, appropriateness, kindness, understanding, and listening – will allow the confidence of customers and health users to be reestablished. Thus, it appears crucial to build an ethical approach to Big Data to better grasp and understand its impact on mankind and to recognize an intimate relationship: "culture ignores in technical reality the human reality, and... to play its full role, culture must incorporate technical beings in the form of knowledge and with a sense of values" [SIM 13]. The cultural side seems then to turn digital technology into a "human reality". The faculty of digital technology to transform our behaviors and to disseminate values through these new reactions should encourage us to develop a correspondence between an ethic of technologies and an ethic of usages.

In addition, the explosion of these huge volumes of data contributes to the emergence of new players, such as manufacturers involved in the production and the "sourcing" of data, as well as in its aggregation and analysis. New players also include users of personal data which will develop services and targeted applications with higher added value, services exclusively based on the visualization and aggregation of data scattered over different services. The reorientation of the organization of our healthcare system, by placing data at its center, requires the creation of new skills.

In most enterprises, the question of the responsibility and governance of this democratization of data could lead to the construction of specific posts such as: "Chief Digital Officer", "Chief Data Officer"[8], or "Chief Analytics

---

8 Responsible for the data of the company; this role would be to transmit to the executive committee observations and analyses based on data, to further support decision-making. For example a head of a clinical department with the administration of the hospital.

Officer", responsible for conducting real "think tanks" to assist the company's strategy.

From now on, the head of an IS will have to integrate and develop skills such as:

– analyzing data, dashboards and justifying the results associated to the activities of its field;

– selecting and using appropriate statistical tools;

– developing, updating, and optimizing a database, relating to the nature of its activities;

– achieving, formalizing and adapting procedures, protocols, procedures and instructions relating to its area of expertise;

– designing, adapting tools and work methods specific to its area of expertise;

– constructing and using pilot tools (criteria, indicators, TB, etc.);

– defining and using techniques and practices adapted to the job;

– developing, writing and operating queries relating to the sector;

– evaluating the appropriateness, the veracity of the data and/or of the information;

– using a procedure, code, language, protocol or regulations specific to the area [BER 15].

Moreover, the usage of Big Data does not purely represent a goal in itself: after processing, the data is simply smoothed, sorted, and have not yet revealed all their potential. It is in this context that the function of specialized analysts such as "Data Scientists" and "Data Analysts"[9] assumes its significance. The latter may interpret the data, cross-reference them, place them back into perspective and propose directly understandable representations for the different decision-making levels. The company will

---

9 These two professions require statistical, technical, computational and operational skills. The Data Analyst is even more exposed to field-work than his counterpart, the Data Scientist, who is rather more engineering-oriented. These two roles operate on activities and prospecting data by associating them to operational business decision-making.

naturally have to address a series of questions: how far can the targeting of messages generated from Big Data go? What are the limits for the use of their knowledge? What interpretation of a body of data combined with previous data can be achieved? How can human organization be harmonized with the ICTs associated with "massive data"? etc.

All this highlights a pronounced separation of the relational organization from the conventional models which have not incorporated this digital shift:

– distribute analytical processes throughout the whole organization of the company;

– recruit from various economic fields to multiply talent, skills, adopt new practices, and promote the heterogeneity of know-how;

– mobilize and accompany the intermediate managers who are implementing the digital revolution;

– confront teams with issues originating from Big Data, making a real difference for the company's strategy;

– implement a single analytical team, under the responsibility of a Chief Strategy Officer, bringing together the skills of various experts previously involved in supporting various businesses (stock management, marketing studies, customer knowledge, pricing, etc.);

– introduce analytics to the center of governance plans and ensure its dissemination throughout the whole organization to support every business process;

– share and accompany the evolution of behaviors and practices by collaborating with multidisciplinary teams (ergonomists, doctors, sociologists, psychologists, etc.);

– work in a collaborative fashion to stimulate creativity centered on data;

– reduce the gap between the ISs and businesses, in particular through sharing skills and expertise;

– integrate the internal social network of the company into business processes, particularly in the context of mobility;

– integrate analytics at the heart of driving change by embedding analytical culture into action.

It should be noted that in implementing a genuine integration of the data, where Big Data fit together with the existing data flow, to be consulted in the same way as all other sources of information and exposed to the other data, the company enhances collaboration among computing professionals, BI professionals and analysts, which creates cooperation and internal partnerships.

A recent report by the European Commission [GUI 13] indicates that the Internet of Things "does not only concern objects; it concerns the relations between everyday objects surrounding humans and humans themselves" [SAN 11]. Furthermore, this report states that the European Group on Ethics of Science and New Technologies claims that the Internet of Things "will radically change the relationship between humans and autonomous interconnected objects, giving them autonomy with respect to their interaction with human beings".

Accordingly, the training of data experts is a challenge in itself. In a large number of countries such as France, schools and universities are just beginning to offer training in connection with BI and Big Data. Companies have difficulty in finding people specialized in this area due to the lack of available profiles.

In addition, there exist asymmetrical relationships between organizations and people who benefit from the usage of their personal data, especially in the control of data. A legal framework dedicated to the protection of the customer's rights notwithstanding, the consumer often finds himself in a situation of incomprehension when facing the processing of the personal data that concerns him. The health and welfare sector is no exception to this. In the 2013 report on health and welfare mobile applications conducted by the American association "Privacy Rights Clearinghouse", the editors reveal that the privacy policies of the applications are particularly prone to risks with respect to the privacy of end-users.

Beyond the blatant lack of available information, the report brings to light the presence of a gap between the privacy policies presented to the user, and the reality of the practices concerning their personal data. The majority of smartphone applications that clearly indicate their confidentiality policy do not describe in a very understandable manner the practices showing potential risks for privacy. The authors of the study further add that:

"the more detailed the confidentiality policy of an application was, the bigger the tendency of the observed practices shown to compromise privacy ". Under these circumstances, it appears difficult for a user to achieve real control over his personal data [CNI 14].

Ultimately, technology is neither good nor bad, nor neutral. The interrelationships between technology and the social and cultural ecosystem are such that technical developments have implications and environmental, human and social consequences that reach far beyond the purposes of the NICTs, of the usages and of the practices themselves [KRA 86]. This reflection, present in the "first law of Kranzberg" about the relationship between technology and the socio-cultural framework, perfectly conveys the importance and the impact of the Big Data revolution in our society today. That is why it appears essential to reposition mankind at the heart of a society governed by data. This requires an in-depth and rigorous knowledge of the structural and the technological dimensions in which Big Data exists.

3.2.3. *Structural and technological aspects*

Large volumes of digital data include technical challenges associated with the structuring and building of knowledge. To be analyzable, reusable, combinable and aggregated, raw data must be structured. The strengthening of the convergence of information resource identification systems with Internet devices, the development of metadata processes, benefit "process" interoperability and computations based on Big Data. We are entitled to raise a question concerning the construction of expertise; what kinds of knowledge are we likely to achieve by crossing data?

As a consequence, the digital metamorphosis has its main roots in technology. Whether at the design, consumption, study, or the data sharing level, technological choices require rethinking the conventional boundaries which exist between operational and decision-making devices. State-of-the-art architectures, by implementing increasingly effective technologies, such as cloud computing and Hadoop, provide consistent and effective responses to these needs for flexibility, for experimentation and for extensibility.

Consequently, it is fundamental that the integration technology of digital data combines Big Data with the various forms of existing data, usually stored in SQL repositories. To this end, it is important to use a technology that integrates the native language of the sources of Big Data equally, such as Hadoop and analytical databases and NoSQL, as well as the traditional SQL language. Documents in plain text and videos are thus included in the data types. Automatic machine learning, the study of texts or videos and a multitude of other techniques, applied to data in Hadoop or in NoSQL databases, can allow that meaning be given to unstructured and disordered data [CIT 13].

That is why Big Data does not encompass only the convergence of an organization, of a team or of various skills. The structural and technological aspect is also crucial in a Big Data project. Technological choices are at the origin of an "analytical democratization", increasingly due to:

– analytical systems integrating business processes;

– economic actors exchanging data, information, and knowledge through technical (API) or economic (Open Data, data monetization) devices.

Under these conditions, NICTs are one of the first challenges of Big Data. Hadoop, NoSQL, analytical databases databases and data warehouses must coexist. The use and the integration of these new technologies (Hadoop, MPP, NoSQL, in Memory, etc.) within the IS of a company then requires the anticipation of their appropriations, to measure the effort of transformation for the organization and the teams set in place. It is also important to find solutions to compensate for the lack of skills within the company.

In addition, companies need tools that help them to avoid the manipulation of Big Data at the granular level, and that offer relational features to identify tendencies. These analytical tools must summarize data in a concrete and accessible manner. As a result, "massive data" can be operated upon through semantic indexing. A Data Analyst, who finds accurate information and wants to deepen his research on a more specific basis, must be able to rely on an analytical tool which is both flexible and adaptive according to the source of the data. This technological solution has to be able to be deployed on-site or in a computing cloud.

Furthermore, today the construction of an efficient algorithm requires machine learning[10] technologies which ought to be at the center of its operation.

The learning mechanism is achieved according to the following three steps: (see Figure 3.2)

– understanding the impact and the repercussions of different data on a specific objective;

– applying the model to predict (see personalized medicine);

– deciding the actions to perform to create value, based on the business and the operational framework, and on the objectives to be achieved.

A system must be able to offer the following two elements:

– the development of operational reports and traditional BI dashboards;

– NICTs such as visualization and predictive analytics.

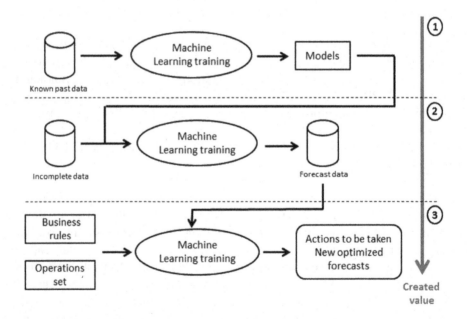

Figure 3.2. *Machine learning functioning*

---

10 Machine learning: a discipline in AI which aims to develop the capacity of machines and of software programs to learn their results.

There is a lack of an urbanization[11] model of the data and of the interfaces allowing the interoperability of devices and connected objects and their dissemination. For example, the remote monitoring of pacemakers and defibrillators is limited because these medical devices differ according to the manufacturer.

It is essential to adopt a sufficiently fluid and highly adaptable data integration technology. An adaptable system must be flexible, customizable and accessible from mobile solutions (laptops, iPads, smartphones, tablets, etc.). It can be observed that data processes "in silos" promote the partitioning of the BI and can be expressed by a flawed analytics operation. Users must be able to integrate only the necessary components for their activity in order to gain access to the only analytical capabilities they need, with the possibility, eventually, to transform these capabilities at any moment. They must also be able to insert the analysis application into other products and other solutions, so that devices and the architecture of the data can be introduced into the new solution.

Customization is also one of the prerogatives for the optimal visualization of the data. The goal of any solution is therefore to provide operational analytics and predictive analysis functions. Ideally, it is important to adopt an intuitive and reactive system, accessible to each user and not just to computer scientists or to analytics experts. End users should be able to use the solution without having to undertake new training. Therefore, ease of use is a key element for success that can be achieved by an interactive Control Panel (CP) integrating performing visualization functions. The implementation must not cause any disruption in terms of employees or activities. Finally, for the sake of efficiency of resources and costs, users must be able to develop and adjust themselves these new analyses without having to resort to computer services at every stage of the system.

On the other hand, one of the major issues related to the explosion of large volumes of data concerns security and confidentiality. By storing critical data upon which it bases its decisions, the company is vulnerable to piracy and cybercrime . This also affects public institutions. From a technical

---

11 By definition, the "urbanization" of the IS of an entity is a discipline of computer engineering, that consists of developing its IS such that it supports and accompanies in an effective and optimal manner the missions of the organization and its transformations.

point of view, a security policy is based on steganography[12], biometrics[13], and cryptography[14], security engineering sciences in the protocols and the architectures of network devices.

Structures must adopt an approach towards the digital threat focused on data, starting with the establishment of more efficient identity and access control management techniques, whether considering data encryption or multifactor authentication procedures, to render the selected information unusable. By introducing the encryption of sensitive data as a basis for computer security, businesses are encouraging cybercriminals to move toward less well-protected targets.

The approach to digital security consists of four dimensions:

– the physical security of places, people and goods, of infrastructures and material resources;

– the security of ISs of personal, technical, office automation or administrative features;

– the security of infrastructures, telecommunications, networks and distributed systems devices;

– the logical security, operational security, and reliability of embedded systems associated with the functioning, strength or survival of a system.

In this context, storage and distribution solutions on servers and in cloud computing must respond to this risk of insecurity to networks. The organizational problem described previously appears once again: how can information feedback be planned and secured?

It is mainly by means of authorization mechanisms that businesses protect themselves against data misuse (for example, *opt-in* for location-based services) but a principal criterion is data anonymization, especially in "profiling" and segmentation activities. In fact, regardless of the actions

---

12 Concealment of a message inside another message.
13 Measurement technique of living entities for recognition, authentication and identification purposes.
14 Protection of messages using codes to ensure confidentiality, integrity, and the authenticity of the data exchanged.

retained by regulatory authorities, it is fundamental for companies and their consumers that data protection be guaranteed. Any flaw in these processes would affect the confidence of users, which would directly limit the impact and innovation power of Big Data.

To fight the risk of leakage and/or loss of data, a set of protection techniques can be implemented, such as DLP (data loss prevention) and/or IRM (information right management) techniques according to several levels:

– in data: through data identification algorithms (keywords, regular expressions) so as to identify and list sensitive data;

– in servers: with the monitoring of information flows, of exposed records and files by indicating to security teams any abnormal activity or any unusual user;

– in networks: by means of gateways for the analysis of data exchange[15].

These DLP techniques and/or IRM make it possible to guarantee part of the conformity of the archiving service in cloud computing with the regulatory framework and the European Union data protection directive [APR 14].

Finally, it seems indispensible to operate processes that do not collect data in the first place. To do this, it is necessary that processing devices be designed by introducing a wide range of privacy policies. There exists a challenge not only in promoting data processing, but also in making the information they have scarce. This paradoxical situation creates a trouble spot which will complicate finding the balance. But "if we want to advocate the right to oblivion, the right to error, the right to access data that transit through us: it will not only be necessary to facilitate their operation, but above all to facilitate their access, their management. We need better access to data collection, better guarantees regarding the rules that govern the processes (so that they cannot be changed unilaterally, for example) and better insurance and protection with respect to the dissemination of the data" [GUI 11]. Such a challenge causes an impact on the methodological and strategic field of enterprises that they have to take into consideration.

---

15 Archive requests via http and https, ftp and ftps file transfer protocols.

3.2.4. *Strategic and methodological aspects*

Big Data are of no use if no one can benefit from them, or if they are not utilized via an automated device designed by individuals. The integration of digital data aim to simplify as much as possible access to data, their understanding and their processing. The reduction of time delays, the removal of bottlenecks due to lack of skills and the fluidity of interactions enable companies to improve in speed and efficiency. From now on, the new sources for creating value around Big Data will refocus on a limited number of data management platforms. Based on this, three levels of strategic challenges emerge:

– carrying out a controlled opening of the architectures;

– establishing data governance resulting in internal and external trust;

– investing in triggering network effects.

Therefore, a part of the ethical issues related to ICTs are conducted with reference to the policy, the strategy and the methodology employed by the company. The infrastructure should "have the obligation, by adopting appropriate policy and code management mechanisms, to avoid ethical questions arising repeatedly" [KAL 96]. Before any development and strategic decision, it is common that a company establishes a SWOT[16] table to study relevance, challenges and consistency for future actions. From this observation, we have performed a SWOT centered on the challenges of healthcare Big Data for a company. Our SWOT matrix consists of 10 items illustrating the strengths, weaknesses, opportunities, and threats respectively (see Table 3.2).

Strengths	Weaknesses
Development of efficient analytical tools at the service of healthcare	Slow management of the organizational change
Emergence of new services to support healthcare	Lack of skills to manage NICTs
Reinforcement of the competitiveness between healthcare manufacturers	Unstable balance between collective interests and protection of people

16 SWOT analysis is a tool of corporate strategy whose mission is to determine the strategic options available at the level of a strategic activity field. The term "SWOT" is an acronym that stands for: strengths, weaknesses, opportunities and threats.

Predictive analysis via processing algorithms	Reliability and integrity of the processed data
Development of analytical environments	Massive data control and traceability
Creation of a single, reusable version of reality	Acquisition of the free and informed consent of the owner of the data
Understanding and anticipation of behaviors and route of the healthcare end-user	Limited data conservation
Medicine customization (finer segmentation and targeting)	Data access control
Predictive, preventive and participatory medicine (Medicine 4.0)	Awareness and training to "data culture"
Automation of healthcare support processes	Medical paradigm shift
Opportunities	Threats
Cloud computing generalization	Unclear regulatory framework and limited regulation
Calls to public research projects (e-health, m-health, etc.)	Non-ethical internal and external uses of medical Big Data
Reduction in health expenditures	Disrespect of citizen rights (to information, to be forgotten, of opposition, of access and of rectification)
Optimization of the healthcare user courses	Non-accountability of health care professionals
Creation of virtual cohort of patients in clinical research	Discrimination, categorization and individualization of society
Rapid detection of weak signals during epidemics or serious adverse effects	Security and protection of medical information
Development of medical self-monitoring (management tool)	Creation of hypochondriacs through the Quantified Self (m-Health)
Implementation of solutions to support medical diagnosis (expert system)	Breach of privacy and of individual liberties
Better understanding of the mechanisms of epigenetics	New wave of medical inequalities and injustices
Continuous improvement of care	Development of less human medical practices and decisions

Table 3.2. *SWOT table of the challenges of healthcare Big Data for a company*

Companies must make human and material investments relatively to a strategy and a policy established involving Big Data. Those who will take advantage of their intangible capital will open new perspectives towards greater competitiveness and innovation. Consequently, infrastructures are considering new unexplored data management and analytical methods to provide them with added value. They are confronted with a series of questions: is it a real opportunity, and what are the challenges of Big Data for them? What choice can be made? Should data processing systems be accumulated or should we choose a device which gathers all the features that meet present and future requirements? Should the technicality or ergonomics and flexibility be favored? How can a coherent whole be obtained?

In the light of this questioning, it appears essential that the strategy and the methodology for the integration of Big Data takes into account the existing data forms and sources in a new device that includes all phases of the data supply chain. Big Data can only constitute value if integrated and merged with existing data. However, the current data and BI integration methods should not be abandoned, because they must adapt themselves to the recent solutions associated with Big Data processing. The optimization of the Return on Investment (ROI) of enterprises is carried out through a highly customizable analytic solution that allows the merging of Big Data with their BI and their application infrastructures. Thus, data integration is influenced by the need for analytics whose purpose is to enable growth and to encourage the adaptation of the company. The integration and study of these huge volumes of data are intrinsically related and are in general inseparable. This digital shift with data at its center must be achieved in enterprises in a progressive way after taking into account the context, the impacts and the changes related to the PER that it causes. The analytical, visualizations processes and the BI must be in phase and be able to interact with each other to work towards a common goal. A lack of integration leads irremediably to a limited value of data.

As a result, it is essential that all the devices involving Big Data in a company share the same language and be in perfect synergy. In these conditions, it is in the best interest of infrastructures to develop solutions that cover the whole of analytics[17]. The platform responsible for processing Big Data must, therefore, be the most complete as possible to allow its users to manipulate all types of data from a single location. The merger between

17 The supply chain, from the data acquisition mechanisms to analyses processing.

the existing data and the massive data is never frozen. It occurs in real time and is never prepared in advance. It becomes fundamental that analytics and visualization systems access data from various sources in a simple and fast manner.

If each data approach implemented in companies present benefits, in our view, it is not necessarily the approach as such that will make the difference, but the consideration of a number of conditions that are key to the success of a strategy centered around Big Data. Companies are entitled to define a Big Data strategy, with data as a strategic axis at the same level as, for example, tariff policy. This methodology centered on data can be summarized in order to quantify and develop strategies around Big Data in 8 Ps: product, price, promotion, place, person, process, performance and profit. These strategies are oriented towards "product-centric" and "customer-centric" approaches.

From this observation, four success factors can be presented for the implementation of a strategy focused on Big Data [PER 14]:

– strong involvement of the general executives of the company to allow optimal adhesion and visibility of all employees. This contributes to the strengthening of a "data culture";

– an indispensible inter-directional transversality from the beginning of the implementation of a Big Data project. To this end, it is paramount to mobilize managements that have different but complementary views. The concept of multi-disciplinarity is, thus, decisive throughout the chain of value originated from data processing. It is essential to strive to communicate as much as possible at the internal level;

– the "by design" confidence based on taking into account, upstream of any project, ethical and legal data-related issues. The guarantee surrounding the security, the confidentiality, the integrity and the utilization of the processed data is therefore a prerequisite to appraise personal data. The structure must answer a series of questions in order to make the use of these Big Data operational and efficient (see Table 3.3);

– the implementation of an "agile analytics program" in which it is important to dedicate time to the identification of the needs and challenges of the company and to its maturity diagnosis, and then to select the technologies most likely to meet only the needs that were identified and qualified. Then, Big Data responds to major challenges for the company, such as: increase the capacity to support its own activity, to gain productivity, but especially to innovate relative to competitors.

Questions	Actions to be taken
What information do we need to innovate and be competitive?	Identify the business opportunities offered by large volumes of data
	Find inspiration in the innovative initiatives of the sector
What is the nature of the data?	Inventory the primary function of data (categorize, calculate, collect, measure, gather, etc.)
	Describe the epistemological nature through their support and supply mode (numbers, codes, tables, texts, databases, etc.)
How to secure data that contain personal information?	Implement the means that make it possible to ensure that the transformation is compatible with the free and informed consent and the anonymization of the owner of the data
	Ensure the technical relevance and rightfulness of the tool, reducing unnecessary or poorly calculated risks
How to integrate Big Data into existing data flows and into repositories?	Identify and list the common areas between Big Data and existing data
	Establish a unique purpose in which Big Data complement and adapt to existing data
What are the under- and unutilized data made available to us?	Know the data sources available to the company
	Know how to interpret the raw data
What legal framework supports the usage of Big Data?	Make an inventory of the regulations relating to the processing of "massive data".
	Internally establish a guide to good practice, a code of ethics or an ethical charter centered on this utilization
What are the major data to manage?	Describe the intrinsic qualities of the data (applicability, ordered, reliable, relevant, universal, unifying, etc.)
	Find the legitimate and reference sources of the data
Are we ready to "extract" useful information from our data?	Be skillful in analyzing data (notably "Data Scientists" and "Data Analysts")
	Be consistent with the associated organizational, ethical, and regulatory transformations
What is the validation device data applied internally?	Internally build a data validation process (criteria and validation metrics)
	Define the profile of the validator, the nature of the tools (if validation is automatic) and the frequency of the device

How is it possible to obtain a good data traceability?	Build a visualization control panel (CP) that allows the monitoring of the whole lifecycle of the data (cartography)
	List the various transformations carried out and identify the intermediate data generated
Who in your organization has access to customer data?	Establish a list of people who have access to the client data according to their professional statuses at each stage of the data processing operation,
What are the surveillance devices implemented to monitor potential violations and damages that data processing may sustain?	Establish a cartography of the various processes that allows the monitoring of the potential damages and violations involving data processing
What management and strategy have to be implemented to correctly complete a digital project?	Establish a clear and flexible action plan
	Favor the "plateau" mode by bringing people together in the same physical space
What management and strategy have to be implemented to achieve a digital project?	Design and implement new collaborative strategies[18]
	Work in "startup" mode, that is with great agility and execution speed, of simplified prototyping, of "test and learn", and also of right to error
Who within your organization has access to customer data?	Not to always rely on and be seduced by a ROI
What are the surveillance devices implemented to monitor potential violations and damages that data processing may sustain?	Generate and obtain the adhesion of users[19]
What are the surveillance devices implemented to monitor potential violations and damages that data processing may sustain?	Implement the conditions for a dynamics of co-innovation[20]
What are the surveillance devices implemented to monitor potential violations and damages that data processing may sustain?	Collaborate with startups in order to progress faster

Table 3.3. *Questions and actions to plan a Big Data project*

18 The development of ecosystems and platform logics, the value chain and the capture modes of the value of a platform, the control conditions of the associated risks, the study of cases of ecosystems, etc.
19 The availability of citizens to disclose their personal data, conditions and actions to establish a trust relationship; the accompaniment of the role.
20 The data governance strategy, internal organizational and cultural sites, the co-design of solutions with users (key determinants, contributors' motivation axes, etc.).

In these circumstances, a rigorous audit of the tools and the processes involved, in Big Data processing within the enterprise, is essential. One can imagine that an audit team oriented towards an ethic of "massive data" will be implemented and will host workshops so as to improve processes that support the way in which data are acquired, processed, secured, managed and used in the company. Using cartography of the devices, auditors will be able to highlight flaws, deficiencies, duplications and overlaps in the processing of these Big Data. Field interviews may be carried out to discover and explore the way in which organizational values are (or are not) put into practice within the practices of data manipulation. These interviews will provide accurate insight into how people deal with data, on the values of the organization regarding these data, and on any weakness or dysfunction points, including at the safety level, of the operational processes on Big Data such as: the sharing, the sale to third parties, its anonymization, or the aggregation of the data. Note that the format and content of the result of these surveys and studies depend on many parameters such as:

– the type of organization;

– the duties and responsibilities of the different actors;

– the duration and the complexity of the devices;

– the nature of the ecosystem of the data and that of NICTs relatively to the latter;

– the sector of the company or of the relevant market [DAV 12].

In addition, as we have previously seen, Big Data bring forward risks which might impair:

– the privacy of the person: storing data on computer media facilitates the speed of the acquisition and of the access to data. Under these conditions, a large volume of personal data is stored on a small support. Privacy risks may include undue access, the misappropriation, the tampering, the disclosure, or the destruction of information;

– individual freedoms: technological solutions make it possible to easily and quickly process data (sorting with one or several criteria, selection, calculation, etc.), thus allowing:

  - the labeling of persons that can lead to discrimination,

- the identity of an individual to be found through triangulation and data cross-reference concerning him namely: the sex, the date of birth, the postal code, the number of children, the occupation, etc.,

- the development of statistics from data compiled from several thousand people allowing the definition of averages that may become norms in our society,

- the utilization of Big Data for purposes other than those originally planned.

It is, therefore, essential to establish strict rules concerning the management of the risks originating from a Big Data project, such as:

– obtaining the informed consent of the consumer during the acquisition of its data;

– giving preference to anonymous data as soon as it is possible;

– stating purposes for the processing which are neither too specific nor too vague;

– ensuring that the profiling of citizens does not cause blatant discrimination;

– giving end users the control over the use of their data;

– guaranteeing that data are accurate and secure;

– not proceeding with the extraction of third-party databases without the permission of consumers;

– highlighting an attractive exchange of value.

It, then, becomes essential to clarify in advance the agreements for the usage of personal data. This necessarily includes:

– the control of cookies: including the acknowledgement from the consumers of the intrusive aspect of cookies that allow the tracking of users during Web browsing;

– the clear transparency of "Opt-In": about the nature and the scope of utilization of personal data;

– formalizing a "permission marketing": by demonstrating to the final consumer the exceptional added value obtained from the use of his personal data , it is a matter of content and context.

– being aware of the latest international regulatory developments: notably on data storage and repatriation conditions that differ between the European Union and the United States, both for reasons of internal security and to ensure a competitive advantage to their strategic enterprises.

In this context, digital data processing must be based on a perfect trust relationship which presupposes some prerequisites such as: knowing each other, appreciating each other but also and especially respecting each other. It thus becomes essential to build the conditions to ensure the confidence in the utilization of the data (and even more if they are collected through connected objects or social networks), because it is not possible to have a digital economy without trust. As a consequence, it must be ensured that people can take ownership and effectively manage their digital identity. The protection and the security of the personal data processed by a company involves among other things a performing process of anonymization of the individual. However, it can be observed that such a device prevents any re-identification, which becomes difficult to obtain and must be assessed according to three major areas [CIG 14]:

– what is the possibility of re-identifying an individual from a set of data?

– what is the possibility of inferring information on an individual from a set of data?

– what is the possibility of linking different data sets belonging to the same person?

The processing of these huge volumes of data is a major issue as soon as they integrate personal data. Now, users (customers, consumers) are increasingly anxious to know what information is held about them and what use is given, therein, by the operator. This problem becomes a slightly bigger with the exponential evolution of NICTs and becomes a major challenge for the reputation of businesses. Thus, since the implementation of the right to oblivion: European Internet users have addressed in 1 year over 250,000 requests to Google (according to Google). They concerned the removal of a million Internet links. 3 requests/5 concern privacy breaches (e.g. address, name, dismissal, embarrassing photos, etc.). As much as 70% of the requests would have been rejected by Google since January 2015[21]. These requests are refused as soon as they concern in particular:

---

21 According to the survey carried out by VIP Reputation in 2015.

– a negative opinion of the professional life (especially for prominent public personalities such as journalists, artists, politicians, TV presenters, etc.);

– an opinion that was expressed and which the author wishes to change following its publication;

– a profile on social networks.

The justification for the request is very important because it is on this basis that Google will make its decision. Note that people have the right to a single attempt only to request the removal of an Internet link. If the request is denied by Google, the user can resort either to the CNIL, or to legal action with a specialized lawyer.

Note that until today, the American giant had kept confidential the subject of these requests. However, the British newspaper "The Guardian" succeeded, in March 2015, to access more than 75% of the deletion requests, by concealing itself in the source code of the Google transparency report. In those circumstances, claiming the right to oblivion raises new conditions to infrastructures and in particular to "pure players".

Now, the company must find a balance between the ethical challenge and the "Business" of the market that covers the usage of personal data, ensuring users the right to digital oblivion. This necessarily implies a greater readability and an effort of transparency from the companies over their policy on the manipulation of personal data. This is why more and more enterprises publish the rules that they are committed to about the use of customer data online. Such an action, thus, proves to be consistent with values that are often present in ethical charters (honesty, respect, integrity, etc.), and with pedagogy values by striving to ensure these rules are understandable by a larger number of people.

From this observation, an approach to information protection can be devised and that can be declined according to the following structuring axes:

– establish a comprehensive and coherent approach (expression of necessity based on a risk analysis throughout the lifecycle of the data);

– rely on the vision and the political, strategic will of the executive management;

– orientate the approach from: people (behavior, management, outreach, etc.), processes (the business purpose, integrate the approach of information protection in business processes), regulations and tools (with the purpose of automation);

– build an approach destined for the long-term (a permanent protection);

– incorporate a perspective of continuous improvement inserting quality processes;

– follow an approach that makes sense and that covers all the REP of the data processing;

– have a safety policy and a structured and explicit risk management policy;

– do not attempt completeness but rather target certain specific areas;

– rely on the development of a mapping that lists all of the risks;

– capitalize on any incidents to reinforce the approach being implemented;

– rely on the executive management, the organization and the shared "data" culture within the company.

A strategic and methodological approach can be established that consists of the following seven steps [CIG 08]:

– perform an audit, a survey and an inventory of the big data process chain. this analysis leads to a set of conclusions and perspectives[22] [DAV 12];

– define the organizational system, the stakeholders, everyone's missions and responsibilities throughout the development cycle of the data. To this end, it is essential to set up a transverse steering committee which directs, leads, validates, and accompanies the actions defined;

– define the major axes, orientations, objectives and priorities of the company about the usage of Big Data;

---

22 The provisional declaration of organizational principles; the conclusions of the audit of security, the policies and data processing devices, The documents describing the sensitivity, the use and the sharing of the data retained. The considerations on the practices of similar organizations (industry standards); the external implications, the current ideas and the perceptions about their level of risk; the gaps, the deficiencies, and the overlaps in the alignment of values with actions.

– build, implement and maintain a reference framework for the protection of information[23];

– inform, raise awareness and empower the management and employees;

– identify and ensure the processing of priority topics[24];

– evaluate and control processes[25].

Ultimately, four major guidelines can be identified that interact between themselves to secure the processing of the Big Data within an infrastructure:

– awareness and education from the earliest age, to inform every citizen on the issues and the risks involving "massive data";

– professional ethics, presented by public institutions and businesses, on the behavior to adopt throughout the Big Data lifecycle. What information (intrinsic criteria) are we looking for? For what use (extrinsic criteria)? What qualitative value can we require – from data?

– the regulatory and legal framework at the international level, accompanied by supranational controls, in particular with regard to the ownership and data control;

– the collective drafting of an international ethical charter of Big Data usage in consensus, with an declaration obligation, for all data users, whether they have correctly respected it or not.

3.3. The data lifecycle: collection, processing and quality control

In raw form, the datum has no usable value in itself. It must be validated, processed (and again controlled after each processing), approximated, studied, in particular, with the aim to be converted into knowledge, into understanding and provide a value for the company. The majority of companies have a "global" approach for their data, ensuring their quality, their protection, and their accessibility at every stage of their lifecycle. This sequence follows five key steps (see Figure 3.3):

---

23 Ethical charter, code of ethics, and guides good practices destined for end-users and ICT administrators, specific and overall policy centered on information security.
24 Establishment of a management cell of vulnerabilities and incidents, protection of written and oral communications, anti-virus protection, network security, access and information management.
25 Integration in the audit program and testing and evaluation approach.

– Generation/Acquisition:

- enlargement of the structured or/and unstructured data sources;

- multiplication of the sources of data (text, Web files, database) and of the types of content external to the company;

- improvement of the information by adding metadata, real-time input, high throughput;

- creation, capture, organization, classification[26] and indexing of the information (topic, source, author, source, keywords, year, and associated business concepts, etc.);

- filtering of the data originated from sensors through advanced signal processing techniques;

- characterization and inventory of the collected data;

- extraction and pattern searching;

- data processing for the reduction of dimensions;

- fusion and interpolation to generate missing or duplicated data;

- automation and massification of exchanges.

– Storage/Conservation[27]:

- development of flexible cloud computing offers less costly services for high volumes of data;

- information stored in different formats, in a unstructured manner and over a long period;

- Hadoop: distributed files storage;

- NoSQL more flexible and faster.

– Analysis/Processing:

- security and access rights, administration, variation and evolution;

---

26 In the context of Big Data, this kind of process becomes complex with external sources because they are often poor in metadata. Therefore, it is necessary to extract the meaning, thereof, to create relevant metadata on the fly.
27 Conservation serves important purposes: prove, memorize, understand and communicate [COU 07].

- parallel algorithmics, "Machine Learning" techniques (or automatic learning), natural language statistical analysis, additions of new directions, new correlations;

- advanced analytics: ability to identify weak signals in large volumes of data;

- deduction and processing of relevant information from available data;

- prototype and build predictive[28] models directly from the data.

– Restitution:

- dissemination[29] and sharing of structured information and most often characterized in "push" mode;

- Dataviz: TB (BSC type), Qlikview, Gephi;

- decision-making.

– Valuation:

- monetization of previously unprocessed data;

- micro-segmentation, consumer loyalty;

- improvement of the operational efficiency;

It can be observed that the data value does not decrease when they are used. They can be processed several times. Information is what economists call a "non-rival" good where the usage by one person does not prevent another to use it. On the contrary, the more it is used, the more new ideas and valuations will appear. The resulting "analyses" can generate additional and feedback data in the data value chain, leading to a new data lifecycle [OEC 13]. Under these circumstances, the notion of data recycling becomes particularly significant and leads us to figure new mechanisms that would give several lives to the "data".

It should be noted that this cycle does not include the "deletion" phase, which is essential for personal data, but is considered to be less important in the context of Big Data, where the default is to preserve data for long periods

---

28 These models must be flexible in order to be applied to data fields in the same development environment to process, in the same manner signals, financial data, images or even videos.

29 The dissemination here encompasses the notion of reversibility, that is to say the restitution aiming at the reintegration into another storage system.

of time, if not indefinitely. However, from a political point of view this phase may deserve a more important role.

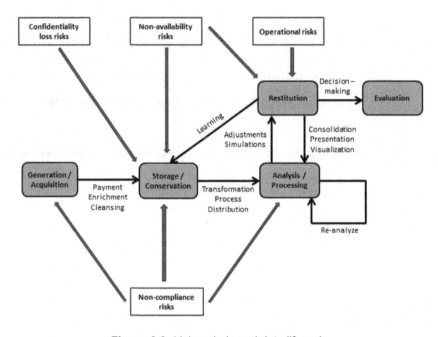

Figure 3.3. *Value chain and data lifecycle*

Big Data analytical processes rely on a set of technological advances throughout the lifecycle of the data. It can be observed that data quality is closely linked to the question of the analytical data workflow. In effect, ensuring data quality, avoiding additional costs associated with the control and the permanent correction of the data assumes the global optimization of the data processing chain, from the acquisition until the outcoming value for the business.

To achieve this, it is essential that the approach to data quality be based on the following actions and rules:

– promote the uniqueness of the data in order to avoid duplication;

– standardize the process;

– take the time to put in place the data quality approach;

– effectively manage authorizations;

– control data quality through performance indicators;

– do not cut corners when it comes to the means that have to be implemented;

– delimit the perimeter of sensitive data;

– accompany the changes with good internal communication about the challenges and the benefits of the initiative of implementing a project about data quality.

As a result, if quality processes are automated and directly integrated as early as the acquisition stages, and if it is possible to ensure that the raw data is not altered throughout the whole information processing chain, then *a posteriori* verifications may be relaxed, and the data can be simply used by the pilot functions of the company.

These data quality control procedures must answer questions such as: who accesses data? What about its availability? What risks do relate to the integrity of the data in the distributed devices? How can these data be manipulated to remain in control of the IS? Is the company ready to safely host Big Data? [COR 12] What can be done in each of the stages of the lifecycle of digital data, from its creation to its conservation, including its management and its presentation? What kind of global approach can be implemented to ensure a good control of the life chain of digital documents?

In effect, the processing of Big Data raises several problems related to the lifecycle of the data:

– protection (loss, mutation, transformation, etc.);

– security (theft, criminal intent, identity theft, etc.);

– the user's reputation (uncontrolled use, litigation, social networks, etc.);

– control (compliance with intellectual property, with privacy, with the protection of sensitive data, with the right to oblivion, etc.);

– dependence (process control, contracts, visibility and changes, etc.).

From this observation, the control of the data lifecycle within a company reveals three major issues:

– a strategic challenge: be able to rationalize Big Data and technical solutions, while controlling the economic impact;

– a tactical challenge: be able to create legal evidence at any time, but also to guarantee access to Big Data;

– an operational issue: ensure sustainability, integrity, security and traceability of Big Data.

Finally, the data lifecycle is subject to a series of risks of: non-compliance, loss of privacy, of non-availability, operational (see Figure 3.3).

To this list, we can add the risks associated with the integration modes of a Big Data platform which can be either internal[30] or external/Cloud[31] (see Table 3.4).

Non-compliance risks	Actions to be taken
Due to the acquisition of non-reported information	Remove as early as the acquisition the data detected as personal through the utilization of known patterns
	Anonymize the data in the collection and storage mechanisms to prevent the identification of people from these data
Due to the duration of storage of personal data	Indicate and describe data with the collection date, and perform "deletion" passes.
Due to the inability to modify/to adjust data Due to the inability to directly access the data	Delete all digital data if the information is questioned
	Anonymize the data in the collection and storage mechanisms to prevent the identification of people from these data
Due to a problem in assigning the liability of the administrators	Identify and trace the actions of administrators: Choose a base that generates log files
	Store secure log files, inaccessible to a unique administrator[32]

---

30 The whole platform is controlled by the company.
31 The company uses a platform shared *through* an outside organization or a cloud-based service.
32 There is the possibility to choose to outsource the storage of logs to prevent an administrator to be able to edit or delete them after a malicious action. It is also possible to store the logs and prevent a lone administrator from accessing the logs, and limiting the risks.

	Authenticate and establish a logical separation of data[33]
Due to an inability to protect data according to the regulations and the standards in force	Encrypt and decrypt data on the fly in case of utilization of these data
	Physically separate the storage processes into distinct infrastructures
Confidentiality loss risks	**Actions to be taken**
Due to theft/transmission/ leakage of confidential information	Secure the infrastructure throughout the lifecycle of the data[34]
Due to the access to confidential data, by an illegitimate person	Establish a regular audit of the permissions database in order to identify the profiles that were left active and forgotten as well as the permissions deemed too large
	Perform a rigorous management of access rights, in particular to allow access to the database only to administration accounts and to applications
Due to mismanagement of the entitlements of an NICT	Perform examinations of the safety of the storage infrastructure by specialists (by means of a technical audit), sub-contracting a consulting company specialized in intrusion tests
	Carefully follow a security guide
Non-availability risks	**Actions to be taken**
Due to a backup policy	Establish a backup policy that integrates a backup technique, the frequency, the restore tests and their frequency
Due to hardware failures	Implement a fully redundant[35] network

---

33 Establish a logical separation of data with mandatory authentication for the use of sensitive data, depending on the storage system being used.

34 It is essential to perform regular infrastructure audits and to verify, notably, the permissions to access data and the configuration of critical systems. Constant monitoring can facilitate, in case of attack, its quick detection and the prevention of information leakage.

35 It is fundamental to enforce redundancy in the network core and in the distribution switches as well as at the level of all intermediate components (VPN, firewalls, and load distribution).

Operational risks	Actions to be taken
Due to the collection of non-relevant or unusable information	Limit the acquisition only to useful data. Therefore, the organization should not start to "capture everything" for a possible development of the data through subsequent correlation[36]
Due to the technological dependency of the company towards a innovative but untested solution	Choose solutions supported by companies whose financial health is good and whose prospect over several years is the continuation of the development of the solution
	Choose de facto standard NICTs to encourage the recruitment of users
Due to a dependency of the other applications to a single technological solution	Use several different technologies in parallel (for different data and usages)
Risks associated with the integration modes	Actions to be taken
Due to the use of a platform beyond the control of the company can cause legal problems[37], risks of loss of confidentiality (information leaks), or risks relative to the dependence on a cloud provider	Internalize the processes and own its personal infrastructure, but this requires advanced technical capabilities and may imply substantial investments

Table 3.4 *Risks and actions to be taken according to the integration modes of a Big Data platform*

Therefore, in the view of these observations, we can list a few rules to manage these risks [NUN 13, BAL 14, MIT 15]:

– give preference to anonymous data as soon as it is possible;

– obtain the informed consent of the consumer during the acquisition of its data;

– ensure that the profiling of consumers does not cause any discrimination;

36 This causes a considerable loss of space, of acquisition time and can unnecessarily saturate the storage infrastructures.
37 Data localization – jurisdiction and platform administrator – membership of the data (see legal and intellectual property).

– state processing purposes neither too specific nor too vague;

– ensure that data are accurate and secure;

– give users the control over the use of their personal data;

– highlight an attractive exchange of value;

– do not proceed to the extraction of various third-party databases without their permission;

– ensure that all the links which allow the identification of the person from the processed data, be deleted;

– obtain information about the source, date, the manner how the data was collected, and where it is stored;

– automatically remove non-structured data, after a defined period of time, if the latter no longer have any commercial or research value.

In addition, the infrastructures wishing to use and process Big Data are faced with a number of identified obstacles. It is possible to list the limits and the following findings, during the processing of these large volumes of data:

– unstructured data constitute the weak link of the study;

– data collection is still largely limited to traditional channels;

– deficiency of data processing tools.

– a lack of analytical skills;

– the absence of measurements of the ROI in Big Data projects;

– the analysis of digital data is still too little oriented towards predictive and real-time considerations;

– a lack of transversality in managing Big Data projects;

– the reluctance to share personal data. This can constitute a major risk for data reliability [PER 14];

– a lack of "sponsorship" from the executive management of the enterprise;

– low awareness of security issues and of the protection of the "massive data";

– the scientific value of digitally processed data;

– storage infrastructures need to be rethought;

– data interoperability and the securing of data hosted on different continents;

– the establishment of personalized decision trees may inflict the risk of practicing medicine without doctors;

– medical data published in the literature do not always reflect the reality of medicine, because they are associated with patients that meet the criteria of the study;

– reading translation and database management tools must be constantly renewed and even invented.

In addition, human factors may also explain the failures surrounding the implementation and the use of Big Data in the field of healthcare, such as [BER 15]:

– the disinterest of health professionals regarding the IS tool;

– the inadequacy of the computing device with the structural organization of the services;

– the bad relationships between the services of a company;

– the lack of motivation and of availability of the players responsible for caretaking;

– the place of the judgment of the practitioner;

– the lack of conviction from the medical officers (chief of service);

– the lack of training of users and health professionals in using ICTs;

– the non-recognition of the hierarchy of specialists in IS (lack of legitimacy);

– the refusal for change in the organization within the structure of healthcare for professional or economic reasons;

– the loss of confidence in computing support;

– denial of change for medical reasons[38];

---

38 Sense of loss of time, of bad luck for the patient, poor quality, unnecessary forensic medical risks and medical rivalries.

– respect for the human dimension in the doctor-patient relationship.

Under these conditions, a good utilization of Big Data necessarily involves accounting for:

– uncertainty management;

– the consideration of major phenomena;

– multidisciplinary Big Data;

– the growing need to apply data quality procedures;

– better knowledge and understanding the digital data;

– the impact of Big Data on organizations is significant;

– define a framework around the proper use of Big Data integrated into the field of healthcare.

– the non-repetition of past mistakes, by applying project management and governance principles, from the beginning;

That is why, based on these various observations and reflections that we have previously seen, we can establish a list of recommendations about the valuation of Big Data, centered on design and management levers. Thus, we were able to list 32 action levers distributed in a balanced way according to our eight design and management criteria for "voluminous data" [CIG 14, IG 14]:

– Strategy & Methodology:

    - unify data management policies with the rest of the IS independently of the format and of the system;

    - establish a reporting mechanism to follow the progress of the data through the IS and the organization, understand their impacts, and to consider possible continuous improvements;

    - follow a scientific assessment of healthcare data;

    - implement a data and processes valuation approach.

– Relationship & Culture:

    - communicate and raise awareness to promote utilizations;

    - mobilize about the security and the confidentiality of the data;

- figure out the new contact points with its targets;

- implement a data management team.

– Organization & Regulatory:

- define rules at the global level for a local application;

- apply rules across various functions and jurisdictions, platforms and applications;

- apply a legal framework and Big Data-specific ethics;

- automatically propose conservation rules directed towards classification plans according to the application domain (business, entity, etc.).

– Structure & Technology:

- make an inventory of the environment of the data (own and those related to the activity in question);

- manage and process Big Data in data sets regardless of the underlying IS;

- the operational capability of Big Data through the available technologies;

- structuring the company so that the information of each service can contribute to the overall development of the activity:

– implementation of computer tools and software programs that simplify the integration and the manipulation of Big Data,

– creation of an organization promoting sharing,

– develop skills and awareness in the collaborators to the information they manipulate.

– Piloting:

- integrate management processes of change in the SI;

- state the initial objectives;

- install and apply proper and adapted managing tools according to the category of the data;

- establish data "liquidity"[39].

– Development lifecycle:

- trace and establish the geographical location of the data in the architecture of the IS;

- develop "tracking" and "reporting" tools to more systematically make use of qualitative data generated from various sources;

- understand how prospects will choose, buy and talk about hand-made products through digital technologies;

- fully manage the data lifecycle according to business needs and/or the laws and regulations in force.

– Shaping:

- manage links and gateways between the description levels of the data;

- apply a constant data quality approach;

- inventory the available data and if necessary accept opening (Open Data, Open Innovation, social Web data, etc.);

- characterize the level of confidentiality (internal, external use, etc.).

– Operations:

- precisely define and identify the datum (structured or not);

- specify the name of the administrator or of the owner of the data;

- apply good approaches and techniques that are not confined to real time;

- classify, categorize, and visualize data (reference, operational and decision-making).

Consequently, the framework around Big Data necessarily requires an impact assessment which relates to the whole lifecycle of the data, from their collection to their destruction or anonymization. In particular, this study includes elements such as:

---

39 That is to say the ability to disseminate data within an organizational structure, but also to exchange it with partners, by means of development efforts focusing on the standardization of the data models (data semantics) around sectoral models.

– a description of the process focusing on the purpose, the legal basis for the utilization, the categories of processed data, the recipients of the data as well as a cartography and a description of the flows;

– an assessment of the associated risks[40] (see Table 3.4);

– a description of the measures and actions designed to prevent these risks and to provide protection against them (see "Privacy by Design");

– a description of the security measures and of the devices implemented with the purpose of protecting personal data and to demonstrate the conformity of the processing, while accounting for the rights and for the legitimate interests of the individuals being concerned.

The analysis must take into consideration the opinion of the persons involved or of their representatives. A balance of interests is carried out of both the infrastructure which organizes the processing and the owner of the data, who has fundamental rights and freedoms.

Ultimately, the typical course begins with the construction of an analysis basis combining the data generated from different sources, and that does not, initially, care too much about their quality or about their homogeneity. These digital data are integrated and cleaned throughout the projects, then operated upon within predictive or descriptive processing algorithms, which will help in the decision-making, and even automate it, within the target process of the company. In effect, because of the huge volume of data, decisions can often no longer be taken by a human being but by machines. The correlations generated by the Big Data can be identified in a much faster fashion (and generally, less expensive) than the causality links coming from reduced and accurate information. This explains that the processing of "mega data" will become preferable in a world of predictions where, for example, clinical constants would not be able to explain the reasons behind medical decisions.

We can imagine that the doctor of the future may decide a medical act just because the data that he/she has collected and then processed, have given indications in this direction, without even understanding the reason why. Therefore, one might ask: what will be the role left to uncertainty, intuition, perception, faith, to free will and to freedom as well as to human

---

40 It may be noted that the framework of the risk assessment goes beyond the scope of the data protection rules as it also relates to the study of potential impacts on privacy, the fundamental rights and freedoms of individuals.

dignity to act in contradiction with evidence, to learning from life and experience? Is taking this decision disconnected from any causation desirable?

As a matter of fact, the more consistent data volumes are, then the better any assumption by segmentation of this data set can be demonstrated "until obtaining a statistically significant correlation" [AME 14]. Thus, the assertion which supposedly claims that more valid conclusions are obtained in a clinical test when we include more patients, or with significant masses of data, is therefore erroneous for someone who has not equipped themselves with the means for controlling the whole analytical system data.

In these conditions, it becomes important, firstly, to not lose sight of the causality by asking the right questions as well as by filtering the responses obtained, and on the other hand, by maintaining control of the process. Such rules may be fully applicable within health care establishments as long as these structures have competent multidisciplinary teams available in this area.

3.4. Towards a controlled regulation of the medical datasphere

Everyone among us is a data producer. However, should we relegate the architecture and the infrastructure, and the manner in which they are used, to specialists and to processing algorithms in front of which we feel helpless and upon which we could no longer apply any governance? In fact, the inflation of the volume of data available to business raises problems such as "information overload" harmful to the extraction of intelligence and the soaring costs of storage, internal organization, regulatory compliance or securing, etc.

Increasingly more companies take these issues into account and make use of them to establish their own regulations and governance upon the data that they operate upon. One of the first stages consists of locating the data, usually scattered between the collaborators, and even retained by partners. Then, it is necessary to determine their current, but also possibly future, value through governance, enquiring: which vision, which strategy, and what metrics are desirable for the processing of digital data? Consequently, it appears essential that the responsibility relative to data must be reassigned to the professionals who process them. Therefore, it is desirable to define responsibilities and a regulatory framework for usage, while promoting innovation and the autonomy of individuals. The real role of computing is to ensure that the people who have control over data can spend longer periods of time to analyzing rather than preparing it.

It is generally possible to identify six business categories which are directly or indirectly associated with Big Data-related challenges:

– "Data Steward" (or "Data Owner"): This is the administrator or data manager. They have knowledge of the data and are responsible for the implementation of the strategy on the ground. They will implement the governance ordered by the chief data officer (CDO), and ensure that it is followed; the same happens with regard to good practices and lifecycles. Data stewards provide methodological know-how[41] and ensure the overall consistency of the documentation of a data set in coordination with the architects and the builders of the information system. They can authorize or deny the access to certain data, and are responsible for the accuracy, integrity and timeliness. The Data Owner's missions include:

- contained data and usage: technical aspect of the data with regard to the importance and the quality of the data and the intended uses;

- algorithms and methods: originated from existing data (see *aggregation*);

- the development and the provision of data.

Finally, the need for the creation of the role of such a position appears essential for businesses that are developing data integration projects such as the construction and the utilization of data warehouses, and the merger of companies.

– The "Chief Data Officer": He or she participates in the executive committee and contributes to the achievement of the company's strategy based on the data, their management, possibly maintaining the level of quality thereof. The CDO's mission is also to implement an operational organization, as well as governance within a "Governance Board". It makes more sense that the latter support the "Chief Executive Officer (CEO)" and do not depend on the IT department of the company. The CDO's formation must consist of a balance between technical and business skills, including a strategic vision and a responsible managerial dimension.

---

41 The Data Steward gives meaning to the documentation elements on definitions, processes, controls, etc.

– The "Data Scientist": He or she analyzes the data using complex statistical and "data mining" tools. Data scientists generate data value from reliable data (by means of the Data Stewart's work), and has the tools to achieve it.

– The "Data Analyst": This is the person who studies data for its own business needs and who constructs the value of the Big Data. They receive part of the Data Scientist's work and bring it closer to other "reporting" and to other available data. The analyst works with "dashboarding", visualization of information and information processing tools similar enough to the ones used for BI but applies them differently depending on the data that is made available and on the business challenges that are to be confronted [BEN 14].

– The "Data Protection Officer" (DPO): Responsible for the protection, the security and the compliance of the company's data. They implement the IT mechanisms to protect data and applications, for example, by developing a control system of the "tokenization"[42] and encryption type[43], strengthened by advanced management keys across the enterprise. The DPO shall also ensures that responsibilities are kept separate, and that security objects (symmetric keys, certificates, encryption codes, lists of passwords, etc.) are protected in a centralized safe.

– The "Chief Privacy Officer" (CPO): A high level executive within a company or an organization who is responsible for risk-management and for the impacts of regulatory affairs, of laws, and of privacy policies. The CPO position is relatively new and was created to address all the concerns of consumers on the use of personal information (notably, about medical data and financial information), and of the laws and regulations. This includes, for example, the legislation concerning the protection of the medical records of patients such as, in the U.S. the HIPAA legislation (Health Insurance Portability and Accountability Act) of 1996. The CPO's role also involves the use and the protection of financial and banking transactions in purchases (notably, through the Fair Credit Reporting Act including its purification rule, and the Gramm-Leach-Bliley Act making backup and confidentiality rules explicit, and the financial management rules, put in place in the United States).

---

42 Tokenization aims to replace sensitive information by a substitution value (Token) in order to protect data such as credit card numbers, account numbers, social security numbers, etc.
43 Application encryption consists in severely managing encryption keys during data capture.

Evolving without damage in a regulatory and legislative environment is not an easy task for the Big Data stakeholders. However, this is a necessary condition to maintain confidence in consumers. But is it enough? In fact, it is necessary to find a balance in the sharing of value between the client who entrusts his personal data to the company and the latter who will make use of it [DES 15].

The privacy non-disclosure and data security guarantees, the transparency in the processing to which they must be subjected and the control by consumers of their use are clearly part of this exchange of value.

This sharing of the value may be clearly explicit (the dissemination of personal data gives rise to financial reward[44]), partially explicit (attribution of reduction coupons or loyalty cards) or moderately explicit (such as the example of Facebook, which does make it clear that the condition to the free use of its services by users is the processing of their personal data).

As a result, it appears essential to look at where the power places of the technical systems are and how programs and algorithms can in the medium-term become more accessible to all. We also have to reflect on the place that the user has in the processing to which we rely upon, and enquire about the usages built by mathematicians, physicists, statisticians, engineers and experts from computer networks. In this context, we are entitled to ask: how does a world covered in data become a world that empowers the user rather than alienates him, and what are tomorrow's regulations? Whereas one knows the regulations surrounding the collection, those that underlie the data processing terms are less known, in particular those that appear in "mash ups" of services, or in exchanges between APIs [GUI 11]. Generally, systems are regulated by four forces: the market, law, social norms, and architecture or, in the case of technology, the code [LES 99].

From our perspective, these must correspond to a combination of technological, procedural and institutional factors, in addition to the vigilance of each individual and good personal practices. It can be seen that more and more European companies put in place "Chief Privacy Officer" (CPO) or/and "Big Data" charters, both human and ethical[45], that work for

---

44 The websites including www.datacoup.com and www.handshake.com.uk.
45 For example, the charter of ethics of the Group Orange on Big Data (See http://oran.ge/SMYku4).

the protection of the personal data of employees, of prospects and of customers and even of sensitive information.

The purpose of a code of ethics is to provide ethical guidelines for professionals, as well as a warning device to help professionals tackle the problems and dilemmas related to Big Data [KEI 85]. It constitues a major element of ethical management [ADA 01, FAR 98, KAP 98, REI 00, STE 08, WIL 00]. The ethical charter favors the construction of an ethics of the environment by introducing fundamental ethical principles that apply to the organization as well as to managers and employees [ADA 01]. Furthermore, faced with hazards and deviations associated with the development, the formatting and the usage of personal health data, it appears essential to properly monitor and supervise these "mega data". This necessarily means a better cleaning and selection of data that supply and circulate in the medical datasphere.

Digital experts and health institutions will seek to expand their presence within the chain of value of the medical data, horizontally (from the production to the use of the "data") and/or vertically (from the Big Data infrastructure to the services destined for users and final customers). The key players of this new data value chain consist of (see Figure 3.4):

– owners and end-users of the data who are the same stakeholders, namely average healthcare users. An effort of awareness and accountability about the use and the fate of their data must be put in place among these stakeholders;

– data producers: they will provide real reliable databases which, through to their trust capital, could be resold to third parties. In this stakeholders category, we are also incorporating institutional collectors. In France, there is a large number of these institutional health data collectors, for example: the CNAMTS, the CNIS, the INSEE, the DREES, the CTNERHI, the INED, the INSERM, the InVS, and the ORS;

– data aggregators: they aggregate, cross-reference and contextualize data for analysis purposes.

– data users: they develop new applications and new services from the obtained analysis. These users can be businesses, start-ups and pharmaceutical industries developing specific and targeted applications for the patient. A positive feedback due to enhanced data is achieved between users and data aggregators.

– Big Data infrastructure operators: new key players in digital technologies, telecommunications operators;

– infrastructure managers: they will be able to rent, in addition to their storage capabilities, calculation capabilities, to companies having one-time Big Data processing requirements;

– trusted stakeholders as an ethical qualitative regulator that ensure the maintenance of the integrity/ethics/data quality, from their "sourcing" to their use, thus reassuring end-users and consumers. These new players would be responsible for organizing the approval of new equipment and would develop protocols to access the data produced by these devices in addition to those originated by other healthcare equipments.

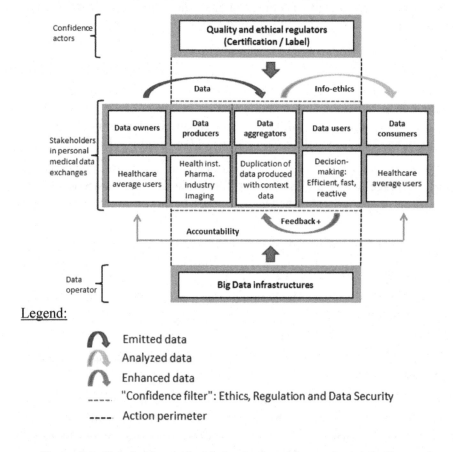

Legend:

Emitted data

Analyzed data

Enhanced data

---- "Confidence filter": Ethics, Regulation and Data Security

---- Action perimeter

Figure 3.4. *Stakeholders in the chain of value of the medical data. For a color version of the figure, see www.iste.co.uk/beranger/data.zip*

All throughout the data chain of value, personal data producers, aggregators, users and consumers move along and position themselves. Such a market should continue to evolve and emerge from new stakeholders and businesses: the "pure players" who will be specialized in the production and the "sourcing" of data, others in the aggregation and the processing of data, and personal data users who will develop services and targeted applications having a higher value-added. All these services will be achieved by means of Big Data infrastructures, involving another category of stakeholders. Therefore, the harmonization and the optimization of the entire digital ecosystem of personal data depends on what we call the "trust filter". The market should therefore evolve towards a separation between data and its use.

The challenge is to meet the problems associated with the reliability of the applications or of the connected objects, based on the correct performance of Big Data processing algorithms, with the security of the personal data, as well as with the rights of the users regarding data privacy matters. To this end, it is important to assess, certify and then label the ethical purposes of these devices. This will consist in a trusted filter centered on ethics, regulation and data security. Its field of action should range from the data producer to its consumer. Personal data protection labels are sources of added value [BON 14]. They constitute factors of confidence, of awareness and transparency. In an equal way, they are sources of quality for customers and employees but also for the organizations whether they are public or private.

The certification is intended to encourage transparency and self-regulation within the organizations. This approach enables them to identify and limit the risks associated with the processing of personal data. It can also accompany the compliance of organizations while delegating part of the load of the control to the bodies issuing the labels. Moreover, the French CNIL is considering the definition of a label to encourage the creators of mobile e-health applications to better inform end-users about the use of their personal data.

Therefore, in France, the creation of a "scholarly society" or a "consortium" could be considered; this could be composed of the ASIP, the ministry, the CNIL, the HAS, the ANSM, healthcare users associations, of unions and committees from the national association of health professionals, to prepare a code of good practice for the protection of data in health and wellness applications. In this context, one can imagine two possible application situations of the regulation:

– a rigorous regulation of higher public authorities through an audit of Big Data processing algorithms and the protection of privacy by certified experts and auditors. These authorities would consult state agencies as well as private enterprises on the optimal usage conditions of algorithms but also throughout the collection process, on information processing and then on its resale;

– controls made by licensed companies, similar to accounting or auditing firms. These organizations would be certified by this "scholarly society" or "consortium".

These trusted stakeholders would represent an ethical qualitative regulator that ensures the maintenance of the integrity, of the ethics, and of data quality, from their "sourcing" to their use, thus reassuring end users and consumers. Such an ethical charter would allow industrialists to engage, if they wish, in the compliance with certain ethical and moral requirements regarding the protection of personal data, in order to demonstrate and guarantee to their customers, their confidence and their commitment in this area. In this context, this code of practice should outline a new framework of confidentiality of personal data, focusing rather on the accountability of the use of data by the agencies which collect, cross-reference, analyze and make use of them, and less on individual consent at the time of the acquisition. Such liability could mean that companies (data aggregators) should give access and rectification rights to average healthcare users (owners and end-users of the data) so that they can have a better control over cross-referencing and over the shelf life of their personal data. However, it should be noted that the transition from "privacy by consent" to "privacy by accountability" will not occur without a significant awareness and without ethical education among these stakeholders.

In summary, we can claim that the ethical charter represents a tool for regulating the use of NICTs which allows:

– the prevention of deviations and illicit behaviors, and the raising of awareness about the safety of digital data [CIG 02, MIR 03];

– efficiency improvement in the use of Big Data by users [TYR 94, VAU 00];

– formalization and the definition of "bilateral" ethical principles around the use of Big Data, notably related to issues of electronic surveillance, in the use of resources for personal purposes and in the protection of privacy.

In this case, the code of ethics establishes a kind of moral contract between the employees and the employer [BOU 99, MER 02]. It, thus, consists of a basis and a decisive framework to raise awareness among all staff of the company on their responsibility, with regard to their use of ICTs that are available to them. It promotes taking ownership of standards and the acquisition of appropriate behaviors. The development of and the compliance to these charters also increases the confidence of the citizen respectively to the Big Data infrastructure. Thus, each employee will know in a clear and accurate manner the obligations that she has towards her employer, organization or society, and finally whom ultimately takes responsibility in the case of an ethical problem [OZ 93].

It can be observed that companies seem to be ready to invest in certification systems, in particular, with regard to the success of the ISO standards. These devices ensure the integrity, reliability and quality of data management. According to Mayer-Schönberger and Cukier (2014), this deluge of data marks the birth of "algorithmists", that is to say of specialists capable of understanding the data in order to control businesses from outside as from within – "in the same manner to companies that have in-house accountants and external auditors to monitor their accounts". For the authors, it is necessary in the near future to create new forms of regulators to better control, monitor and verify the source codes and integrated processing algorithms in Big Data NICTs. These external auditors would then correspond to these "algorithmists". Nevertheless, if increasingly more actors imagine the certification of algorithms through external experts, no one truly knows on what basis and on what rules this will be carried out.

The difficulty is also to acknowledge what is certified: a company, a specific data processing device, or a product? It is important to not certify an isolated technological block but everything that is based on data, namely the whole chain of values of the data. A process that would pair "a standard and a measure of this type, as well as the awareness of consumers to their personal data might encourage businesses to improve their transparency, their excellence when it comes to data processing" [CNI 12]. Under these conditions, "business models", stakeholders and galaxies of innovative services will emerge and develop as, for example:

– "sourcing" (producer of reliable data);

– the specialization in the development of highly-targeted mobile and connected healthcare;

– the "Privacy by Design" which consists of accompanying the industry during the development of their services so that they integrate the issues related to personal health data upstream;

– the certification and the ethical qualitative audit related to the security, the privacy, the integrity and the quality of data throughout the value chain, in order to meet the transparency and confidence requirements of consumers and end users.

Such initiatives would provide users with solid reference systems and referential bases in their selection of applications, and this is not only concerning the reliability but also the protection and the security of its personal data. This would have the merit of raising awareness, of educating and of empowering the average healthcare user (as the owner and the consumer of the data) with respect to the ethical issues relating to the confidentiality of their medical data and their privacy in their uses.

Finally, there is the concern that a lack of controls added to too weak sanctions, does not encourage companies to invest in labels or in "Privacy Impact Assessments". Some experts, such as Dr. Leslie Saxon from the University of South Carolina, appealed for the creation of an international organization similar to the United Nations, to regulate healthcare data privacy and security issues.

3.5. Can medicine remain human?

NICTs and the "mathematization" of systems have invaded the world of today, to the extent that they memorize, calculate and project themselves on our behalf. The ubiquity of these ICTs shifts our representations of humans and of the relationships to others. For millennia, intelligence has always been linked to consciousness. However, since the emergence of digital technologies and AI, this couple is attempting to split in all areas. Computers play chess, cars can drive on their own and expert systems diagnose diseases, etc. We are, therefore, legitimately inquiring what will be the usefulness and the place of man in such a universe. And what will be the economic and societal model for such a situation? At the present moment, we still do not know!

Despite this uncertainty, individuals continue to create their digital identity at the center of multiple networks paving the way for communication flows of a new kind, giving emphasis to present and instantaneous aspects. This digital universe is animated by actions which all produce data in a voluntarily as well as in an unintended fashion. Any movement, action or word is due to become data contributing to the emergence of new modes of production, and as consequence new producers of Big Data. Thus, the huge masses of data will be co-produced by sensors and mobile applications through the Internet, and by users and "internauts" whose numbers are increasingly higher. This avalanche of data has become the nourishing sap "of knowledge, of representation, of discussion, of decision, of production, of evaluation, etc." [GUI 11]. An algorithmic approach then becomes a necessity to make this impressive volume of information intelligible and to decide what is relevant (or not) for the user.

In these conditions, with the standardization of Internet technologies, connected objects will all soon become interoperable and will be able to be crossed with the measured data. One can imagine that in a decade, Web platforms will emerge, bringing together the measured healthcare and welfare data in a person notably through mobile health. Consequently, by confronting this data and identifying the similarities and the patterns of Big Data, processing algorithms (data mining) will be able to notify the individual when there will be a high probability of falling ill. We can consider the example of a person who has been geolocalized in an area where a flu epidemic is circulating. The connected measurement objects associated with the patient have enabled the abnormally high measurement of temperature, loss of appetite, and an abnormally low respiratory activity. The processing platform will be able to inform the person, via SMS on a smartphone, that the latter has a very high probability of contracting the flu.

Furthermore, this vision of machines is used increasingly in medicine with tasks and actions once only performed by health professionals. For the majority of people, new technologies are perceived favorably once they have an auxiliary role in the management of healthcare. From the moment they become the source of malfunctions and deviations, they raise concerns about their good intentions. Based on this observation, the power of these mathematical formulas drives one to question the role of humans in the organization of the world. It then appears crucial to investigate the role of the acquisition, collection, processing and data conservation in this complex lifecycle which ranges from the discretization of the data[46] up to the "programmability" of the data[47] [GUI 11].

It may seem contradictory to question the place of humans in a sector of activity such as medicine which has what is most valuable for humans, namely health and life. Yet, with the emergence of Big Data and technological developments that have become a credible response to the reduction of health costs and to the optimization of the quality of administered care, this is a real present issue nowadays. For [BAB 14], "having machines which considerably predict and organize our lives, that create effective and coherent human societies, is certainly an interesting temptation, but if the emergence of these must be done at the price of alienating our freedom, and as a matter of fact, our humanity, this is a question which at least deserves to be debated".

Would the intrusion of engineering and electronic material in the human anatomy dare to transgress the laws according to which the human body is inviolable? Are we heading towards a dehumanized medicine and a "uberisation" of the latter? A process medicine? A medicine in which the healthcare professional will become a "Data Manager" executing orders and decisions originating from protocols and statistics similarly to the expert system Watson from Google? Where the user's health will be permanently controlled, monitored and forced by all kinds of connected tools; and sensors that will be implanted even in the human body? Will we become connected objects or producers of data at the service of an "algorithmized" healthcare system? Will people be willing to transfer their data to a data management platform (DMP) that overwhelms them? Is the hyper-connectivity of the Internet an enslavement or a liberation for us humans? Should we wish or fear the transhuman, this hypothetical man with increased intellectual and physical capacities to the point of replacing us in evolution? Can humanists be reconciled with transhumanists[48]? Does the balance between technological maturity, algorithmic rationality and human consciousness not

---

46 In other words, how data is produced and collected.
47 That is to say how data is exploited, programmed, "algorithmized".
48 The transhumanist is a person who adheres to the intellectual and cultural world movement advocating the use of science and technology to develop physical and mental abilities, and to overcome the adverse aspects of the human condition, such as suffering, pathology, old age and death.

imply transiting through an ethics of digital technology? Is the algorithmic rigor of machines going to substitute experience and human sensibility? How will the players of the medical ecosystem react? Will society accept to believe in an the algorithm to determine our lifestyle and guide our health? Will new Medtechs[49] based on the utilization of Big Data be added to those already present in monitoring and processing segments such as pharmaceutical laboratories and medical equipment manufacturers? Will it instead concern partnerships or competition?

A human being who is recently born will benefit from many innovations in nano-biotechnology still unimaginable today. Stem cells, gene therapy, DNA sequencing and future innovations will be the ones that will radically change a person's life expectancy.

We can consider the example of the cost of DNA sequencing which has dramatically fallen in just 10 years. The first sequencing took 13 years, mobilized 22,000 researchers around the world and cost 3 billion USD. In the near future, it will take a few hours and will only cost 100 dollars. The accurate readings of our biological identity make it possible to have a precise idea of the pathologies that will be available and of the treatments to be applied. We are gradually entering the era of transhumanity where we will be able in the medium term to change the DNA of a person in order to roll back death, or insert implants to meet the problems related to deafness, or even diseases such as Parkinson's or Alzheimer's.

With the massive arrival of connected objects (watches, bracelets, thermostats, connected cars, etc.), one can observe a magnification of gigantic flows of data and of intimate knowledge of our behaviors, actions, intentions, opinions, cognitive styles and preferences. Novel solutions to complex problems are created and reach beyond the threshold of the limited rationality of human judgment. In the end, we are witnessing a humanization of the data where all information[50] are involved in the real-time analysis and decision-making and in the convergence of the "BRING" (biology, robotics, IT, neuroscience and genetics).

For humanists, transhumanism must not overlook the adverse effects of ICT on humans.

---

49 Companies specialized in medical devices and equipment.
50 Texts, voice, images, video, data, relationships, feelings, activities and interactions.

With regard to decision-making, these ICTs tend to ignore human interpretation and evaluation, as well as the public debate focusing on necessity, free will, charity, merit, non-maleficence, desirability, fairness and justice indicators in favor of real-time operational management, systematic rather than systemic of events. In such context, "a vision and an ethical approach of ICTs are therefore more than needed" [ROU 13]. Yves Poullet also notes that the "reduction" of the person is becoming stronger: "the individual is today reduced to its data and to constructs made from these data, the profiles of the algorithmic avatars. It is a dangerous statistical construction of people" [CNI 12].

"Algorithmic governmentality" is explored therein in the way where it concentrates three types of closely intertwined issues that alter our certainties [ROU 12]:

– *Dominance and influence challenges*: How does Big Data affect the doctor–patient relationship, and medical decision-making? How do profiling and data mining correspond to the new tools of power? Power invests an impersonal, statistical and virtual body to represent a model of behavior and profiles.

– *The epistemological and semiotic issues*: What kind of knowledge emerges from "massive data"? How can we criticize, adjust and qualify them? The knowledge revealed by processing algorithms is inductive and statistical, removing all concepts of causality. The information is disconnected from any human empathy.

– *Individuation and subjectivization challenges*: How can we keep hold of human identity when faced with this galaxy of data? How do we ensure that human beings remain the main topic of technological purposes? The operational capability of digital governance ignores all human accounting, opinion, testimonials and experiences collections.

This is why "algorithmic governace" marks the advent of a system that will contribute to the suppression of institutional, temporal, human, emotional, affective, spatial and language conditions of subjectivization in favor of an objective, operational, regulation of the actions to be taken. According to [HAR 15], "computer algorithms are catching up with humans in increasingly more numerous cognitive areas. It is expected that, in the coming decades, computers and other robots will become better than us in yet more tasks and that, in doing so, they replace us in even more roles".

The intermediaries who were making data categories will disappear, due to the fact that we can now bring together singularities. This optimization of life is not neutral! The vision of the world of utilitarianism (from Jeremy Bentham) appears thus at the center of Big Data. Moreover, it is necessary to take into consideration the principle of inspection associated with the principle of utility. Therefore, inspection and optimization of data have an impact on transparency and individual liberties (so believed John Stuart Milles) among the owners of the latter.

In addition, with the evolution of technology, machines can make accurate diagnoses safer and simpler to achieve (especially in medical imaging or in biology), gradually replacing the hand of the technician (in particular, in tumor stereotaxic destruction, or robot-guided operations). Big Data processing also provides new evaluation and support forms made possible by the monitoring of the patient on a daily basis and using everyday tools.

Expert systems that produce AI and simulate the thinking of the doctor have begun to multiply, for example in the decision-making of certain anti-cancer chemotherapies or in the choice of an antihypertensive drug. These expert systems operate with rules, facts, databases, and an "inference engine". This intelligent knowledge acquisition system[51] is designed to search for, discover and remember useful information, through its large memorization and calculation capacity.

In the medium-term, one can legitimately think that the post-operative monitoring of a patient will be ensured in real-time by specific sensors or that a virtualization process can provide remote monitoring of dozens of patients by a doctor who will monitor and manage remotely their personal health data. One can imagine that such an approach will cause legal-medical problems once an accident considered as avoidable will not have been announced because of the inattention of the operator. This new "multi-technological therapeutic approach" will modify the relationship of the patient not only with respect to the treatment and the doctor, but also with respect to health.

---

51 This procedure attempts to predict by means of experience the attitude that must be adopted and the decisions to take when facing facts which we do not know yet the nature of, and through the results obtained, to enrich the knowledge.

Ultimately, this issue of human and political algorithmic construction has today become essential due to the fact that algorithms have penetrated many areas of our daily lives and structure our access to information. Medicine 4.0 relying on Big Data processing among others must give meaning to this data. This necessarily involves ethical and semantic algorithms, as well as the construction of ontologies that consist of representing the risks and must train computers to work for the well-being of people towards an ethics of computing. The human dimension associated with ethical values must never be underestimated and forgotten by the potentials offered by NICTs.

In our opinion, it will still be necessary to wait for a decade before ICTs in healthcare are sufficiently standardized, robust and reliable to be accepted by regulatory bodies, public institutions, healthcare professionals and end-users. It is important to not forget that the relationship of trust between a physician and the patient is still strongly rooted in our society, further playing a predominant role in the good recovery of the patient. Finally, a large number of people will prefer to provide their personal data to their doctor rather than to a technological entity. In any case, the medical profession will have to evolve with these technologies that can measure the health status of the patient on a daily basis in order to make a medical decision.

Moreover, the development and the implementation of these ethical algorithms may incur the risk of being complex and may cause not only latency but also bottleneck areas in the data value chain. To address and resolve these complications, it appears crucial to identify the potential blocking areas, to study them, and then to implement a solution to streamline the procedures to operate on Big Data. It would be interesting to associate healthcare stakeholders (healthcare professionals and users, in particular) to the design and development of mechanisms capable of valuing and improving Big Data at the service of an optimized care course. To this end, we can consider the example of the "living labs", real participatory innovation and "design" environments. In our opinion, this ethical valuation of "mega data" is a fundamental prerequisite to the development of medicine 4.0 so that technological creation can incline towards nature and human kindness.

Conclusion

Big Data is not just a simple question of volume and scale. NICTs that allow them to be operated upon, particularly in the healthcare sector, are achieving a radical change of the medical paradigm in the physician–patient relationship through the processing of personal health data. From now on, Hippocrates's traditional medicine has given way to a medicine 4.0, which is at the same time, personalized, participatory, preventive, prognostic and also predictive based on the analysis of digital data. The development of consumerism of medical information reveals an important evolution in the legitimate request of patients [FAI 06]. They naturally require accounts of the manner they are treated and how health personal data are being used. For this reason, health professionals, information producers and providers are obliged to adapt the way they work and their performance taking this new situation into consideration.

Contemporary medicine brings a better understanding of chronic diseases, infectious diseases, of new approaches to diagnosis and therapeutic treatment, of disease monitoring and health risk factors in public health, according to our habits and our behavior on the Internet, health-related application programs on smartphones and connected objects.

Digital performance concerns at the same level the volume of data under study, the diversity of the sources and the search for a real-time response. This new approach raises new strategies of data analysis based on probabilities, and the manipulation of complete distributions. This allows the translation of the problems in the process of automatic decision-making and the development of new visualizations from new rules of interaction with the data. Big Data, therefore, alleviates our relationship to the datum, allowing us to behave in a permanent exploratory mode. Therefore, "massive data" has built a growing presence within companies, thus achieving a milestone in the strategy and organization of the latter. The history of innovation proves that the more ICTs there are, the more humanity there is. Technologies and humanities correspond to complementary assets that interact with one another. The debate on the dehumanization of medicine is, in our perspective, a false debate which has no place. Let us look at the example of the first revolution of NBICs which occurred in the aerospace sector with the appearance of a new generation of aircraft in the 1980s. Since this revolution, airline pilots still exist, but their activities are no longer the same.

However, this deluge of data raises some ethical concerns about their uses and about the deviations that may result therefrom. The computerized management of personal health data calls for increased vigilance, in particular, for its protection and will be considered only in compliance with certain conditions. This brings us to the question concerning the recovery and the protection of healthcare data.

This is the reason why the search for meaning that underlies this digital shift necessarily brings about reflection about the values that guide our behaviors and our actions both as individuals and as a collective [SAI 02]. This ethic, located at the heart of Big Data, is all the more important that it concerns the health sector. Under these conditions, the awareness of the value of ICT-generated data becomes essential, as well as a better supervision of the use of processing algorithms with respect to individuals. In effect, if we want to live harmoniously in this new world governed by the "algorithmic governance", we must intensify our efforts focusing on the use of data that allow "Machine Learning" to learn from their control by the user and from the transparency of their uses.

It is based on this observation that we have established a risk study resulting in a translation of the ethical issues of the medical datasphere based on ontologies. This has resulted in the development of neo-platonic ethics systemic modeling (Ψ, G, Φ), of a technical and ethical guide system, as well as of a selective hierarchization of healthcare data. As a result, each individual must think, sort and render each datum in a range of rational values to be able to assume his choices and his decisions on its use with particular concern to healthcare. The implementation of our "Ethical Data Mining" approach throughout the stages of the lifecycle of the data is illustrated by our "Infoethics Management" tool that identifies and analyzes the ethical value of unstructured data. One of the challenges consists of demonstrating clarity about the rules for the use of our personal health that stakeholders have available, by facilitating in particular their traceability and their security in compliance with dignity and human freedom.

One of the main aspects of this book is to develop a capacity that allows the incorporation of questioning and an ethical approach in the daily life of a company that operates with Big Data. The recognition of the decision and ethical value points is one way to start the construction of this ability. As a consequence, an alignment of the ethical values with concrete actions will reduce the risk of misuse of personal data and will enable a better control of the latter.

In our perspective, the proper use and the protection of these data is inevitably undergoing an ethical reflection about the control and the supervision procedures of the latter to reserve a predominant place for privacy and confidence among producers and information providers, and thus to contribute to a certain control of the risks and deviations from these. Therefore, anonymity through Big Data has become algorithmically impossible. That is one of the reasons why "algorithmic ethics" has become decisive so that Big Data professionals are finding a fair balance between rational and measured data processing, respectful of one's privacy, and an over-processing that would be particularly counter-productive in the doctor–patient relationship. These ethics will provide some sense of direction to the management of these huge volumes of data by notably restoring a causal link between the correlations that are revealed by these usages.

It would be interesting to evaluate the exponential phenomenon of substitution of processing algorithms in the place of human interaction between users and professionals of healthcare in the context of counseling, recommendations, or medical decisions, and especially to estimate the risks and benefits, to consider the need for a regulatory and ethical guidance around well-defined actions. Furthermore, it is essential that these new ethical choices presented to us be apprehended by all the key players involved in this digital transformation, such as philosophers, public administrations, researchers, health professionals, health users, etc. and not just software vendors who will model them as they wish.

Ultimately, we hope that our ethical vision will aim to strengthen public partnerships/private when it comes to sharing and processing personal medical data, while maintaining the security of personal data in trusted networks.

Stakeholders must be aware that Big Data can help them in the optimization of the healthcare system but also that the latter must primarily rely on human relationships and genuine emotions. The players involved in the lifecycle of personal data will have to agree with this ethical valuation model so that responsibilities are clearly defined and stated. The intensification and the complexity of the information development chain must be subject to appropriate regulation. It must take into account the major role played by algorithms and by the design of a form of regulation focused on verification by a certified third-party making it possible to fluidify the market while preserving the confidence of users.

Similar to MIT in the United States, academic research around Big Data must be an important lever of innovation for organizations as well as in debates about the data and regulation with special focus on healthcare. Note that all our reflections and ethical approaches expressed in this book can be applied and adapted to other areas of activity to trigger a similar dynamic of awareness and establish a universal frame of reference about the design, the use and the control of personal digital data.

Finally, it is possible to anticipate that in the years to come all "mega data" processing, which was previously impossible, will become effective. The synergies and collaborations that were only imagined will become real and will change the role of the person facing the usage of health-related data of a personal nature. Therefore, this brings about the reflection of whether the use of health data records stored by institutional organizations (like the CNAMTS in France) should not be open and free to access to external actors who wish to use them in a research context based on epidemiology and prevention, in compliance with the law in force and an ethical charter with regard to health-related Big Data? On the same principle of autonomy, would it not be beneficial to provide ownership of data to their original producers – that is to citizens – and thus to shift towards a heritage logic of personal data? For the philosopher Gaspard Koenig[1], "we have invented the

---

[1]"L'utopie numérique est-elle dangereuse pour l'individu?", *Les Assises de la Sécurité et des Systèmes d'Information*, Monaco, 1 October 2015.

law of intellectual property during the industrial revolution. With the advent of digital technology, it is essential to create a right of ownership of individual data". That would, perhaps, allow people to better protect themselves and take responsibility with regard to their personal data, while benefiting from a part of the financial value originated from their usages. One can imagine the construction of a medical social network allowing the health user to access its data and the definition of rights of access and processing; this would include a system of financial compensation for health industrial manufacturers, and a free system of "data donation" for research and science. This platform would reveal the patient as a key player in the process, allowing them to regain control over their own information, which they could access and share as they please, according to a system similar to the American "Blue Button" previously seen.

In this context, the healthcare user and the doctor would see their statutes respectively evolve towards "Data Trader" and "Data Manager" of personal health data. Such an evolution of the doctor–patient relationship must create a culture of data which is, today, still lacking. It must also redefine the notion itself of justice and of digital heritage to ensure people's freedom, namely of knowing what can be done with our own data and under what conditions we can share their value? A delicate balance and contract of trust between all these stakeholders thus remains to be found.

Finally, machine learning algorithms powered by Big Data often generate unexpected results, and their functioning may even not be completely understood by those who have built them. Furthermore, we should also consider the problem related to the transparency of the recommendation and processing algorithms. Do the mechanisms of expert systems themselves drive us to the point that the ethical decisions will be transferred to the people who will create the software? How can a tool designed by humans be neutral and objective? It would be unrealistic to believe so, if we remember the algorithm of the manufacturer Volkswagen! That is why it appears essential to verify their content and their functionality by means of a rigorous framework, and implement redressment procedures. Our society must therefore develop ways to systematically assess the purposes, impact and repercussions of these algorithmic devices. This, necessarily, relates to algorithmic ethics that we will develop in depth in an upcoming book.

Appendices

Appendix 1

Advantages of Big Data Technologies According to Data Sources and Stakeholders

Data sources	Processing technologies	Marketing Profits	Utilities for consumers	Values for businesses
Of usages through connected objects: geolocation, RFID, etc.	Hadoop, noSQL, semantic, analysis, more or less structured information base			
Of content disseminated from devices: videos, photos, reviews, blogs, Tweets, status, etc.	Hadoop, noSQL, semantic, analysis, more or less structured information base		Expectation and practice anticipation Innovation products	Anticipation/Organization and means optimization New business opportunities Reaction speed
	Cookie bases, RTB, MDM	Predictive marketing		
Of references and explanatory data: reliable, Open Data, third-party data (mapping, weather, etc.)	Hadoop, noSQL, semantic, analysis, more or less structured information base		Navigation recognition and customization & customer route Personalized product recommendation Targeted and customized banners	ROI, recruitment action organization & conversions & loyalty Profitability improvement and Website turnover
	Cookie bases, RTB, MDM	Web analytics		

Of anonymous online behaviour: Web browsing, searches in engines	Hadoop, noSQL, semantic, analysis, more or less structured information base			
	Cookie bases, RTB, MDM			
Of information and of identified behaviors	Nominative basis (relational database), campaign managers, Data Mining, MDM	Multi-channel relational marketing	Segments and targeting optimization Customer relationship customization: phone, SMS, mail, email, Web identified Channel and promotional mechanism customization Product personal recommendation Adapted pressure management	Action automization Relational marketing campaign ROI optimization Reduction of the costs associated with Bad Data

Appendix 2

Issues Involving a Data Management Platform (DMP)

Technological challenges
A single data management platform (DMP) concentrates, consolidates and enriches all customer data in real time
One single control panel (BSC)
Integrated management and multi-channel piloting
Operational challenges
Knowledge of the client, relevance of campaigns, advertising pressure control
Permanent efficiency growth by data enrichment at each action and utilization of self-learning algorithms
Free creativity due to the power of personalized messages
"Anonymized" data: only targeted profiles are used
Security challenges
The data are protected against unwanted access and technical failures
The value of these data justify their protection against theft, hijacking and piracy
Customer data are hosted on the territory of the advertiser and not in cloud computing services

Financial challenges
The data remains the property of the advertiser: she has a fully evolving and growing capital "data"
Balance between short-term performances and maximizing client value in the long term
Short-term outcomes: increase in campaigns performance and of their ROI
Trade challenge
Evolutive knowledge of the behavior of the audience, that is throughout the lifecycle of the data
Campaigns calibration, regardless of the channel through this detailed knowledge of the targets
Availability of all data on the audience, gathered and analyzed in their entirety

Appendix 3

Evaluation Criteria on the Ethical Evaluation of Personal Health Data

Axes	Evaluation criteria on the ethical appraisal of personal health data
	In your perspective, the exploitation of these personal health data must be for purposes of:
Charity	1) To help medical decision-making established by the healthcare professional (HP)?
	2) To promote the quality, organization, management and planning of patient care?
	3) To contribute to the welfare of the patient?
	4) To share transparent and accessible information between the patient and the HP?
	5) To ensure the quality and the choice of information transmitted to the patient?
	6) To improve the continuity of care?
	7) To assist the ministry of health to respond to the user's expectations and medical care?
	8) To establish the patient's legal and information processing legitimacy?
	9) To establish a safety, integrity, traceability and protection of medical data duty?

Justice	10) To evaluate the performance and identify areas where action is needed by listing the points of failure?
	11) To allow epidemiological analysis or statistics (SEA)?
	12) To improve and strengthen the interactivity with stakeholders external to the healthcare structure?
	13) To strengthen the availability of HPs?
	14) To equitably distribute the disadvantages and advantages of such a tool in the workload of the HP?
	15) To develop and share accurate and adapted information to the entire population?
Non-maleficence	16) To follow the legislative regulation of medical data?
	17) To comply with the storage, hosting and dissemination rules established by the CNIL?
	18) To minimize or eliminate wrong-doing to patients due to bad information?
	19) To minimize unnecessary or poorly calculated risks?
	20) To ensure the reliability of the medical data collection and its permanence?
	21) To ensure the technical relevance and the rightfulness of the tool?
Autonomy	22) To replace the patient at the center of the decision by providing him with more complete and rapid medical information: Better patient autonomy?
	23) To respect the privacy and the right to medical confidentiality and privacy?
	24) To adapt technology to the HP's knowledge and know-how?
	25) To ensure the consent and adhesion of the owner of the data?
	26) To respect the right to prior information, rectification and opposition described to the owner of the data?

	27) Are these health data easily applicable to be analyzed?
	28) Are these health data rich in resulting information?
	29) Are these health data sufficiently adapted to its users?
	30) Are these health data well ordered?
	31) Are these health data flexible enough to be used as such?
Strategy & Methodology	32) Can these health data be evolutive in time?
	33) Are these health data performing in terms of transmitted information?
	34) Are these health data reusable as they are?
	35) Are these health data pragmatic?
	36) Have these health data been consolidated by health professionals?
	37) Are these health data functional and operational as such?
	38) Are these health data relevant?
	39) Do these health data comprise a certain stability and continuity in its outcoming results?
	40) Do these health data contribute to a guarantee for fair information?
	41) Do these health data originate from a multidisciplinary activity of care?
	42) Do these health data systematically transmit the same information?
Organization & Regulation	43) Are these health data references in the sector?
	44) Are these health data standards for a given health status?
	45) Can these health data maintain themselves as such in time?
	46) Have these health data been accompanied by a precise and rigorous regulation?
	47) Do these health data correctly provide evidence of good care services?
	48) Do these health data originate from the coordination of several care services?

Structure & Technology	49) Are these health data consistent and do they have meaning?
	50) Are these health data sufficiently accurate?
	51) Do these health data show integrity?
	52) Are these health data comprehensive?
	53) Are these health data sufficiently authentic?
	54) Are these health data reliable?
	55) Are these health data fairly robust and solid?
	56) Are these health data legitimate?
	57) Are these health data nominal designating a category within an existing database?
Relationship & Culture	58) Are these health data secured?
	59) Are these health data confidential?
	60) Are these health data unifying?
	61) Can these health data be easily disseminated?
	62) Can these health data be easily accessed by all?
	63) Are these health data user-friendly as such?
	64) Are these health data universal?
	65) Can these health data be easily made available?
	66) Can these health data allow for a better cooperation in the management of care services?
Control	67) Is there a policy and management strategy for these health data?
	68) Are the responsibilities and tasks of each actor clearly defined with regard to health data management?
	69) Is there an organization specifically dedicated to the management of health data implemented?
	70) Is there a prospective management of the required skills from health data users implemented?
	71) Is there a specific and developed management of reference health data?

Layout	72) Have a health data categorization and hierarchization by relevance been carried out?
	73) Have the so-called essential health data been modeled?
	74) Has a health data sharing mechanism been implemented?
	75) Is there a directory of essential health data?
	76) Are flows and localizations of health data mapped?
Development lifecycle	77) Is the same health data collected only once?
	78) Are unstructured health data stored in an organized manner?
	79) Is there a device for the identification of useful unstructured sources of health data?
	80) Has a lifecycle monitoring policy of health data been implemented?
	81) Have all health data collected been subjected to specific control?
	82) Have all health data that have been processed undergone controlling?
	83) Are the problems about the quality of health data managed until they are corrected?
	84) Is there a health data "reporting" approach available?
Operations	85) Are there systems for the preparation of health data in order to build consistent data sets?
	86) Has a health data processing and usage mechanism been put in place?
	87) Are databases administered?
	88) Are databases access modules developed (connectors, Web services, APIs, etc.)?
	89) Are Big Data applications implemented?
	90) Are health data archived, potentially replicated, and are they backed up?
	91) Is there a control of the quality approach of health data backups?
	92) Are health data restored on request?
	93) Are activity continuity tests involving health data regularly operated?

Appendix 4

OECD Guideline Principles Governing the Security of the Systems and Information Networks

The following nine principles complement each other and should be considered as a whole. They concern stakeholders at all levels, including political and operational ones. Under the terms of the guidelines, the responsibilities of the stakeholders vary according to their role. All stakeholders can get support through awareness, education, information sharing and training actions so as to facilitate a better understanding of security issues and the adoption of the best practices in this area. The efforts aiming to strengthen the security of the systems and information networks must comply with the values of a democratic society, in particular, with the need for a free and open circulation of information and the basic respect principles targeting the privacy of individuals[1].

---

1 In addition to these safety guidelines, the OECD has developed a series of additional recommendations concerning guidelines for other important aspects of the world information society. These relate to privacy (guidelines governing the protection of privacy and transborder flows of data of personal nature, OECD, 1980) and cryptography (guidelines governing cryptography policies, OECD, 1997). Safety guidelines ought to be read in conjunction with these other guidelines.

A4.1. Awareness

Stakeholders must be aware of the necessity to ensure the safety of information systems and networks and of the actions they can undertake to enhance security.

Awareness of the risks and the available countermeasures is the first line of defense to ensure the security of the systems and information networks. Systems and information networks can be exposed to both internal and external risks. Stakeholders must understand that security failures may seriously adversely affect systems and networks under their control but also, because of the inter-connectivity and interdependence, those of others. Stakeholders should reflect on the configuration of their system, on the updates available for the latter, to the place it occupies in networks, on the good practices that can be implemented to enhance the security, as well as the needs of other stakeholders.

A4.2. Responsibility

Stakeholders are responsible for the security of the systems and of the information networks.

Stakeholders are reliant on interconnected local and world information networks and systems. They must understand their responsibility in the security of these systems and of networks and be, depending on the role that they are responsible for, individually accountable thereof. They must regularly review and assess their own policies, practices, measures and procedures to ensure that they are adapted to their environment. Those who develop, design and supply products and services must take into account the safety of systems and networks and disseminate appropriate information; this includes updates in a timely manner so that users can better understand the security features of products and services and their responsibilities regarding this matter.

A4.3. Reaction

Stakeholders must act promptly and in a spirit of cooperation to prevent, detect and respond to security incidents.

Due to the inter-connectivity of the information systems and networks and the propensity of damages to quickly and massively propagate, the stakeholders must respond promptly and in a spirit of cooperation to security incidents. They must exchange information on threats and vulnerabilities in an appropriate manner and implement procedures for a rapid and effective cooperation to prevent and detect security incidents and respond thereto. Where permitted, this may involve cross-border exchange of information and cooperation.

A4.4. Ethics

Stakeholders are required to respect the legitimate interests of other stakeholders.

Systems and information networks are ubiquitous in our societies and stakeholders should be aware of the harm they can cause to others by their action or their inaction. An ethical conduct is, therefore, essential and stakeholders should make an effort to develop and adopt model practices and to promote behaviors that take into account security requirements and do respect the legitimate interests of other stakeholders.

A4.5. Democracy

The security of information systems and networks must be compatible with the fundamental values of a democratic society.

Security must be ensured in compliance with the values recognized by democratic societies, in particular with the freedom to exchange thoughts and ideas, the free flow of information, the confidentiality of information and communications, the adequate protection of personal information, with openness and transparency.

A4.6. Risk analysis

Stakeholders should perform risk analysis.

Risks analyses allow the identification of threats and vulnerabilities and should be broad enough to cover all of the main internal and external factors such as technology, physical and human factors, third-party policies and services having implications about the security. Risk analysis will allow that the acceptable level of risk be determined and will facilitate the selection of appropriate control measures to manage the risk of possible prejudice in systems and information networks taking into account the nature and the importance of the information that must be protected. Risk analysis must account for prejudice to the interests of others or caused by others made possible by the increasing interconnection of information systems.

A4.7. Safety design and implementation

Stakeholders should integrate security as an essential element of information systems and networks.

Systems, networks and policies must be appropriately designed, implemented and coordinated to optimize safety. A major, but not exclusive, axis of this effort must be the design and adoption of protection measures and appropriate solutions in order to prevent or limit the potential harm associated with the identified threats and vulnerabilities. Protection measures and solutions must be both technical and non-technical and be proportionate to the value of information in the organization's information networks and systems. Security must be a fundamental element of all products, services, systems and networks and be an integral part of the design and architecture of the systems. For the end user, the design and implementation of security measures consist essentially of selecting and configuring products and services for their systems.

A4.8. Security management

Participants are required to adopt a comprehensive approach to security management.

Safety management must be based on the assessment of the risks and be dynamic and comprehensive to cover all levels of activities of the stakeholder and all aspects of their operations. It must also include, by anticipation, responses to emerging threats and cover the prevention, detection and solution of incidents, systems recovery, ongoing maintenance, control and audit. Security policies of information systems and networks, the practices, the measures and the security procedures must be coordinated and integrated to create a coherent security system. The safety management requirements are based on the level of participation, on the role of the stakeholder, on the risks involved and on the characteristics of the system.

A4.9. Reevaluation

Stakeholders are required to review and re-evaluate the security of the information systems and networks; and introduce the appropriate modifications in their policies, practices, measures and safety procedures.

New or evolving threats and vulnerabilities are constantly discovered. All stakeholders must continually revisit, reassess and modify all security aspects to address these evolving risks.

Glossary

A2B	Administration to Business
ADPS	Automated Data Processing System
AFDEL	*Association Française Des Editeurs de Logiciels et solutions Internet* – French association of software publishers and Internet solutions
ANSM	*Agence Nationale de Sécurité du Médicament et des produits de santé* – French National Agency for Medicines and Health Products Safety
AP-HP	*Assistance Publique – Hôpitaux de Paris* – French Public Assistance – Paris Hospitals
API	Application Programming Interface
ARC	Clinical Research Assistant
ASIP	*Agence des SI Partagés de santé* – French Health Shared IS Agency
B2B	Business to Business
B2BC	Back to Basics Compliance
BAT	Baidu Alibaba Tencent
BI	Business Intelligence
BRING	Biology, Robotics, Information Technology, Neuroscience, Genetics

BSC	Balanced ScoreCard
CDC	Center for Disease Control and prevention
CDM	Clinical Data Manager
CDO	Chief Data Officer
CESC	Computer Engineering Services Company
CIL	Data Protection Officers
CIO	Chief Information Officer
CNAMTS	*Caisse Nationale de l'Assurance Maladie des Travailleurs Salariés* – French National Health Insurance Fund for Salaried Workers
CNIL	*Commission Nationale de l'Informatique et des Libertés* – French National Commission on Information Technology and Liberties
CNIS	*Conseil National de l'Information Statistique* – French Statistical Information National Council
CNOM	*Conseil National de l'Ordre des Médecins* – French National Council of the Order of Doctors
CP	Control Panel
CPO	Chief Privacy Officer
CRM	Customer Relationship Management
CTMS	Clinical Trial Management System
CTNERHI	*Centre Technique National d'Etudes et de Recherches sur les Handicaps et les Inadaptations* – French National Technical Center for the study and the research on Disability and Indaptations
DBMS	Database Management System
DICOM	Digital Imaging and Communications in Medicine
DIKW	Data Information Knowledge Wisdom
DLP	Data Loss Prevention
DMP	Data Management Platform

DNA	Deoxyribonucleic Acid
DPO	Data Protection Officier
DREES	*Direction de la Recherche, des Etudes, de l'Evaluation et des Statistiques* – French Research, studies, Evaluation and Statistics Administration
EC	European Convention
ECG	Electrocardiogram
ERP	Enterprise Resource Planning
ESA	Epidemiological or Statistical Analysis
ETL	Extract Transform-Load
FDA	Food and Drug Administration
FNRS	*Fonds National de la Recherche Scientifique* – French National Fund for Scientific Research
GAFA	Google, Apple, Facebook, Amazon
GDP	Gross Domestic Product
HAS	*Haute Autorité de Santé* – French Health High Authority
HIPAA	Health Insurance Portability and Accountability Act
HIS	Hospital Information System
HP	Healthcare Professional
HPC	High Performance Computer
ICT	Information and Communication Technology
IDC	*Observatoire des Données* – French Data Observatory
IMEI	International Mobile Equipment Identity
INED	*Institut National d'Etudes Démographiques* – French National Institute of Demographic Studies

INSEE	*Institut National de la Statistique et des Etudes Economiques* – French National Institute of Statistics and Economic Studies
INSERM	*Institut National de la Santé et de la Recherche Médicale* – French Health and Medical Research National Institute
InVS	*Institut de Veille Sanitaire* – French Institute for Public Health Surveillance
IQ	Information Quality
IRM	Information Right Management
IS	Information System
ISO	International Organization for Standardization
KPI	Key Performance Indicators
MDM	Mobile Device Management
MIT	Massachussetts Institute of Technology
NATU	Netflix Airbnb Tesla Uber
NBIC	Nanotechnologies, Biotechnologies, Information Technology and Cognitive Sciences
NHS	National Health Service
NIH	National Institutes of Health
NoSQL	Not Only SQL
NTIC	New Information and Communication Technology
OECD	Organization for Economic Cooperation and Development
ORS	*Observatoire Régional de la Santé* – French Regional Health Observatory
PER	Reality Environmental parameters
PRO	Patient Reported Outcome
R&D	Research and Development
RC	Relational and Cultural

RFID	Radio Frequency IDentification
RIS	Radiology Information System
RO	Regulatory and Organizational
ROI	Return On Investment
RTB	Real Time Bidding
SCM	Supply Chain Management
SIM	Subscriber Identity Module
SM	Strategic and Methodological
SNIIRAM	*Système National d'Information Inter Régimes de l'Assurance Maladie* – French Inter Regime Health Insurance National Information System
SQL	Structured Query Language
SRE	Social Responsibility of Enterprises
SSID	Service Set Identifier
ST	Structural and Technological
SWOT	Strengths Weaknesses Opportunities Threats
TPS	Toyota Production System
UID	Unique Identification Autority
UN	United Nations Organization
URI	Uniform Resource Identifier
URL	Uniform Resource Locator
VICT	Virtual Imaging Clinical Trials
VPN	Virtual Private Network

Bibliography

[ABB 01] ABBAD J., *Organisation et management hospitalier*, Berger-Levrault, Paris, pp. 25–103, 2001.

[ABO 13] ABOULICAN W., Big Data: enjeux, perspectives et incertitudes d'une omniscience en devenir, 3 June 2013.

[ACH 13] ACHIARY A., HAMELIN J., AUVERLOT D., Cybersécurité, l'urgence d'agir, La note d'analyse, Centre d'analyse stratégique, no. 324, March 2013.

[ADA 01] ADAMS J.S., TASHCHIAN A., SHORE T., "Codes of ethics as signals for ethical behavior", *Journal of Business Ethics*, vol. 29, pp. 199–211, 2001.

[AIM 13] AIM, Big data: les défis de la gestion des volumes des données de santé à caractère personnel, Les Etats généraux du Cloud, 22–24 May 2013.

[ALB 12] ALBERTS C., DOROFEE A., Managing Information Security Risks: The OCTAVE (SM), 2002.

[AME 14] AMELINE P., "Big data: Pourquoi (pas) à l'hôpital?", *DSIH*, vol. 1, no. 13, pp. 54–55, October 2014.

[APR 14] APROGED, "Archivage sur le Cloud: pratiques et perspectives", *Livre Blanc*, vol. 1, p. 45, January, 2014.

[AVE 12] AVENIER M.J., GENELOT D., *Agir et penser en complexité avec Jean-Louis Le Moigne*, L'Harmattan, Paris, p. 87, 2012.

[AYA 09] AYACHE N., "Informatique et imagerie médicale: le patient numérique personnalisé" *Les défis scientifiques du 21ème siécle*, Académie des Sciences, Paris, 2009.

[BAB 14] BABINET G., *Big data, penser l'homme et le monde autrement*, Le Passeur, Paris, 2014.

[BAD 15] BADILLO P.Y., PÉLISSIER N., "Usages et usagers de l'information numérique", *Revue Française des Sciences de l'Information et de la Communication*, vol.1, no. 6, p. 4, 2015.

[BAI 14] BAIL C.A., "The cultural environment: measuring culture with big data", *Theory and Society*, vol. 43, nos. 3–4, pp. 465–482, 2014.

[BAL 14] BALTASSIS E., STRAGIER F., TELLE N. *et al.*, Le Big Data face au défi de la confiance, The Boston Consulting group, DLA Piper, pp. 1–24, June 2014.

[BAR 10] BARONE D., STELLA F., BATINI C., "Dependency discovery in data quality", *Proceedings of the International Conference in Advanced Information Systems Engineering (CAISE)*, pp. 53–67, 2010.

[BAT 06] BATINI C., SCANNAPIECA M., *Data Quality: Concepts, Methodologies and Techniques*, Springer, 2006.

[BEA 01] BEAUCHAMP T.L., CHILDRESS J., *Principles of Biomedical Ethics*, 5th ed., Oxford University Press, New-York/Oxford, 2001.

[BEA 13] BEAUCHAMP T.L., CHILDRESS J.F., *Principles of Biomedical Ethics*, 7th edition Oxford University Press, New York, 2013.

[BEC 13] BECK M., "Next in tech: app helps patients track care", *Wall Street Journal*, p. 1–2, December 2013.

[BEC 14] BECKER S., MIRON-SHATZ T., SCHUMACHER N. *et al.*, "mHealth 2.0: experiences, possibilities, and perspectives", *JMIR MhealthUhealth*, vol. 2, no. 2, p. e24, 2014.

[BEH 96] BEHAR R., GORDON D.A., *Women Writing Culture*, University of California Press, Berkeley, 1996.

[BEL 73] BELL D., *The Coming of Post-Industrial Society*, Boston Press, 1973.

[BEL 08] BELKADI F., "Démarche de modélisation d'une situation de conception collaborative", *Document numérique*, vol. 8, pp. 93–106, 2008.

[BEN 13] BENHAMOU B., "Les mutations économiques, sociales, et politiques de l'internet des objets", *Cahier français*, no. 372, January–February 2013.

[BEN 14] BENSABAT P., GAULTIER D., HOARAU M. *et al.*, "Du Big Data au Big Business, Livre 1: Phénomène de mode ou facteur de performance?", *Business & Décision*, vol. 1, pp. 1–40, October 2014.

[BER 15] BÉRANGER J., *Medical Information System Ethics,* ISTE, London, and John Wiley & Sons, New York, 2015.

[BIR 13] BIRMELÉ B., BOCQUILLON B., PAPON R., "Le dossier informatisé: entre partage des données pour une prise en charge optimale du patient et risque de rupture de la confidentialité", *Médecine & Droit*, no. 121, p. 137, 2013.

[BLO 13] BLONDEL V., *La Recherche*, no. 482, p. 30, December 2013.

[BOI 03] BOISVERT Y., JUTRAS M., LEGAULT G.A. *et al.*, Raisonnement éthique dans un contexte de marge de manoeuvre accrue: clarification conceptuelle et aide à la décision. Rapport de recherche, Secrétariat du Conseil du trésor, Gouvernement du Québec, Centre d'expertise en gestion des ressources humaines, Québec, p. 31, 2003.

[BOL 10] BOLLIER D., *The Promise and Peril of Big Data*, The Aspen Institute, Washington, p. 13, 2010.

[BON 14] BONNET F., "La protection des données personnelles face aux nouvelles exigences de sécurité", *Revue Banque*, no. 769, p. 3, 2014.

[BOU 98] BOURCIER D., "Les profils, le marketing et la gestion du risque: vers l'ordinateur-indic?", *Colloque "Surfichés, ne vous en fichez plus..."*, 25 April 1998.

[BOU 02] BOUCHET H., MATHON S., MACKER J-P. *et al.*, La cybersurveillance des salariés sur les lieux de travail, Rapport d'étude et de consultation publique, available at: www.cnil.fr, 2002.

[BOU 03] BOUNFOUR A., *The Management of Intangibles, The Organisation's Most Valuable Assets*, Routledge, London, NY, 2003.

[BOU 06] BOULLIER D., "Prises et emprises dans les systèmes d'aides homme-machine: Pour une anthropologie de l'appropriation", *Intellectica*, vol. 2, no. 44, pp. 17–44, 2006.

[BOU 09] BOUCHET-LE MAPPIAN, Propriété intellectuelle et droit de propriété en droit anglais, allemand et français, thesis, Nantes, 2009.

[BOY 12a] BOYD D., CRAWFORD K., "Critical questions for big data: provocations for a cultural, technological, and scholarly phenomenon", *Information Communication & Society*, vol. 15, no. 5, pp. 662–679, 2012.

[BOY 12b] BOYE N., "Co-production of health enabled by next generation personal health systems", *Studies in Health Technology and Informatics*, vol. 177, pp. 52–58, 2012.

[BRA 13] BRASSEUR C., *Enjeux et usages du big data. Technologies, méthodes et mises en œuvre*, Hermes-Lavoiser, Paris, p. 30, 2013.

[BRE 02] BRETON P., PROULX S., *L'explosion de la communication, à l'aube du XXIème siècle*, Editions La Découverte, Paris, 2002.

[BRU 06] BRUGUIÈRE J.-M., "L'immatériel à la trappe", *Recueil Dalloz*, no. 2, p. 2804, 2006.

[BUI 03] BUIN Y., "Normopathie. Le Passant Ordinaire", *Revue Internationale de Création et de Pensée Critique*, pp. 45–46, 2003.

[BUI 13] BUIJINK A.W.G., VISSER B.J., MARSHALL L., "Medical apps for smartphones: lack of evidence undermines quality and safety", *Evidence-Based Medicine.*, vol. 18, no. 3, pp. 90–92, 2013.

[CAI 81] CAIN M., FINCH J., "Towards a rehabilitation of data", in ABRAMS P., DEEM R., FINCH J. *et al.* (eds), *Practice and Progress: British Sociology 1950–1980*, George Allen and Unwin, London, p. 105–119, 1981.

[CAL 12] CALLEBAUT W., "Scientific perspectivism: a philosopher of science's response to the challenge of big data biology", *Studies in History and Philosophy of Science Part C: Studies in History and Philosophy of Biological and Biomedical Sciences*, vol. 43, no. 1, pp. 69–80, 2012.

[CAN 08] CANARY H.E., JENNINGS M.M., "Principles and influence in codes of ethics: a centering resonance analysis comparing pre- and post-Sarbanes-Oxley code of ethics", *Journal of Business Ethics*, vol. 80, pp. 263–278, 2008.

[CAR 00] CARLEY K.M., "Organizational change and the digital economy: a computational organization science perspective", in BRYNJOLFSSON, ERIK, KAHIN B. (eds), *Understanding the Digital Economy: Data Tools, Research*, MIT Press, Cambridge, MA, pp. 325–351, 2000.

[CAR 01] CARRÉ D., LACROIX J.G., *La santé et les autoroutes de l'information*, L'Harmattan, Paris, 2001.

[CAR 13] CARTER M.C., BURLEY V.J., NYKJAER C. *et al.*, "Adherence to a smartphone application for weight loss compared to website and paper diary: pilot randomized controlled trial", *J. Med. Internet Res.*, vol. 15, no. 4, p. e32, 2013.

[CAR 14] CARMES M., NOYER J., "L'irrésistible montée de l'algorithmique. Méthodes et concepts en SHS", *Les Cahiers du numérique,* vol. 10, no. 4, pp. 63–102, 2014.

[CAS 10] CASILLI A., *Liaisons numériques, vers une nouvelle sociabilité*, Éditions La Martinière, 2010.

[CAT 83] CATALA P., "Ebauche d'une théorie juridique de l'information", *Revue de droit prospectif,* vol. 1, p. 185, 1983.

[CAT 85] CATALA P., *La "propriété" de l'information*, Mélanges Pierre Raynaud, Dalloz-Sirey, 1985.

[CHA 09] CHANNIN D.S., BOWERS G., NAGY P., "Should radiology IT be owned by the chief information officier?", *Journal of Digital Imaging*, vol. 22, no. 3, pp. 218–221, June 2009.

[CHA 14] CHAZALON F., "Gouvernance de l'information: Comment ça marche? 4 clés à découvrir!", *Aproged*, 4 November 2014.

[CHE 11] CHERFI S., THION-GOASDOUÉ V., "Assessment and analysis of information quality: a multidimensional model and case studies", *Intl. Journal of Information Quality*, vol. 2, no. 4, pp. 300–323, 2011.

[CHO 14] CHOUDHURY S., FISHMAN J.R., MCGOWAN M.L. *et al.*, "Big data, open science and the brain: lessons learned from genomics", *Frontiers in Human Neuroscience*, vol. 8, p. 239, 2014.

[CHR 03] CHRISSIS M., KONRAD M., SHRUM S., *CMMI: Guidelines for Process Integration and Product Improvement*, 2nd ed., Addison-Wesley, Boston, 2003.

[CIG 02] CIGREF, "Sécurité des Systèmes d'Information, quelle politique globale de gestion des risques?", available at: www.cigref.fr, 2002.

[CIG 08] CIGREF, "Protection de l'information: Enjeux, gouvernance et bonnes pratiques", available at: www.cigref.fr, 2008.

[CIG 14] CIGREF, "Enjeux business des données: comment gérer les données de l'entreprise pour créer de la valeur?", available at: www.cigref.fr, October 2014.

[CIT 13] CITO RESEARCH, *Guide d'achat sur l'intégration du Big Data*, September 2013.

[CNI 12] CNIL, "Vie privée à l'horizon 2020. Cahiers IP", *Innovation & Prospective*, vol. 1, no. 1, pp. 1–60, 2012.

[CNI 13] CNIL, Décision no. 2013–025 de la présidente de la CNIL mettant en demeure la société GOOGLE INC, 10 June 2013.

[CNI 14] CNIL, "Le corps, nouvel objet connecté. Cahiers IP", *Innovation & Prospective*, vol.2, no. 2, pp. 1–64, May 2014.

[CNO 15] CNOM, Santé connectée: de la e-santé à la santé connectée, Livre Blanc, vol. 1, pp. 1–36, January 2015.

[COL 13] COLLIN P., COLIN N., Mission d'expertise sur la fiscalité numérique, report, January 2013.

[COL 14] COLL S., "Power, knowledge, and the subjects of privacy: understanding privacy as the ally of surveillance", *Information Communication & Society*, vol. 17, no. 10, pp. 1250–1263, 2014.

[COS 14] COSTA F.F., "Big data in biomedicine", *Drug Discovery Today*, vol. 19, no. 4, pp. 433–440, 2014.

[COU 07] COUDERC B., PREVEL L., "La maîtrise du cycle de vie du document numérique", *Aproged*, vol. 1, pp. 1–4, October 2007.

[COR 12] CORINUS M., DEREY T., MARGUERIE J. *et al.*, "Rapport d'étude sur le Big Data", *SRS Day*, pp. 1–54, 5 October 2012.

[CUM 13] CUMMINGS E., BORYCKI E.M., ROEHRER E., "Issues and considerations for healthcare consumers using mobile applications", *Stud. Health Technol. Inform.*, vol. 183, pp. 227–231, 2013.

[CUR 13] CURRIE J., ""'Big Data" Versus "Big Brother": on the appropriate use of large-scale data collections in pediatrics", *Pediatrics*, vol. 131, (Supplement), pp. S127–S132, 2013.

[DAL 01] D'ALMEIDA N., *Les promesses de la communication*, Presses Universitaires de France, Paris, 2001.

[DAR 98] DARAGON E., *Etude sur le statut juridique de l'information*, Dalloz, no. 63, 1998.

[DAV 12] DAVIS K., PATTERSON D., *Ethics of Big Data: Balancing Risk and Innovation*, O'Reilly, Media, Sebastopol, CA, pp. 16–17, 28 September 2012.

[DEF 05] DE FEO J.A., BARNARD W., JURAN Institute's Six Sigma Breakthrough and Beyond – Quality Performance Breakthrough Methods, McGraw-Hill Professional, 2005.

[DEL 14] DE LA VEGA R., MIRÓ J., "mHealth: a strategic field without a solid scientific soul. A systematic review of pain- related apps", *PLoS One*, vol. 9, no. 7, e101312, 2014.

[DEM 12] DEMIDOWICH A.P., LU K., TAMLER R. *et al.*, "An evaluation of diabetes self-management applications for Android smartphones", *J. Telemed. Telecare*, vol. 18, no. 4, pp. 235–238, 2012.

[DES 15] DESCHAUX H., "Data: les 5 tendances qui préoccupent les entreprises mais qui créent de la valeur", *Prospective*, p. 2, 3 February 2015.

[DEV 00] DE VAUJANY F.X., "Usage d'un intranet et processus de structuration de l'organisation", *Systèmes d'Information et Management*, pp. 79–105, 2000.

[DEV 14] DE VILLEMANDY A., "Santé numérique: le Big Data et l'analytique en tête des investissements", *L'Atelier*, p. 1, 3 October 2014.

[DHE 07] DHERSE J.-L., MINGUET D.H., *L'éthique ou le chaos?*, Presses de la Renaissance, Paris, pp. 1–448, 2007.

[DOU 13] DOUEIHI M., *Qu'est-ce que le numérique?*, PUF, Paris, 2013.

[DSI 11] DSIH, Big Data en santé: oser le doute, 24 May 2015.

[DUP 13] DUPERRIN B., "Le Big Data demande de l'éthique et une culture spécifique", *Cognitive Computing – BI – Big Data*, pp. 1–2, 27 August 2013.

[ENG 13] ENGOHAN T., Les enjeux du Big Data pour l'Entreprise, professionnelle thesis, MBA, ISC Paris, 3 March 2013.

[ERT 15] ERTZSCHEID O., "Usages de l'information numérique: comprendre les nouvelles enclosures algorithmiques pour mieux s'en libérer", *Revue française des sciences de l'information et de la communication*, no. 6, p. 1–13, 2015.

[EUB 12] EUBANKS V., *Digital Dead End: Fighting for Social Justice in the Information Age*, MIT Press, p. 288, 2012.

[EYN 12] EYNARD J., "L'éthique à l'épreuve des nouvelles particularités et fonctions des informations personnelles", *Éthique Publique, Revue Internationale D'Éthique Sociétale Et Gouvernementale*, vol. 14, no. 2, p. 8, 2012.

[FAI 06] FAINZANG S., *La relation médecin-malades: Information et mensonge*, PUF, Paris, 2006.

[FAR 98] FARRELL H., FARRELL B., "The language of business codes of ethics, implications of knowledge and power", *Journal of Business Ethics*, vol. 17, pp. 587–601, 1998.

[FED 08] FEDAOUI S., La protection des données personnelles face aux nouvelles exigences de sécurité, University of Rouen, Master 2 – Droit public, 2008.

[FES 01] FESSLER J.M., GRÉMY F., "Ethical problems in health information systems", *Methods Inf. Med.*, vol. 40, no. 4, pp. 359–361, 2001.

[FIS 14] FISCHER F., Ethique et Numérique: une éthique à inventer?, Rapport CIGREF, pp. 1–40, June 2014.

[FLO 98] FLORIDI L.,"L'éthique télématique", *L'Agora*, vol. 5, no. 4, North-Hatley (Québec), 1998.

[FLO 02] FLORIDI L., "Ethique dans l'infosphère", *Blesok*, no. 24, January–February 2002.

[FLO 04] FLORIDI L., "Information", in FLORIDI L. (ed.), *The Blackwell Guide to the Philosophy of Computing and Information*, Blackwell, Oxford, UK, 2004.

[FLO 07] FLORIDI L., "A look into the future impact of ICT on our lives", *The Information Society*, vol. 23, no. 1, pp. 59–64, 2007.

[FLO 09] FLORIDI L., "The information society and its philosophy: introduction to the special issue on The philosophy of information, its nature, and future developments", *The Information Society: An International Journal*, vol. 25, no. 3, pp. 153–158, 2009.

[FLO 13] FLORIDI L., "Information quality", *Philos. Technol.*, vol. 26, pp. 1–6, 2013.

[FOU 08] FOURNIER T., "Ethique et cancérologie: Donner un sens au soin", *ONCORA*, p. 12, 29 January 2008.

[FRA 94] FRANSMAN M., "Information, knowledge, vision and theories of the firm", *Industrial and Corporate Change*, vol. 3, no. 3, pp. 1–45, 1994.

[GAD 76] GADAMER H.G., *The Historicity of Understanding*, Penguin Books Ltd, Harmondsworth, 1976.

[GAL 94] GALLOUX J.C., *Ebauche d'une définition juridique de l'information*, Recueil Dalloz-Sirey, 1994.

[GAR 97] GARRO O., Contribution à la modélisation de la conception des systèmes mécaniques, *thesis*, Grenoble I, University Joseph Fourier, p. 82, 1997.

[GAR 14] GARCÍA-GÓMEZ J.M., DE LA TORRE-DÍEZ I., VICENTE J. *et al.*, "Analysis of mobile health applications for a broad spectrum of consumers: a user experience approach", *Health Informatics J.*, vol. 20, no. 1, pp. 74–84, 2014.

[GFI 12] GFII, Big data: exploiter de grands volumes de données: quels enjeux pour les acteurs du marché de l'information et de la croissance?, Dossier de synthèse de la journée d'étude du GFII, 2012.

[GHI 00] GHITALLA F., "L'espace du document numérique", *Communication et langages*, no. 126, p. 76, December 2000.

[GOO 14] GOODMAN E., "Design and ethics in the era of big data", *Interactions*, vol. 21, no. 3, pp. 22–24, Accessed 1 October 2014.

[GUI 11] GUILLAUD H., *Un monde de données*, Publie.net, Paris, p. 314, 2011.

[GUI 13] GUIMARAES PEREIRA A., BENESSIA A., CURVELO P., *Agency in the Internet of Things*, Publication Office of the European Union, Luxembourg, p. 5, 2013.

[HAB 84] HABERMAS J., *The Theory of Communicative Action. Volume 1: Reason and the Rationalization of Society*, Beacon, Boston, 1984.

[HAB 87] HABERMAS J., *Théorie de l'agir communicationnel. Tome 1; Rationalité de l'agir et rationalisation de la société*, Fayard, Paris, p. 101, 1987.

[HAM 07] HAMID N., *Information Security and Computer Ethics, Tools ,Theories and Modeling*, Igbi Science Publication, North Carolina University, pp. 543–568, 2007.

[HAM 13] HAMEL M.P., MARGUERIT D., "Analyse des big data. Quels usages, quels défis?", *La note d'analyse* no. 8, Commissariat général à la stratégie et à la perspective, pp. 1–12, 2013.

[HAR 15] HARARI Y.N., *Sapiens: Une brève histoire de l'humanité*, Albin Michel, Paris, 2015.

[HER 97] HERVÉ C., *Ethique médicale ou Biomédicale? L'éthique en mouvement*, L'Harmattan, Paris, 1997.

[HOF 91] HÖFFE O., *La justice politique: fondement d'une philosophie critique du droit et de l'Etat*, PUF, Paris, pp. 38–40, 1991.

[HOF 13] HOFFMAN S., PODGURSKI A., "Big bad data: law, public health, and biomedical databases", *Journal of Law, Medicine and Ethics*, vol. 41, no. 1, pp. 56–60, 2013.

[IKI 13] IKILIOSSANA G., FAVIER M., COAT F., "Codes éthiques et usages des TIC: analyse des chartes d'utilisation des TIC de trois universités de l'Isère", *Cahier de recherche*, no. 2012 – 04 ES, CERAG, pp. 1–16, 2013.

[IMI 13] INSTITUTE OF MULTILINGUAL AND INFORMATION MULTIMEDIA TECHNOLOGIES, Ethical Charter and Big Data: Facilitating the Creation, Exchange and Dissemination of Data, IMMI-CNRS, available at http://wiki.ethique-big-data.org, 2013.

[INS 14a] INSTITUT G9+, Big Data, l'accélérateur d'innovation, Livre Blanc, pp. 1–122, December 2014.

[INS 14b] INSTITUT DE L'ENTREPRISE, Faire entrer la France dans la 3ème Révolution Industrielle, p. 19, May 2014.

[ISO 03] ISO, PN ISO/IEC 17799, 2003.

[JAC 15] JACQUIN J.B., "IBM s'associe à Apple pour analyser les données de santé", *Le Monde*, 14 April 2015.

[JEA 13] JEANNE W., ROSS C.M., "You may not need big data after all", *Harvard Business Review*, available at: https://hbr.org/2013/12/you-may-not-need-big-data-after-all, 2013.

[JOH 85] JOHNSON D., *Computer Ethics*, 1st ed., Prentice-Hall, Englewood Cliffs, NJ; 1985.

[JOL 12] JOLY Y., DOVE E.S., KNOPPERS B.M. *et al.*, "Data sharing in the postgenomic world: the experience of the international cancer genome consortium (ICGC) data access compliance office (DACO)", *PLoS Computational Biology*, vol. 8, no. 7, p. e1002549, 2012.

[JUL 04] JUILLET A., "Du renseignement à l'intelligence économique", *Défense Nationale*, no. 12, pp. 7–20, 2004.

[KAL 96] KALLMAN E.A., GRILLO J.P., *Ethical Decision Making and Information Technology: An Introduction With Cases,* 2nd ed., McGraw-Hill, New York, 1996.

[KAP 96] KAPLAN R.S., NORTON D.P., "Using the balanced scorecard as a strategic management system", *Harvard Business Review*, vol. 74, pp. 75–85, January–February 1996.

[KAP 98] KAPTEIN M., WEMPE J., "Twelve gordian knots when developing an organizational code of ethics", *Journal of Business Ethics*, vol. 17, pp. 853–869, 1998.

[KEI 85] KEITH-SPIEGEL P., KOOCHER G.P., *Ethics in Psychology: Professional Standards and Cases*, Random House, New York, 1985.

[KEP 12] KEPEKLIAN G., WIBAUX G., Quels modèles économiques pour le Big Data?, ATOS, Transactional services, Powering progress, pp. 1–54, July 2012.

[KIN 09] KINNEY S.K., KARR A.F., GONZALEZ Jr. J.F., "Data confidentiality: the next five years summary and guide to papers", *Journal of Privacy and Confidentiality*, vol. 1, no. 2, pp. 125–134, 2009.

[KRA 86] KRANZBERG M., "Technology and history: Kranzberg's laws", *Technology and Culture*, vol. 27, no. 3, p. 545, 1986.

[KUH 99] KUHLTHAU C., "The role of experience in the information search process of an early career information worker: perceptions of uncertainty, complexity construction and sources", *Journal of the American Society of Information Science*, vol. 50, no. 5, pp. 399–412, 1999.

[LAM 11] LAMBERT S.M., *Tableaux de bord dynamiques: Une approche à base d'ontologies*, Editions Univ. Europ., December 2011.

[LAM 12] LAMARI M., "Le courtage de connaissance à l'ère du numérique. Recherche collaborative d'information", *Les Cahiers du Numérique*, vol. 8, nos. 1–2, pp. 97–130, 2012.

[LAN 01] LANEY D., 3D data management: controlling data volume, velocity, and variety, Rapport Gartner, p. 4, 2001.

[LAU 97] LAUFER W.S., ROBERTSON D.C., "Corporate ethics initiatives as social control", *Journal of Business Ethics*, vol. 16, pp. 1029–1048, 1997.

[LAZ 14] LAZER D., KENNEDY R., KING G. et al., "The Parable of Google Flu: Traps in Big Data", *Science*, vol. 343, pp. 1203–1205, 2014.

[LEB 01] LEBRATY J.F., "Comprendre le concept d'information pour mieux appréhender les Technologies de l'information et de la communication", *Colloque du CRIC, La communication d'entreprise–Regards croisés Sciences de Gestion Sciences de l'Information et de la Communication*, Nice, p. 2, 6–7 Dcemeber 2001.

[LEC 07] LE COZ P., *Petit traité de la décision médicale*, Le Seuil, Paris, 2007.

[LEC 10] LE COZ P., "Cancer et fertilité: les aspects éthiques", *Colloque: 1ère journée d'éthique de l'Institut Paoli-Calmettes*, Marseille, 19 November 2010.

[LEM 95] LE MOIGNE J.L., *Les épistémologies constructives*, PUF, 1995.

[LEM 07] LE MOIGNE J.L., *Les épistémologies constructives*, PUF, 2007.

[LEM 13] LE MONDE, Les données puissance du futur, 7 January 2013.

[LER 08] LÉRY L., COLLOC J., "Prise de décision dans l'éthique au quotidien, comment décider dans le soin?", *SDM, Médicament, éthique et Pays en Développement*, p. 245, November 2008.

[LES 99] LESSIG L., *Code and Other Laws of Cyberspace*, Basic Books, Inc., New York, p. 241, 1999.

[LES 13] LESAULNIER F., "Internet, santé et données personnelles", *Médecine & Droit*, no. 118, pp. 1–2, 2013.

[LUC 13] LUCAS J., "Les freins à lever pour structurer la médecine de premier recours avec la télémédecine", *6ème congrès européen de l'ANTEL: Le parcours de soins: rôle et place de la Télémédecine*, 16 November 2013.

[LUC 15] LUCAS J., La santé connectée pose-t-elle des problèmes éthiques? Interview recueilli par Pierre Bienvault, Livre Blanc sur la "santé connectée", Ordre national des médecins, Paris, 3 February 2015.

[LUP 14] LUPTON D., "The commodification of patient opinion: the digital patient experience economy in the age of big data", *Sociology of Health & Illness*, vol. 36, no. 6, pp. 856–869, 2014.

[LYO 03] LYON D., *Surveillance as Social Sorting: Privacy, Risk, and Digital Discrimination*, Routledge, London, 2003.

[MAC 07] MACINTYRE A., *After Virtue: A Study in Moral Theory*, 3rd ed., Gerald Duckworth & Co Ltd, London, 2007.

[MAJ 05] MAJUMDER M.A., "Cyberbanks and other virtual research repositories", *Journal of Law, Medicine & Ethics*, vol. 33, no. 1, pp. 31–39, 2005.

[MAK 13] MAKAZI GROUP, Livre blanc du data marketing, pp. 1–26, 2013.

[MAL 97] MALLET-POUJOL N., *Appropriation de l'information: l'éternelle chimère*, Dalloz, Chron., 1997.

[MAL 13] MALLE J.P., "La triple rupture des Big data", *ParisTech Review*, 15 March 2013.

[MAR 12] MARÇAL DE OLIVEIRA K., THION V., DUPUY-CHESSA S. *et al.*, "Limites de l'évaluation d'un Système d'Information: une analyse fondée sur l'expérience pratique", *INFORSID*, p. 395–410, 2012.

[MAR 14] MARKOWETZ A., BŁASZKIEWICZ K., MONTAG C. *et al.*, "Psycho-informatics: big data shaping modern psychometrics", *Medical Hypotheses*, vol. 82, no. 4, pp. 405–411, 2014.

[MAS 86] MASON R., "Four ethical issues of the information age", *MIS Quarterly*, vol. 10, no. 1, pp. 5–11, 1986.

[MAT 05] MATTEI J.F., "De l'indignation", *La Table Ronde*, Paris, 2005.

[MAT 13] MATHAIYAN J., CHANDRASEKARAN A., DAVIS S., "Ethics of genomic research", *Perspectives in Clinical Research*, vol. 4, no. 1, p. 100, 2013.

[MAY 99] MAY Y.C., "Web mining technology and academic librarianship: human-machine connections for the 21st century", *Peer-Reviewed Journal on the Internet*, vol. 4, no. 6–7, June 1999.

[MAY 13] MAYER-SCHÖNBERGER V., "Big Data: nouvelle étape de l'informatisation du monde", *Le Monde*, p. 2, 24 May 2013.

[MAY 14] MAYER-SCHONBERGER V., CUKIER K., *Big Data: A Revolution That Will Transform How We Live, Work, and Think*, Robert Laffont, 2014.

[MCK 08] MCKINNEY J.A., MOORE C.W., "International bribery: does a written code of ethics make a difference in perceptions of business professionals", *Journal of Business Ethics*, vol. 79, pp. 103–111, 2008.

[MCK 13] MCKINSTRY B., "Currently available smartphone apps for asthma have worrying deficiencies", *Evid. Based Med.*, vol. 18, no. 5, pp. e45–e45, 2013.

[MCG 08] MCGUIRE A.L., COLGROVE J., WHITNEY S.N. *et al.*, "Ethical, legal, and social considerations in conducting the Human Microbiome Project", *Genome Research*, vol. 18, no. 12, pp. 1861–1864, 2008.

[MCL 77] MCLUHAN M., *La galaxie Gutenberg: La genèse de l'homme typographique*, Gallimard, Paris, 1977.

[MCN 14] MCNEELY C.L., HAHM J., "The big (data) bang: policy, prospects, and challenges", *Review of Policy Research*, vol. 31, no. 4, pp. 304–310, 2014.

[MEL 13] MELLO M.M., FRANCER J.K., WILENZICK M. *et al.*, "Preparing for responsible sharing of clinical trial data", *New England Journal of Medicine*, vol. 369, no. 17, pp. 1651–1658, 2013.

[MER 02] MERCIER S., COULON R., ISAAC H., LEDR M., JOSSERAND E. "Le développement des technologies de l'information: comment préserver la vie privée des salariés?", in KALIKA *et al.* (ed.), *E-GRH: révolution ou évolution?,* Editions Liaisons, pp. 171–194, 2002.

[MIR 03] MIRCHANDANI D., MOTWANI J., "Reducing Internet abuse in the workplace", *S.A.M Advanced Management Journal,* vol. 68, no. 1, pp. 22–26, 2003.

[MIT 11] MITTELSTADT B.D., FAIRWEATHER N.B., MCBRIDE N. *et al.*, "Ethical issues of personal health monitoring: a literature review", *ETHICOMP 2011 Conference Proceedings*, Sheffield, UK, pp. 313–321, 2011.

[MIT 13] MITTELSTADT B.D., FAIRWEATHER N.B., MCBRIDE N. *et al.*, "Privacy, risk and personal health monitoring", *ETHICOMP 2013 Conference Proceedings*, Kolding, Denmark, pp. 340–351, 2013.

[MIT 14] MITTELSTADT B.D., FAIRWEATHER N.B., SHAW M. *et al.*, "The ethical implications of personal health monitoring", *International Journal of Technoethics*, vol. 5, no. 2, pp. 37–60, 2014.

[MIT 15] MITTELSTADT B.D., FLORIDI L., "The ethics of big data: current and foreseeable issues in biomedical contexts", *SciEng. Ethics*, vol. 13, pp. 1–39, 2015.

[MOO 65] MOORE G.E., "Cramming More Components onto Integrated Circuits" Electronics Magazine, vol. 38, no. 8, p. 114, 19 April 1965.

[MOO 85] MOOR J., "What is computer ethics?", *Metaphilosophy*, vol. 16, no. 4, pp. 266–275, 1985.

[MOR 77] MORIN E., *La méthode 1: La nature de la nature*, Le Seuil, Paris, 1977.

[MOR 91] MORIN E., *La Méthode 4: Les idées*, Le Seuil, Paris, 1991.

[MOR 04] MORIN E., *La Méthode 6: Ethique*, Le Seuil, Paris, 2004.

[MOR 05] MORIN E., "Complexité restreinte, complexité générale", *Colloque "Intelligence de la complexité: épistémologie et pragmatique*, Cerisy-La-Salle, 26 June 2005.

[NIE 10] NIEMEIJER A.R., FREDERIKS B.J., RIPHAGEN I.I. *et al.*, "Ethical and practical concerns of surveillance technologies in residential care for people with dementia or intellectual disabilities: an overview of the literature", *International Psychogeriatrics*, vol. 22, pp. 1129–1142, 2010.

[NON 94] NONAKA I., "A dynamic theory of organizational knowledge creation", *Organization Science*, vol. 5, no. 1, pp. 14–37, 1994.

[NON 00] NONAKA I., TOYAMA R., KONNO N., "SECI, Ba, and leadership: a unified model of dynamic knowledge creation", *Long Range Planning*, vol. 33, pp. 5–34, 2000.

[NOR 92] NORTON D., KAPLAN R., "The Balanced Scorecard-mesures that drive performance", *Harvard Business Review*, pp. 44–45, 1992.

[NYE 08] NYE D.E., *Technologie & civilisation: 10 questions fondamentales liées aux* technologies, FYP, Limoges, 2008.

[OEC 80] OECD, Recommendation of the Council on Guidelines Governing the Protection of Privacy and Transborder Flows of Personal Data, Paris, 23 September 1980.

[OEC 13] OECD, Exploring Data-Driven Innovation as a New Source of Growth: Mapping the Policy Issues Raised by "Big Data", OECD Digital Economy Papers, no. 222, OECD Publishing, 2013.

[OMA 02] OMARJEE S., "Le Data Mining: "Aspects juridiques de l'intelligence artificielle au regard de la protection des données personnelles. Mémoire universitaire", *ERCIM*, pp. 1–51, 2002.

[OST 10] OSTP, Blue Ribbon Task Force on Sustainable Digital Preservation and Access, Sustainable Economics for a Digital Planet: Ensuring Long Term Access to Digital Information. available at: http://brtf.sdsc.edu/biblio/BRTF_Final_Report.pdf, February 2010.

[OZ 93] OZ E., "Ethical standards for computer professionals: a comparative analysis of four major codes", *Journal of Business Ethics*, vol. 12, no. 9, pp. 709–726, 1993.

[OZD 12] OZDALGA E., OZDALGA A., AHUJA N., "The smartphone in medicine: a review of current and potential use among physicians and students", *J. Med. Internet Res.*, vol. 14, no. 5, p. e128, 2012.

[PAS 15] PASQUALE F., *The Black Box Society: The Secret Algorithms That Control Money and Information*, Harvard University Press, Cambridge, MA, 2015.

[PAT 12] PATEL B.K., CHAPMAN C.G., LUO N. *et al.*, "Impact of mobile tablet computers on internal medicine resident efficiency", *Arch. Intern. Med.*, vol. 172, no. 5, pp. 436–438, 2012.

[PER 09] PERRIN B., NAIM D., "(Big) data: où en sont les entreprises françaises?", *EY*, pp. 1–44, 2009.

[PON 09] PONÇON G., "Système d'information: Vers une éthique de l'usage?", *Revue hospitalière de France*, vol. 531, pp. 74–7, 2009.

[POR 14] PORTER M., HEPPELMANN J.E., "How smart, connected products are transforming competition", *Harvard Business Review*, vol. 1, p. 2, November 2014.

[POS 14] POSTEL-VINAY N., BOLBRIE G., TOPOL E., "Livre Blanc de la santé connectée: pour entrer dans la médecine 2.0", *Withings Inspire Health*, pp. 13–14, 2014.

[PRA 13] PRAINSACK B., BUYX A., "A solidarity-based approach to the governance of research biobanks", *Medical Law Review*, vol. 21, no. 1, pp. 71–91, 2013.

[PRE 06] PREUSS-LAUSSINOTTE S., "Bases de données personnelles et politiques de sécurité: une protection illusoire?", *Cultures & Conflits*, vol. 1, no. 64, pp. 77–95, 2006.

[RAV 13] RAVIX V., Réflexions éthiques attachées à la dématérialisation des données de santé, *Mémoire pour l'obtention du Master 2 d'Ethique, Sciences, Santé, Société, Espace Ethique Méditerranéen*, University Aix-Marseille, 2013.

[RAY 14] RAY M., CHANG ROBERT J., KAUFFMAN YOUNGOK KWON C., "Understanding the paradigm shift to computational social science in the presence of big data", *Decision Support Systems*, vol. 63, pp. 67–80, 2014.

[RED 98] REDMAN T.C., "The impact of poor data quality on the typical enterprise", *Communications of the ACM*, vol. 41, no. 2, pp. 79–82, 1998.

[REI 00] REICHERT A.K., WEBB M., THOMAS E., "Corporate support for ethical and environmental policies: a financial management perspective", *Journal of Business Ethics*, vol. 25, pp. 53–64, 2000.

[REI 02] REIX R., *Systèmes d'information et management des organisations*, 4th ed., Vuibert, 2002.

[REY 00] REYNOLDS M.A., "Professionalism, ethical codes and the internal auditor: a moral argument", *Journal of Business Ethics*, vol. 24, pp. 115–124, 2000.

[REY 12] REYNAUDI M., SAUNERON S., "Médecine prédictive: les balbutiements d'un concept aux enjeux considérables", *La note d'analyse,* Centre d'analyse stratégique, no. 289, October 2012.

[RIC 90] RICŒUR P., *Soi-même comme un autre*, Le Seuil, Paris, 1990.

[RIC 91] RICŒUR P., "Éthique et morale", *Lectures 1: Autour du politique*, Le Seuil, 1991.

[ROC 10] ROCHFELD J., "Les nouveaux défis du droit des personnes: la marchandisation des données personnelles: en collaboration avec R. Perray", in *Les nouveaux défis du commerce électronique*, L.G.D.J. 2010.

[ROS 14] ROSKI J., BO-LINN G.W., ANDREWS T.A., "Creating value in health care through big data: opportunities and policy implications", *Health Affairs*, vol. 33, no. 7, pp. 1115–1122, 2014.

[ROT 04] ROTH F., "Des mécanismes de gouvernance informationnels aux mécanismes de gouvernance cognitifs: une grille de lecture et quelques conséquences pour la communication financière des entreprises", *Congrès Gouvernance et juriscomptabilité*, HEC Montréal, p. 19, June 2004.

[ROU 12] ROUVROY A., "Face à la gouvernementalité algorithmique, repenser le sujet de droit comme puissance", *The Selected Works of Antoinette Rouvroy*, vol. 3, p. 3, 2012.

[ROU 13] ROUVROY A., BERNS T., "Gouvernementalité algorithmique et perspectives d'émancipation. Ledisparate comme condition d'individuation par la relation?", *Réseaux*, vol. 1, no. 177, pp. 163–196, 2013.

[RUL 99] RULE J., HUNTER L., "Towards property rights in personal data", *Visions of Privacy: Policy Choices for the Digital Age*, University of Toronto Press, Canada, p. 168, 1999.

[RUS 11] RUSSOM P., Big data analytics, best practices report, Fourth Quarter, The Data Warehouse Institute, Renton, WA, 18 September 2011.

[SAF 06] SAFRAN C., BLOOMROSEN M., HAMMOND W.E. *et al.*, "Toward a national framework for the secondary use of health data: an American medical informatics association white paper", *Journal of the American Medical Informatics Association*, vol. 14, no. 1, pp. 1–9, 2006.

[SAI 02] SAINT-JEAN A., *Ethique de l'information*, Les presses de l'Université de Montréal, Québec, p. 22, 2002.

[SAM 00] SAMUELSON P., "Privacy As Intellectual Property?", *Stanford Law Review*, 1125, 2000.

[SAN 11] SANTUCCI G., "The internet of things: the way ahead", in VERMESAM O., FRIESS P. (eds), *Internet of Things – Global Technological and Societal Trends*, River Publishers, Aalbord, pp. 53–99, 2011.

[SAV 58] SAVATIER R., *Essai d'une présentation nouvelle des biens incorporels*, RTDC, 1958.

[SAV 15] SAVIN P., TESSALONIKOS A., "Big data, santé et droit: quelle combinaison idéale?", *Techniques Hospitalières*, no. 753, pp. 26–30, September–October 2015.

[SCH 00] SCHWANDT T.A., "Three epistemological stances for qualitative inquiry: interpretivism, hermeneutics, and social constructionism", *Handbook of Qualitative Research*, Sage, Thousand Oaks, CA, pp. 189–214, 2000.

[SCH 12] SCHADT E.E., "The changing privacy landscape in the era of big data", *Molecular Systems Biology*, vol. 8, no. 612, pp. 1–3, 2012.

[SHA 48] SHANNON C., "A mathematical theory of communication", *Bell System Technical Journal*, vol. 27, pp. 379–423 and 623–656, July and October 1948.

[SIM 13] SIMONDON G., *Du mode d'existence des objets techniques*, Aubier, 2013.

[SPR 13] SPRANZI M., "Clinical ethics and values: how do norms evolve from prastice ?", *Med. Health Care and Philos.*, vol. 16, pp. 93–103, 2013.

[STE 08] STEVENS B., "Corporate ethical codes: effective instruments for influencing behavior", *Journal of Business Ethics*, vol. 78, pp. 601–609, 2008.

[STE 13] STEINSBEKK K.S., URSIN L.Ø., SKOLBEKKEN J.A. *et al.*, "We're not in it for the money-lay people's moral intuitions on commercial use of "their" biobank", *Medicine, Health Care and Philosophy*, vol. 16, no. 2, pp. 151–162, 2013.

[SUC 11] SUCHMAN L., "Consuming anthropology", in BARRY A., BORN G. (eds), *Interdisciplinarity: Reconfigurations of the Social and Natural Sciences*, Routledge, London/New York, 2011.

[TAH 11] TAHERDOOST H., SAHIBUDDIN S., NAMAYANDEH M. *et al.*, "Propose an educational plan for computer ethics and information security", *Procedia – Social and Behavioral Sciences*, vol. 28, pp. 815–819, 2011.

[TEN 13] TENE O., POLONETSKY J., Big data for all: privacy and user control in the age of analytics, available at: http://heinonlinebackup.com/hol-cgi-bin/get_pdf.cgi?handle=hein.journals/nwteintp11&section=20, Accessed 2 October 2014, p. 246, 2013.

[TER 12] TERRY N., "Protecting patient privacy in the age of big data", *UMKC L. Rev.*, vol. 81, p. 385, Accessed 2 October 2014.

[TER 14] TERRY N., "Health privacy is difficult but not impossible in a post-hipaa data-driven world", *Chest*, vol. 146, no. 3, pp. 835–840, 2014.

[TOD 07] TODOROVA G., DURISIN B., "Absorptive capacity: valuing a reconceptualization", *Academy of Management Review*, vol. 32, no. 3, p. 776, 2007.

[TOU 53] TOULMIN S., *The Philosophy of Science: An Introduction*, Hutchinsons University Library, pp. 1–176, 1953.

[TYR 94] TYRE M., ORLIKOWSKI W., "Windows of opportunity: temporel patterns of technological adaptation in organizations", *Organization Science*, vol. 5, no. 1, pp. 98–118, 1994.

[UMH 14] UMHOEFER C., ROFÉ J., LEMARCHAND S., Le Big Data face au défie de la confiance, The Boston Consulting Group, June 2014.

[VAL 41] VALÉRY P., *Les carnets de Léonard de Vinci*, Traduits de l'anglais, Gallimard, collection TEL, 1941.

[VAL 48] VALÉRY P., *Vues*, La Table Ronde, Paris, 1948.

[VAL 02] VALENTINE S., FLEISCHMAN G., "Ethics codes and professionals' tolerance of societaldiversity", *Journal of Business Ethics*, vol. 40, no. 4, pp. 301–312, 2002.

[VAS 12] VASQUEZ M., LAMMARI N., COMYN-WATTIAU I. et al., "De l'analyse des risques à l'expression des exigences de sécurité des systèmes d'informations", *30ème conférence INFORSID (INFormatique des ORganisations et Systèmes d'Information et de Décision)*, Montpellier, pp. 337–362, May 2012.

[VIC 98] VICK S., SCOTT A., "Agency in health care: examining patients' preferences for attributes of the doctor–patient relationship", *Journal of Health Economics*, vol. 17, no. 5, pp. 587–605, 1998.

[VIS 12] VISVANATHAN A., HAMILTON A., BRADY R.R.W., "Smartphone apps in microbiology–is better regulation required?", *Clin. Microbiol. Infect.*, vol. 18, no. 7, pp. E218–E220, 2012.

[VIT 12] VITALIROSATI M., "Une éthique appliquée? Considérations pour une éthique du numérique", *Éthique publique*, vol. 14, no. 2, p. 13-32, 2012.

[WAN 95] WANG R.Y., STOREY V.C., FIRTH C.P., "A framework for analysis of data quality research", *IEEE Trans. on Knowl. and Data Eng.*, vol. 7, no. 4, pp. 623–640, 1995.

[WAN 96] WANG R.Y., STRONG D.M., "Beyond accuracy: what data quality means to data consumers", *Journal of Management Information Systems*, vol. 12, no. 4, pp. 5–33, 1996.

[WAN 98] WANG R.Y., "A product perspective on total data quality management", *Communication of the ACM*, vol. 41, no. 2, pp. 58–65, 1998.

[WAS 96] WASKUL D., DOUGLASS M., "Considering the electronic participant. Some polemical observations on the ethics of on-line research", *The Information Society*, vol. 12, no. 2, pp. 129–139, 1996.

[WIL 00] WILEY C., "Ethical standards for human resource management professionals: a comparative analysis of five major codes", *Journal of Business Ethics*, vol. 25, pp. 93–114, 2000.

[WLA 14] WLADAWSKY-BERGER I., "Science des données Vs statistiques", *DSIH*, vol. 1, p. 54, October 2014.

[WOR 12] WORLD ECONOMIC FORUM, Big Data, Big Impact: New Possibilities for International Development, 2012.

[YAH 14] YAHIA O., "Vade-mecum des objets connectés", *APSSIS*, p. 1–102, 2014.

[YAS 15] YASINI M., MARCHAND G., "Toward a use case based classification of mobile health applications", *Digital Healthcare Empowering Europeans*, pp. 175–179, 2015.

Index

Printed in the United States
By Bookmasters